A model of a globe made in 1492

Man, Civilization, and Conquest

From Prehistory to World Exploration

Margaret Sharman

WORLDSPAN I

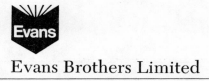

Evans Brothers Limited

List of Maps

Published by Evans Brothers Limited
Montague House, Russell Square
London, WC1B 5BX

Evans Brothers (Nigeria Publishers) Ltd
PMB 5164, Jericho Road
Ibadan

© Margaret Sharman 1971
First published 1971

illustrations   Maurice Wilson
maps   Edgar Holloway
picture-maps and charts   Leslie Haywood

Cover:
Model of the Martin Behaim globe from the Science
Museum, London. Photograph by Simon Dell.

Printed by Kenya Litho Ltd., Nairobi
SBN 237 28764 1   PR 1738

Contents

Acknowledgements

Several people have very kindly read chapters in this book and advised me on points of history. I should especially like to thank Richard Leakey and Jean Brown for information on East African prehistory; James Kirkman and Neville Chittick on the Arab and Portuguese periods in East Africa; Dr Ahmed Salim for reading the chapters on Islam; and E. W. Young for drawing me sketch-maps to show the difficulties the Atlantic explorers had to face.

Most of my other helpers I have not met—they are the authors of the dozens of books that I have read during the past two years while writing this history.   M. S.

For permission to reproduce copyright illustrations, the author and publishers gratefully acknowledge the following: Ashmolean Museum; page 32. Baghdad Museum; page 18. Biblioteca Nazionale, Florence; page 163. Curators of the Bodleian Library; page 111, taken from *MSS Marsh 144*. British Institute of History and Archaeology in East Africa; page 136. Trustees of the British Museum; pages 11 (top), 14 (top), 14 (bottom), 15 (top), 15 (bottom), 19 (top), 19 (bottom), 25 (bottom-right), 29, 34, 41 (bottom), 44, 47, 53, 54 (top), 60, 78 (top), 90, 96, 97 (top), 102, 105, 112, 115, 120, 138, 141 (top), 146, 169, 174 (top). British Museum (Natural History); page 4 (top). École Française D'Archéologie D'Athènes; page 78 (bottom). Editions Payot, Paris; page 10 (bottom), taken from *La Chase Prehistorique* by Lindner. The Executors of the late Mary Houston; page 26, taken from *Ancient Egyptian, Mesopotamian and Persian Costume*, by Mary Houston. Institute of Ethnology of the University of Paris; page 165. James Kirkman; page 139. Dr L. S. B. Leakey; pages 5 (top), 6 (top). Frank Lane; page 155. Lehnart and Landrock; pages 23, 28 (top) 28 (centre). The Louvre, Paris; page 20. The Mansell Collection; pages 35, 40, 49, 50, 54 (bottom), 57, 58, 66, 68, 73, 75, 79, 82, 83, 85 (top), 86, 95, 97 (bottom), 99, 105, 109, 118 (top), 119, 121, 122, 123, 127, 131, 132, 151, 173, 174 (bottom), 175, 176, 177. By courtesy of the Trustees of The National Gallery, London; page 100. National Museum of Wales; page 77. National Portrait Gallery; pages 125, 129, 166. Nigeria Museum; page 152. Popperfoto; page 104. Radio Times Hulton Picture Library; pages 42, 55, 56, 65, 69, 72, 87 (top), 87 (bottom), 91 (top), 91 (bottom), 92, 98, 103, 106, 110 (top), 110 (bottom), 114, 124, 126, 128 (top), 128 (bottom), 132 (bottom), 144 (top), 148, 149, 158, 161 (top), 161 (bottom), 170. Science Museum, London; pages 51, 118 (bottom),/By courtesy of the Lovell Observatory, U.S.A.; page 41 (top),/Crown Copyright; page 144 (bottom). The Victoria and Albert Museum, London; pages 89, 93, 116 (top).

Preface

In the days before there were any history books, people passed on to their children stories about events that happened to themselves and to their ancestors. When the children grew up, they passed on these same stories to *their* children, and added other tales about events they had themselves experienced or heard of. People have always been interested in stories, and it makes them more exciting if they are true, or partly true.

When they learnt how to write, people liked to record stories about the glorious victories they won against their enemies. The people they fought against were (to them) always 'bad', while they themselves were 'good'. This attitude still persists today, of course. We all think of ourselves, our family, or our nation, as being right, while anyone with very different views must be wrong.

It is therefore very difficult to write a history book that is fair to everybody. 'Who won the battle?' is an easy question to answer; it is much more difficult to say which of the two different ways of life that led to the battle was right, and which was wrong. Both sides say things from their own point of view, while the history writer has to try to see and understand both sides.

Sometimes we are helped by having written accounts from several different people who were actually there at the time. We then use these accounts to try to find out what really happened. We can never be absolutely certain that we have found out the whole truth, but we try to get as complete a picture of historical events as we can.

The second thing that anyone studying history has to try to do is to put himself into the past. People living say, 400 years ago were very much like ourselves in many ways—we have only to read the plays of Shakespeare to know that this is true. There have always been love and hate,
ambition, greed, goodness, poverty and so on. People's motives have probably not changed very much; but their surroundings and the things they take for granted differ from country to country and from age to age. In the sixteenth century men and women dressed differently from us, they ate different kinds of food, they had different ideas about religion, and it took them much longer to travel from one town to another, or to exchange information and news. All these changes mean that they thought about themselves, and about their neighbours, in a very different way from the way we think today. Even in primary schools our children learn things about the Universe that the wisest men of Shakespeare's time did not know; but on the other hand, even if they were less well-informed about the 'outside' world, each man and woman in a sixteenth-century village knew a lot more than most of us do now about how to weave cloth, or preserve meat or make pottery.

So these two things have to be kept in mind— that people in the past thought differently from us, and that what they wrote about themselves was likely to be one-sided. The very early history of our Earth, before people knew how to write at all, is even more difficult to discover. Yet, as you will see, there are people who spend their lives finding out about this very early history—or prehistory, as it is called. Each year that goes by, we learn a little more about our own ancestors and their lives, while we ourselves are making 'history' to pass on to our descendants. Perhaps one day they will say of us twentieth-century peoples, 'Well, they must have been like us in some ways—but look at the primitive radios they had! How slowly their aeroplanes travelled!'

We keep on learning more and more about the Universe in which we live. Does this make us better people than those of past ages?

In the Beginning

5,000
million
years ago

The Earth was spinning in space *millions* of years before there were any living plants or animals on it.

200
million
years ago

There were plants, animals and birds on Earth *millions* of years before men appeared. Some of the animals were very strange, and died out long ago.

2
million
years
ago

There were also—the apes.

Some of the apes, after countless generations and more millions of years, became man-like. Many kinds of man-apes (we call them 'hominids') lived on earth at the same time. Only the more cunning ones survived. Their brains became larger, and their intelligence grew.

The scientific words used to describe ancient apes and hominids come from Latin and Greek. Here are some of the English meanings:

Zinjanthropus = East African man
Australopithecus = southern ape
Homo sapiens = 'thinking' man
Homo erectus = upright man
Which two words mean 'man'?

1

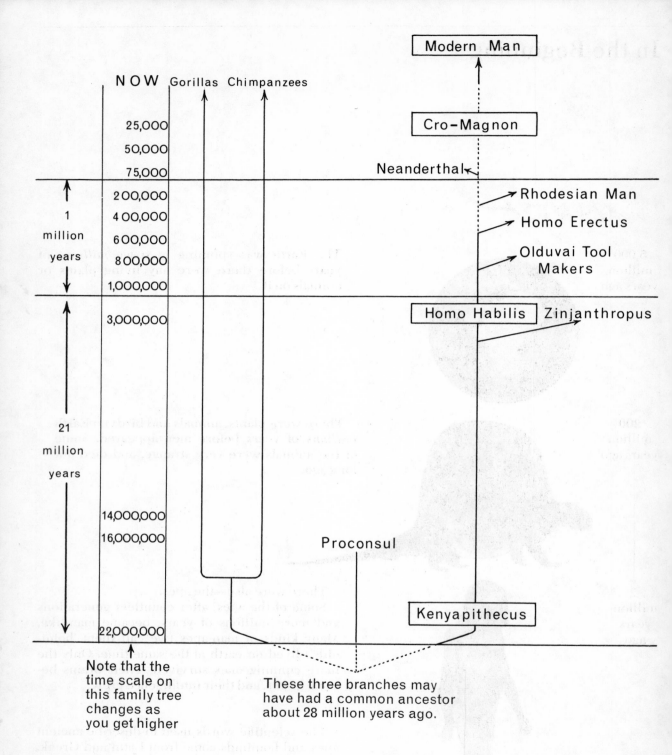

NOW Gorillas Chimpanzees

25,000	
50,000	
75,000	

Modern Man

Cro-Magnon

Neanderthal

1 million years

200,000
400,000
600,000
800,000
1,000,000

→ Rhodesian Man

→ Homo Erectus

→ Olduvai Tool Makers

3,000,000

Homo Habilis Zinjanthropus

21 million years

14,000,000
16,000,000

Proconsul

Kenyapithecus

22,000,000

Note that the time scale on this family tree changes as you get higher

These three branches may have had a common ancestor about 28 million years ago.

Our Family Tree

This kind of diagram is called a 'family tree'. This one is the family tree of Man, stretching right back for more than 22 million years. At the bottom are the very earliest types of men, and at the top, *Homo sapiens*—you and me. The gorillas and chimpanzees are put into our family tree because they are remote 'cousins'.

The little lines leading from the main branch show kinds of men who probably died out altogether. There were many many other kinds not shown here—the ones in the diagram are those we are going to talk about now.

We are uncertain about some of the stages which came before *Homo sapiens*, and at these points there is a dotted line in the diagram.

Part I The First Men
Chapter 1 The Ancestors of Man

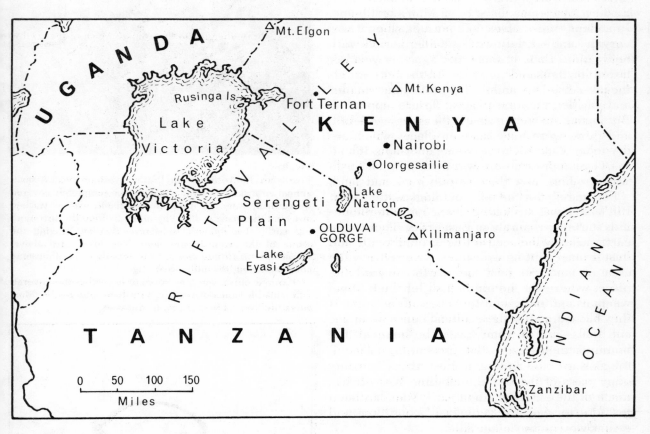

In 1859 a scientist named Charles Darwin published a book called *The Origin of Species*. In this book, he put forward the theory that all creatures on Earth had developed from more primitive forms. The book shocked the Christian world. Previously most Christians had believed in the Genesis story in the Bible, which says that every creature was created in its present form. But gradually the idea of 'evolution' (change and development over many years) was accepted; and in the last 100 years we have found out a great deal about the creatures that inhabited the Earth thousands and even millions of years ago.

But 100 years has not been long enough to find out about *all* the stages that took place. Palaeontologists* are searching all the time for more clues to Man's ancestors. Perhaps even before you finish reading this book, we may be told about some new discovery.

The Cradle of Man
We now believe that Africa was the starting-place of Man. The early apes, and hundreds of

---

*People who study the way in which men and animals evolved from primitive origins.

other different kinds of animals, first lived in Africa, probably around what is now the Rift Valley and Lake Victoria. Millions of years ago, some of them went northwards into Europe and Asia. Here their descendants went through similar stages of development to those who were left behind in Africa.

Near the Equator, in Central and West Africa, there were thick forests; in East Africa, near the Great Lakes, the forest was not so thick as in lands to the west. And this 'savannah' country (grassland with scattered trees and bushes) of Eastern Africa may have been Man's first home. In ancient times, Africa had periods when it was very dry and hot, followed by colder periods with heavy rain. Each of these two types of weather lasted for thousands of years. In the hot periods the lakes dried up and the forests became smaller and smaller; in some places, deserts appeared. But during the wetter years, the rivers were full, and there were huge lakes in places which are dry today. Lake Victoria was an enormous inland sea. Grass and shrubs grew in wide areas of North Africa, where now there is only rock and sand.

Fortunately for the palaeontologists, the Great Rift Valley was still taking shape long after hominids started to roam about East Africa. There were earthquakes which caused the ground to tilt, and dust from erupting volcanoes covered a wide area of land. So dust and earth covered the places where the hominids had left their stone weapons and tools, and the bones of the animals they had eaten. It is these animal bones, weapons and tools — and in some cases the bones of the hominids themselves — that present-day palaeontologists are now finding in East Africa. In many other parts of the world, including West Africa, much of the evidence about early Man has been lost for ever, because geological* conditions and events were not so favourable.

Proconsul

Our earliest East African evidence comes from a small creature's skull, squashed sideways by the weight of the covering earth. This little creature has been named 'Proconsul', and his skull was found on Rusinga Island, at the north-eastern end of Lake Victoria, in present-day Kenya.

'Proconsul' may sometimes have left the forests and scrambled around on open ground; but they were still not men, but apes. The canine

*Geology is the study of the Earth's crust.

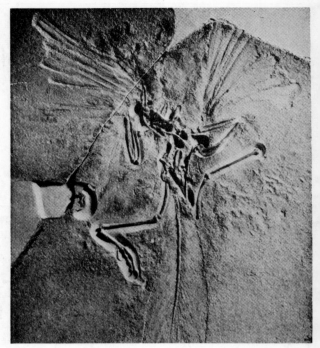

Fossils

Fossils are the result of long burial by ash or rock. A small animal, or a skull, or even a leaf may be completely covered by earth or water. In time the perishable part is washed away and the space is filled by minerals from the surrounding earth. The mineral substances harden, leaving the shape of the original specimen. The fossil bird above, *Archaeopteryx lithographica*, was fossilised in limestone and water about 180 million years ago.

Of course only a very few bones or leaves become covered with suitable kinds of earth to turn them into fossils. Most animal and vegetable remains just rot away.

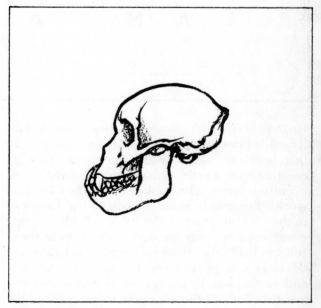

Skull of Proconsul

4

teeth (the pointed teeth on each side of the four front 'incisors', the cutting teeth) were long, as in most animals. They could be used for tearing flesh, or stripping the bark off trees. Our human canine teeth are very little different in length from the rest of our teeth. This is one of the signs palaeontologists look for when they are deciding whether a skull belongs to an ape or to a near-man.

Kenyapithecus

Not far away from Lake Victoria, there is a very small prehistoric site called Fort Ternan. (Prehistory is the time before there were any written records.) Here there are thousands of fossils (ancient bones and traces of bones preserved in the Earth) in a very small area, no larger than an average classroom. They are all between 12,000,000 and 14,000,000 years old. Dr L. S. B. Leakey and his wife, Mrs Mary Leakey, are Kenya palaeontologists who have been working on the prehistory of the Earth for many years. Dr Leakey believes that there was once a watering-place at Fort Ternan, where animals came to drink. But near the spring of water there was a crack in the rock, through which a poisonous gas sometimes came to the surface. Some of the animals who came to drink the water were killed by the gas. Carnivores (meat-eating animals) ate the dead animals and left the bones on the ground. They were then covered with ash from an erupting volcano, and preserved until now. Most of the bones on this site are of small animals, but there is evidence of one more man-like than the rest. We call him *Kenyapithecus*. This kind of hominid may in fact have been a very, very remote ancestor of us all. They also lived between 12,000,000 and 14,000,000 years ago. We do not know what they looked like, because the palaeontologists have so far found only the jawbone. The canine teeth were smaller than those of true apes, yet these creatures were still more like apes than men. Man-apes like *Kenyapithecus* have also been found as far away as India and China, so already these animals had wandered far.

Zinjanthropus

There is a gap in our knowledge of hominids here, until about 1,700,000 years ago—that is, a gap of 11 to 13 *million* years.*

---

*This does not mean that there are no skulls or bones waiting to be found, but that there has not yet been time, money or enough trained palaeontologists to look for more evidence.

Proconsul, remains of skull found in Kenya

Reconstruction of Zinjanthropus

hominid we know about from finds in East Africa is today called *Zinjanthropus*. The first *Zinjanthropus* skull was discovered by Mrs Mary Leakey, when she was looking for prehistoric evidence in Olduvai Gorge, in Tanzania.

In the days when *Zinjanthropus* lived, the cool waters of rivers and lakes attracted many animals and birds to Olduvai. *Zinjanthropus* ate small animals when he could catch them; he also ate vegetable foods, and he developed a huge jaw for grinding up the tough stringy leaves and stems. Although the skull that was found belonged to quite a young hominid (whose 'wisdom-teeth' had only just come through his gums*), his huge molar teeth were already worn down because of constant chewing. He has been nicknamed 'Nutcracker Man'. This Nutcracker Man's skull is about 1¾ million years old; in 1969 Dr Leakey's son Richard found another one at Lake Rudolf, which was 2 million years old! They belong to a family of African hominids all of which are called 'Australopithecines'. They lived in scattered places in East and South Africa.

The Australopithecines were probably hairy all over; they were short and strong, with low foreheads and deep-set eyes. They had very strong muscles on both sides of the head, a sloping brow, and a brain of about one-third the size of ours.

The skull Mrs Leakey found at Olduvai was incomplete: there was no bottom jaw. So it was great good fortune that 50 miles away, near Lake Natron, there lay on a shelf of rock a bottom jaw belonging to another Nutcracker Man. The two fossils together show us how Nutcracker Man's skull differed from ours.

Dr Leakey
Ranged in front of Dr Leakey are the skulls of *Australopithecus* (left), *Zinjanthropus* (centre) and that of a modern ape (right).

*In humans these teeth, at the back of the jaw, normally appear when we are 18–20 years old.

Australopithecus with animals in the background
Here are some of the animals that roamed over the African plains and were even found in Europe and Asia nearly 2 million years ago. There are crocodiles and hippos in the lake. An odd-looking elephant and a pig graze in the background.

Homo Habilis

Olduvai Gorge had further surprises in store: Richard Leakey's brother Jonathan found the broken fragments of the skull of a very young hominid. With painstaking care the pieces were stuck together to form the back part of the head. Later a lower jaw, and the bones of a hand were found. Dr Leakey has always been certain that this is a true ancestor of Man, and other experts now agree. The shape of the skull is very like ours, the teeth are in the same positions on the jaw as ours are; the finger bones show that this creature, now called *Homo habilis*, 'the man with ability', could grasp an object as we do, between fingers and thumb. *Homo habilis* and Nutcracker Man both lived in Africa about $1\frac{3}{4}$ million years ago. Nutcracker Man died out somewhere between that date and the coming of *Homo sapiens*. He could not compete against the later men, with their larger brains and their 'ability'.

Homo habilis made rough stone tools called 'pebble tools'. Examples of these tools have been found together with the skulls on the very lowest 'living-site' at Olduvai.

Homo Erectus

After another long gap in time, we find that a new hominid has taken the place of the earlier ones. His face was still very ape-like, but his leg and thigh bones show that he could stand up straight. This hominid is one member of a world-wide family which has been called *Homo erectus*, the 'upright man'. *Homo erectus* was much cleverer than Nutcracker Man or *Homo habilis*. He was capable of patiently spending hours chipping away at pieces of stone and bone in order to make for himself a really efficient weapon or tool. One type of tool we find in very large quantities—it is called a 'hand-axe', though in fact it was not used like a modern axe, but as a knife and scraper. From then onwards for thousands of years, hominids used hand-axes for all sorts of jobs that required a sharp-edged or pointed tool. Before long, these men had also learned how to make spear-heads, which they tied to long wooden handles. They hunted in groups, and with great cunning; they had a primitive form of speech. Their brains were about the size of the smallest of ours today. In Europe and parts of Asia, some of these groups of people could use fire, but they had not

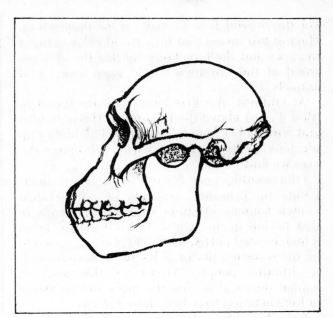

Skull of Australopithecus

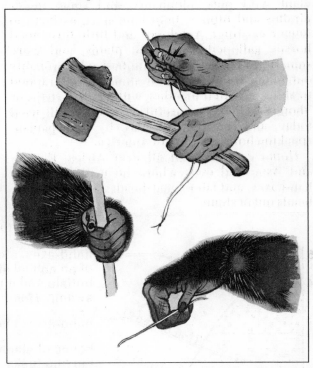

'Man the toolmaker'

What makes a man different from an ape? A long time ago people used to say 'Man is a tool-maker'; but many apes can make simple tools (an ape can hold a stick in a very similar way to man). There is no really good definition of the difference between an ape and early man. Perhaps we can say that man is a creature that uses tools to make other tools.

Notice the way the man is holding the needle and thread. Why is his grip more efficient than the chimpanzee's?

7

yet discovered how to make it for themselves. Having fire meant that they could relax at night in caves and shelters, knowing that the glowing wood at the entrance would keep away wild animals.

At Olduvai, the first hand-axes are found in 'Bed 2', just above the remains of *Homo habilis* and Nutcracker Man (see below). The higher up we look in the layers of earth, the better the axes we find.

Olorgesailie, near Nairobi, and Isimila near Iringa in Tanzania, are two of the greatest known sources of stone weapons and tools of that period in the world. In both places, lakes which existed perhaps 100,000 years ago, used to be the watering places of bands of these nomadic, hunting people. There are thousands of animal bones alongside the tools, but no skulls or human bones have been found so far.

Side by side with the hunters there lived giant wild pigs, elephants, and some queer giraffes and hippos, both long since extinct (no longer existing). Antelopes and little three-toed horses galloped across the plains, and were sometimes caught by the hunters, who probably entangled their legs with stone balls wrapped in skins, and tied together with leather strips or 'thongs'. This very useful weapon is still used today, and is called a 'bolas' by the Spanish-speaking hunters of South America.

Homo erectus lived all over Africa, Europe and Asia, and everywhere he made beautiful hand-axes, and later spear-heads and even arrow heads out of stone.

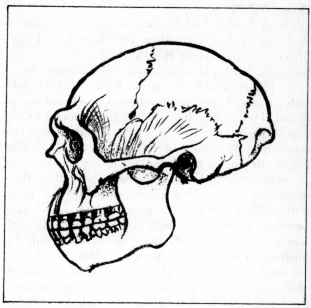

Skull of Homo erectus

How a gorge-site like Olduvai may be formed

I   1,750,000 years ago: hominids leave thigh bones of animals, fish bones and round pebble tools near a lake.

II The lake floods and covers the tools and bones and later retreats. This happens many times.

III Other animals use the lakeside and leave *their* bones and tools above those of the first hominids.

IV Eventually, after many layers of ash and mud have been deposited the ground level has risen about 300 feet.

V   After severe earth movements a river is formed; it wears away the soil. Steep banks appear on both sides of the river.

VI The river dries up, leaving a deep gorge. Some of the ancient bones and tools are washed away by the river. Others are exposed in the sides of the gorge after rain and soil erosion.

These were found at Olduvai Gorge:

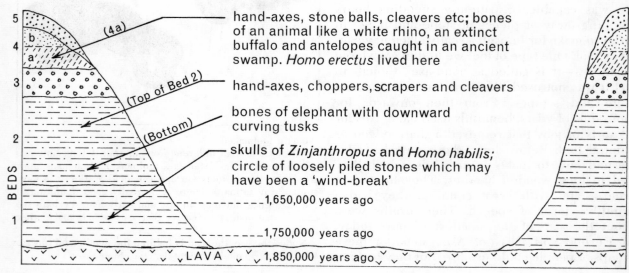

hand-axes, stone balls, cleavers etc; bones of an animal like a white rhino, an extinct buffalo and antelopes caught in an ancient swamp. *Homo erectus* lived here

hand-axes, choppers, scrapers and cleavers

bones of elephant with downward curving tusks

skulls of *Zinjanthropus* and *Homo habilis*; circle of loosely piled stones which may have been a 'wind-break'

1,650,000 years ago

1,750,000 years ago

LAVA 1,850,000 years ago

BEDS

Other early hominids

If you look at the diagram on p. 2, you will see that the next step in human evolution is 'Rhodesian Man'. He was given this name because his skull was found in Northern Rhodesia (now Zambia). But he, or other hominids very like him, also lived in many other places. Rhodesian Man was nearer to us than *Homo erectus* was. He had straight legs and could walk with a long stride, as we do. His brain was nearly as big as ours, but he still looked very ape-like, with great ridges over his eyes, and a backward-sloping forehead.

'Neanderthal Man' (named after the Neander Valley in Europe in which his bones were first found) comes almost at the top of our family tree. Traces of him have been found all over Europe and the Near East. Neanderthal Man was powerful and broad, with heavy brow-ridges and a receding chin. He was intelligent, and skilled with his hands. He had a very large brain. Like all the hominids before him, he was a nomad. He hunted the mammoth (a kind of hairy elephant), and the woolly rhinoceros, both of which were common in Europe and Asia. He relied for his meat on smaller kinds of animals like deer, pig and wild sheep. Some Neanderthal skulls seem to be almost man-like; others are much more like those of apes. Perhaps the more man-like ones are the result of breeding

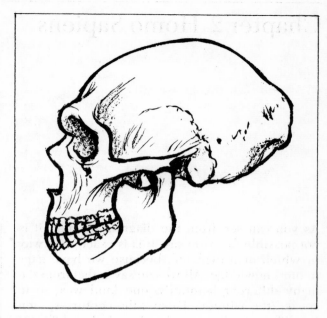

Skull of Neanderthal Man

with European and Asian hominids who were as advanced as Rhodesian Man. We do not yet know.

Long before Neanderthal Men disappeared for ever, another and more important creature was also making tools and weapons, and hunting the same kinds of animals for his food. He is the only hominid who has not yet died out. His name is *Homo sapiens*.

Stone-age hunting scene

In order to live at all men must have water. Without water plants could not grow and without plants there would be no animals and no men. You will always find stone-age sites near rivers or lakes, where the vegetation and animal life were at their richest.

Chapter 2 Homo Sapiens

As you can see from the diagram on p. 2, it is not possible for us to say 'this is exactly the way in which man evolved', because we have gaps in our knowledge. All we can say is that from the many different hominids, one kind was, so to speak, 'the winner'. During the centuries, men in different climates developed the different characteristics that we call 'race'. But all the races of Man belong to the same species, or type—*Homo sapiens*.

Early *Homo sapiens* (we will now just call them 'men') made weapons and tools of flint, stone, bone, ivory, wood and horn. He caught fish with bone harpoons; he used scrapers for cleaning animal hides, and sewed them together with bone needles to make clothes, and even small boats.

Cro-Magnon Man and cave art

The Cro-Magnon people were taller and probably stronger than modern men. They believed in magic and were superstitious. We think they drew animals and people on cave walls as a magic spell to give them good fortune in hunting.

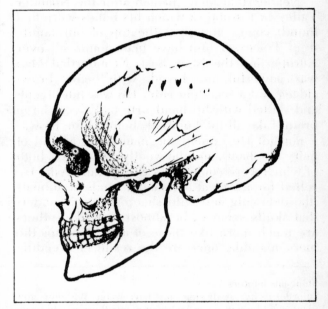

Skull of Cro-Magnon Man

There were very few people living in each continent. The way of life of ancient men did not allow them to live for very long, and most of them died before they were 30. In the days before medicines of any kind, and when wild animals killed men for food, their 'expectation of life', that is the length of time they could expect to live, was not very high.

Man is an inventor. He likes to find out about the things around him. His enquiring mind has led him to discover more about the universe than Nutcracker Man ever learnt—although he has only been on Earth a fraction of the time that Nutcracker Man was here. His first really big discovery was how to make fire by striking sparks into wood shavings and dried leaves. After that, each new invention led to another. Now that everybody could make fire when and where he liked, men (or more likely, women) made pots to put on the fire. The old way of roasting meat on sticks, or between stones was wasteful, and much of the fat and the nourishing juices were lost. Soon the clay pots were in every hut, some reserved for cooking, and others for storing water, grain, honey, milk or berries.

A long time later the hunters captured some of the wild dogs that lived in the bush country, and trained them to help catch larger animals. Hunting, and collecting wild wheat, berries and leaves took up most of their time.

In North Africa parts of the Sahara became inhabited during the long wet periods of ancient times. Here early men hunted all the animals that today live much farther south—ostriches, giraffes, elephants, and buffalo. We know this because they painted pictures of these animals on the walls of caves and rocks.

By about 10,000 B.C., the Sahara area had started to dry up, and men were forced to follow the more fertile valleys either to the north or to the south. The southern part of Africa gradually became cut off from the north by a wide belt of rock and sand. In the north-east, the mighty river Nile attracted many of the refugees from the drying Sahara. They joined the people who already lived by the river banks, and together built huts, and hunted for their food.

As far as we know, nobody had the idea of actually sowing grasses for grain until about 9000 B.C. By that time *Homo sapiens* may have been on the Earth for as long as 100,000 years. The first grain planters probably lived in Asia. They improved the quality of the wild crop by

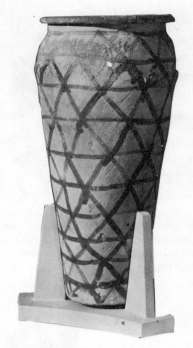

Pottery
Wood, leather and woven grasses do not survive as well as bone and stone, so we are not always certain about which kinds of people plaited baskets or made wooden bowls. But we do know that baskets were made before pots. Some baskets were plastered with mud inside so that flour, small berries and seeds did not fall through. When people started making pots of clay only, without the basket-work outside, they often made patterns on them imitating basket-work plaiting.

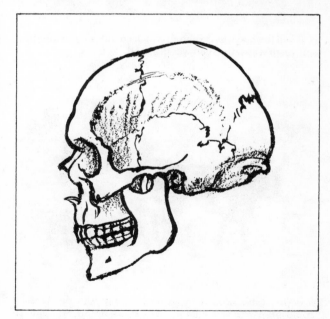

Skull of Homo sapiens
Trace this drawing and then put your tracing over the pictures of the skulls on pages 4, 7, 8, 9 and 10. How has evolution affected the shape of the face?

1. In very early times men took handfuls of seed and just threw them on to the ground. Much of the seed which was 'broadcast' like this was eaten by birds, so it was not a very good method of sowing. (But it was still used in many parts of the world until quite recently.)

2. Some people improved on this method by making holes in the ground with a pointed stick, but this was very slow.

3. Then the hoe was invented, which cut up and loosened the soil, on to which the seed was dropped.

4. The first ploughs were just pieces of bone or wood with long handles and the farmers pulled them along the ground making a furrow, a long cut in the ground, into which they dropped the seed.

5. When cattle were tame enough to pull ploughs, farmers could prepare a much larger area of ground in a day and so could enlarge their fields and grow more food.

6. Improvements were invented to make the job of a farm-worker easier at harvest time. Sickles were made out of sharpened flint or bone with a wooden handle. Later came the idea of using a curved bone and the sickle became the shape it is today. Why is this a better shape than the earlier straight sickle?

Early Agriculture

planting only the biggest and best seeds each year. While they tended the crops, they had to live near the fields. So small settlements grew near to fertile ground.

The hunters still went after wild animals for meat, but even they were soon able to stay at home for longer periods, because the new farmers had learnt how to build stockades, protective places made of wood, in which to keep wild animals, and fatten them for food. They could then choose the beast they wanted to kill, and they could eat meat even when the wild herds had migrated elsewhere. So a new occupation was invented—that of a herdsman. As time went by, the domestic animals improved in the same way as the grain improved for the agriculturalists—by clever selection and breeding.

Men were now able to 'control their environment', that is, their surroundings and the conditions under which they lived. They no longer had to live at the mercy of wild animals, storms and cold, or famine. The coming of agriculture meant that they need no longer be nomads. They built permanent houses to shelter them from the weather, wore clothing to keep out the cold, stored grain to eat all the year round, and made efficient weapons for protection. The groups of people grew, as one group joined another to share their crops. Only a few people had to grow food; the rest could hunt, or make tools, or repair houses, or sew skins. Men began to specialize in the jobs they were best at, and as they now had more leisure, they became more skilled. They decorated their pots with coloured paint, and with interesting patterns. They carved wood and ivory into beautiful shapes, and set precious stones into gold to make decorative drinking vessels, jewellery and ornaments. Each community had its own special ways of decorating pottery. Archaeologists* can tell how old a society is by the type of pottery the people made or imported.

When the villagers had a surplus of goods (that is, more than enough for their own needs), they exchanged them with the next village for *their* surplus goods. This was the beginnings of trade, and competition between the villages led to each craftsman trying to become more skilled than his neighbour. The basket-weavers

*Bones, tools, pottery and even the ruins of complete cities are sometimes found deep underground. Archaeologists are people who find out about the past by a careful study of buried evidence.

Boats
Tree trunks were probably the first form of boats used by man. He could get across streams and rivers by simply sitting astride a log. Early settlers used to hollow out the trunks to make canoes, and string logs together to make rafts. In countries where there were no large trees available, rafts were made from reeds or rushes. In time, animal skins were stretched over a framework of wood. What advantages would this type of boat have over the log or raft?

developed their art and invented the weaving of cloth. In Asia and North Africa they used the fibres of a kind of grass called flax—the first grass grown not for its grain, or flour, but for clothing. The new settlements became self-supporting. Some of them were on the very brink of becoming what we now call 'civilized'.

13

Part II Early Civilizations
Chapter 3 Mesopotamia

We are now going to jump in time to about 3500 B.C., when the earliest civilizations we know about were already flourishing. Up to that date, archaeologists rely on examining bones, tools and weapons, baskets, and pots, in order to find out about man's past. But from around 3500 B.C. their work is helped enormously by a great invention—writing. Prehistory now becomes history, because for the first time we have actual records from the people themselves.

Writing

It is true that very early writing was only concerned with such things as lists of kings, lists of goods in a storeroom, the measurements of fields, and so on. But from this time onwards men relied less and less on memory, and more and more on written records. Of course, if someone living 6000 years *later* than us—in about A.D. 8000—were to find a page of your exercise book, he would not (if he were wise!) immediately assume that everything written in it was true; the same applies to all the written evidence from the past. The writer of a letter may have been wrongly informed; an account of a battle is almost always one-sided; and an inscription cut in stone or metal praising a king may have been written more to flatter than to tell the truth. Therefore, historians read all these writings with an open mind, hoping that some other evidence—perhaps the discovery of a ruined building, or a weapon, or a second piece of writing—will agree with the evidence they already have.

So—the early civilizations had writing: that was an enormous step forward. Without it, perhaps they would not have been civilizations at all.

Writing

The earliest kind of writing was in pictures so at first people could only write down information about *things*. Then gradually pictures came to mean abstract words as well—for instance, a picture of a leg might mean 'walk' or 'travel' as well as being the symbol for the leg itself. The people of Sumeria and the Near East simplified the pictures into horizontal and vertical strokes. This is called cuneiform writing.

The Egyptians wrote on a kind of paper made of papyrus stems, with a pen cut from the hard part of a feather—a quill—and ink. We call their writing hieroglyphics.

This is what the two kinds of writing looked like in about 2000 B.C.

Above: Cuneiform.   *Below:* Hieroglyphics

Learning to live together

We know that in several places around the Mediterranean Sea, and in the area we now call the 'Fertile Crescent', between Palestine and the Persian Gulf, people lived together in large towns, with well-built houses, good drainage, and sometimes town walls to protect them from their nomadic neighbours. (Many communities have remained as nomads, or as small village dwellers, right up to the present.)

In these towns, each person had his own rights in the community, and to protect their rights, they had to have laws. The farmers had to know where their fields ended, and where their neighbours' fields began; the tax-collectors had to have rules about how to calculate each man's contribution to the state; there had to be some way of stopping crimes like theft or murder. This was the beginning of government, and of laws — laws that everyone helped to keep, so that they could all live peacefully together in these large communities.

The gods look on

The lives of people in all the early civilizations was coloured by their religion. 'Religion' means 'binding together'. And religious ideas have to do with the way people live together, as well as their feelings about their god or gods. Primitive religions were all concerned with nature — there was a god of the sun, a god (or goddess) of the moon, a sea-god, a fire-god, a god of thunder, and so on. The gods were all around, on this Earth.

Then people began to believe in a life beyond this Earth, a life after death. And so they thought it was important to bury people in the right way, to ensure that their souls lived on. It is because of these burial customs that we know so much about the lives of people in the early civilizations — and indeed in some of the village communities as well. For most of these people did not simply bury the dead body. They included in the graves the dead person's goods — his pottery, his ornaments, his furniture, and his weapons. Much of the early pottery and ornaments you can see in museums today was once part of the grave-furniture of ancient people.

Sumeria — the land between two rivers

In about 3500 B.C., there were many small towns in the land between the two rivers called Tigris and Euphrates, in Mesopotamia. Nowadays the

Metals

Gold was probably the first metal used by ancient peoples because it was easy to find, in tiny bits, among river sand and even just lying on the surface of the earth. It is a very soft metal, suitable for making cups, plates and ornaments but not for tools and weapons.

A much more useful metal was copper, which people had started to use for knife blades and tools by about 5000 B.C. As the early civilizations had no copper in their own lands they sent prospectors (people who look for metals) to foreign lands. This meant there was contact between peoples of far-away places from very early times. The bison pictured above is of copper. It is Sumerian, about 2300 B.C.

Copper alloyed (mixed) with tin is called bronze. Bronze is a harder metal than copper by itself, but it is not as hard as iron. People had found lumps of iron that had come from meteorites and the Egyptians called it 'the metal from the sky'.

We can no longer find metals in exposed rocks or in the sand. Our miners have to dig for gold, copper and iron in deep mines far below the surface of the earth.

Burial Scene, 4500 B.C.

area round the Persian Gulf is desert or semi-desert, and the ruins of the old towns are buried in sand; but 5500 years ago the towns were situated in a broad, fertile plain at one end of the Fertile Crescent. Each town in the plain had its own ruler, but all the towns were loosely connected, all speaking the same language and obeying the same laws. The rulers often quarrelled with each other, but their towns also carried on a lively trade. The whole country we call Sumeria, and one of its most important towns was called Ur.

The river Euphrates was the life-blood of Sumeria. The Tigris was not so 'manageable'. Fishing boats, pleasure boats and barges loaded with cargo sailed up the Euphrates to the towns north of Ur, linking them all together. The river was the main highroad for the transport of market produce—barley and dates, goat-cheese and wine. In winter, when the two rivers flooded the plain, the effects on the farmlands could be disastrous. One of the first great works in which all the towns joined was the building of canals and ditches to control the overflowing waters. Without canals, the fields would have been water-logged, that is, soaked with water, and the crops completely ruined. After this, every year when the waters went down, the land was ready for planting the Sumerians' staple* crop, barley. (Wheat did not grow well in the land of the two rivers, because the ground was very salty.) Once the barley crop had ripened, men and women cut it with flint-and-wood sickles, and piled the golden grain on to heavy wooden carts. These were probably the first wheeled vehicles in the world, and their solid wheels clattered along the stone-paved streets of the towns as the tame oxen pulled them to the store-rooms, or to the market stalls.

Just outside the walls of Ur, archaeologists have found some very interesting graves, dating from about 3200 B.C. There are 16 of them, and they are known as 'royal' graves, although we are not absolutely certain that they were the graves of kings and queens.

The Sumerian burial customs were unusual: the priests and the people brought their dead king (we will assume he was a king) on a chariot to the top of a long sloping roadway, or ramp, which led to the underground tomb. They carried him down the ramp, through large limestone-

*A staple crop is the principal crop on which people depend for food.

Clothing

The early Sumerians wore clothes made of lambs' skins. Then later they wove woollen cloth, and wore a kind of skirt with fringes. The women wore a one-piece dress leaving one shoulder bare. Sometimes they added a shawl with a jewelled pin. In old statues and pictures kings and gods are sometimes shown wearing a long robe, fastened on one shoulder.

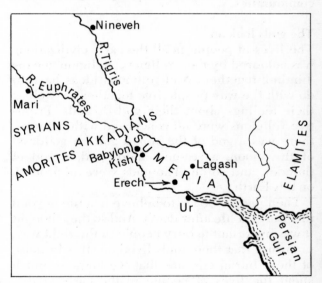

Ur

Ur was once a busy town and port on the shores of the Persian Gulf. But year by year the rivers brought fresh earth down from the highlands, and the sea built up ridges of sand along the coast. Ur was left high and dry, with its wharves and boat-sheds far inland.

Compare this map with a modern map of Iraq. You will see that Ur is now buried under an uninhabited desert about 150 miles from the sea. The sand of the desert has completely swallowed it up, and the only people who go to Ur now are archaeologists and historians. Ur might have been forgotten completely, had it not been mentioned many times in the Old Testament of the Bible. This encouraged archaeologists to dig in the sands for traces of the old cities of Sumeria. All our knowledge of Sumeria has been gained during this present century.

lined chambers, into the burial place itself. His drinking cups and bowls were put on the ground nearby. Then a curious (and to us, horrible) ceremony took place. Dozens of young men and women, all dressed in their best clothes, wearing gold and silver ornaments, and jewels made of precious stones, came down the ramp into the tomb. To the music of a harp they took their places in the chambers of the tomb. The king's chariot, decorated with gold and precious stones, was backed down the ramp, and the groom and driver led in the asses which had pulled the king's body from his palace to the tomb. Six of the king's soldiers, wearing their copper helmets, and with their copper daggers in their belts, marched down the ramp, and lined up near the opening. Then when everyone was ready, someone filled over 60 little cups with poison, one cup for each person. All these people, the attendants of the king in his lifetime, had come into the pit to die, so that they could continue to serve the king in his future life. In accepting the honour of becoming a king's or queen's servant or lady's-maid, a young man or woman knew that one day he or she might have to die by this kind of suicide.

Archaeologists can reconstruct the lives of ancient peoples from bones, broken pottery, beads, and even grains of wheat! So from these graves, we get a picture not only of the burial customs of the Sumerians, but also of the way they dressed, the musical instruments they played, their games, their food, and their chariots.

As we have seen, the thousands of ordinary citizens of Ur, Erech, Lalash, Kish, Mari, and all the other towns in the plain, lived the busy life of thriving agricultural communities. The town was the centre where all the produce from the neighbouring farms, and all the work of the craftsmen, were exchanged by barter. It was also the home of the scholars, among them mathematicians who worked out the number of days in a year, and who divided the day into hours, minutes, and even seconds. We still use the old Sumerian system, with its divisions based on 12's and 60's.

King Sargon

After about 500 years of civilization, the townsmen of Sumeria started to be worried by threats from outside their borders. The years were not always peaceful, and nomads from beyond the

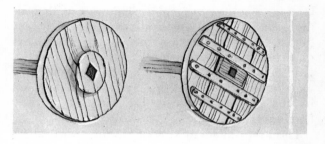

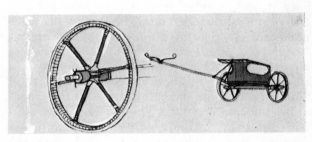

Wheels

Perhaps the invention of the wheel began when someone rolled a log under a heavy object, in order to move it from one place to another. The oldest wheel discovered so far comes from Sumeria, and dates back to 3000 B.C. It was made of three pieces of wood joined together. Painted clay models found in the Near East show that the spoked wheel has been known to mankind since about 2500 B.C. The Egyptians were using spoked wheels (as in the bottom picture above) from about 1500 B.C. They made Chariots much lighter and faster.

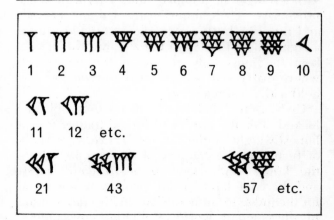

Sumerian numerals

17

rivers often tried to raid the rich cities. The townspeople built stout walls to keep them out, and they organized an army—the first in the world—for their defence. But to the north of Sumeria lived a people called the Akkadians. They copied the Sumerians' idea of an army, and in time they became stronger than the Sumerians. They invaded the country and took the whole land for themselves. They united the two kingdoms under one ruler. This meant that all the various towns owed allegiance, or loyalty, to the same king; they no longer had local quarrels about water-rights, or claims to fertile land, as they used to do in the days when there were many kings. But the taxes forced on them by the new rulers were far higher than they had been in the past.

The first Akkadian king of Sumeria was called Sargon, and he ruled from the northern town of Babylon in about 2380 B.C. The Akkadians were not as advanced as the Sumerians, but they wisely adopted the existing laws and system of government. They employed Sumerians as clerks in the government offices, and they used Sumerian writing, changing it to suit their own quite different language. The two peoples gradually came to accept one another as partners in one country. Both languages were spoken in the towns; but Sumerian very gradually died out. In time it was only used as a religious language in the temples.

Sumeria's Golden Age

In about 2150 B.C., 200 years after Sargon died, a great king named Ur-Nammu ruled in Sumeria. He was one of the strongest and most just rulers the Sumerians had ever known. This was the 'Golden Age' of Sumeria, and a time of great prosperity. Ur-Nammu made Ur his capital, and there he built a magnificent temple, called a ziggurat. At the top of the ziggurat the priests kept the most holy shrine of the moon-god, where every year a New Year's ceremony was held with great rejoicing.

Ur-Nammu dismissed dishonest officials, looked after the poor, and forced traders to use honest weights and measures. There were Halls of Justice at the gateway of the temple, where the king's representative heard court cases, and the complaints of the people. It was usual for the judge to 'sit in the gate to give judgement' in the ancient world. Religion, government, law and political power were all linked together,

King Sargon

and the Sumerians must have thought of them all as parts of one whole.

The priests, law-givers, and government servants were the most highly educated men in the community. The priests were greatly respected because they seemed to know all the right magic words to bring rain, or to stop plague, or to send away the swarms of locusts that sometimes ate the crops. Of course the priests could do none of these things, but they could use their knowledge of the weather, or of astronomy, to predict when rain, or famine, or a flood would come. They were the first real scientists in the world. Some of them were the first doctors, who no doubt relied on magic a good deal, but who also

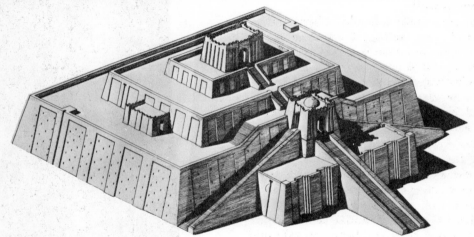

Ziggurat, present-day ruins and reconstruction
The centre part of the ziggurat at Ur was made of solid mud-brick. The outer walls were mud-brick with bitumen (tar) to bind them together. (There were no suitable rocks in Sumeria, so all stone for building had to be imported. The Sumerians used mud-brick for most of their buildings.)

The three staircases each had 100 steps, leading to the lower platform. The walls were painted black and red, with blue tiles on the walls of the topmost shrine.

We think the priests planted trees and flowers on the terraces, and that the slits in the walls were drainage holes for the water, which would otherwise have caused the centre of the ziggurat to swell and crumble.

used herbs, poultices, and ointments. They even performed surgical operations — though we cannot say how many of their patients lived!

The Babylonians
Then suddenly everything changed. Two new tribes, called the Elamites and the Amorites, invaded Sumeria. The ancient ways of the southern Sumerians were taken over by their conquerors, who recognized that the people in these old towns were superior in knowledge and in art

and in government. But in the north, the Sumerians refused to submit to the foreigners' rule, and they set up a king of their own at Babylon.

King Hammurabi
The sixth king of the new Babylonian line was called Hammurabi. He reigned in about 1780 B.C. He took his armies into southern Sumeria, and he conquered the Amorite and Elamite kings. He reunited the country into one great kingdom, stretching from Nineveh to the Persian

Gulf, and from the Elamite Mountains in the east to the borders of Syria. From this time onwards we call the Sumerians 'Babylonians', because the capital city was Babylon. The old capital, Ur, gradually lost importance until it became just a small market town.

In the wars against the Amorites and Elamites, Hammurabi destroyed a great many of Sumeria's ancient buildings; but when peace was restored he organized the rebuilding of towns, and encouraged the farmers to clear the canals and water-works. He built a marvellous new ziggurat in Babylon—the legendary 'Tower of Babel' mentioned in the Bible. In the book of Genesis we read that the labourers working on the Tower spoke many different languages. Certainly by then the Babylonians were a very mixed people, and no doubt they were using slave-labour from other countries as well.

Hammurabi also built schools, where young scholars copied texts, telling them how to be good citizens. The exercise books of Babylonia were squares of dried mud, or clay. The boys wrote on the clay with their wedge-shaped 'pens'. (The Latin for 'wedge' is *cuneus* from which we get the word 'cuneiform'.) The hardened clay was thrown away afterwards, and some of the exercises were found hundreds of years later, in the ruins of the old Babylonian towns.

One of these exercises said: 'He who shall excel in tablet-writing shall shine like the sun'. The schoolboys' task was by no means easy, for whereas we have between 20 and 30 letters in our alphabets, *they* had to learn between 600 and 700 different symbols! Hammurabi himself was a fine letter-writer, and we have found many writings on literature and science dating from his time.

Hammurabi's tablet
Here are some of the laws which scribes wrote on stone for all to read. Some were very harsh. Do you think they were just?

- If a house falls down and kills someone, the builder's son shall die.
- If a man steals from the temple, he must pay back ten times the value of the stolen article.
- If a man breaks your tooth, you may break his in return.
- A careless or spend-thrift wife, [one who spends too much money], may be made into a slave, or drowned.
- If a carrier loses a man's goods, the man may claim five times the value of the goods.
- If a doctor kills his patient while using a bronze knife, his hand shall be cut off.

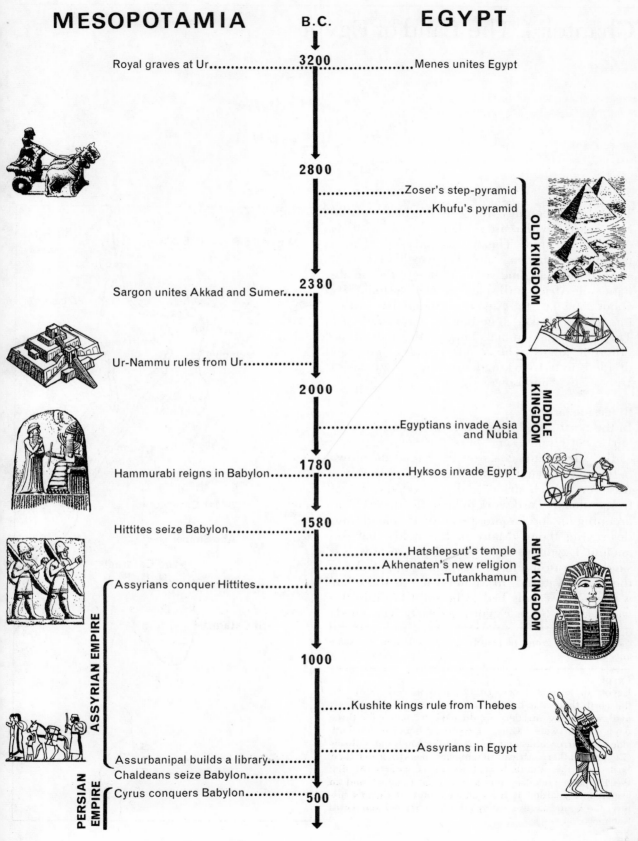

MESOPOTAMIA

B.C.

EGYPT

3200 — Royal graves at Ur .... Menes unites Egypt

2800

.... Zoser's step-pyramid

.... Khufu's pyramid

2380 — Sargon unites Akkad and Sumer ......

OLD KINGDOM

Ur-Nammu rules from Ur ....

2000

.... Egyptians invade Asia and Nubia

MIDDLE KINGDOM

1780 — Hammurabi reigns in Babylon .... Hyksos invade Egypt

1580 — Hittites seize Babylon ....

.... Hatshepsut's temple

.... Akhenaten's new religion

.... Tutankhamun

Assyrians conquer Hittites ....

NEW KINGDOM

1000

.... Kushite kings rule from Thebes

.... Assyrians in Egypt

Assurbanipal builds a library ....

ASSYRIAN EMPIRE

Chaldeans seize Babylon ....

Cyrus conquers Babylon 500

PERSIAN EMPIRE

Chapter 4 The Land of Egypt

The various peoples living by the banks of the Nile were divided into 'clans*', each with its own animal-sign. There was a jackal clan, a falcon clan (a falcon is a bird of prey like a hawk), a crocodile clan, and so on. (Some of the inhabitants of Africa still have a clan-system.) By about 3500 B.C., the Egyptian villages had grown into towns, linked together by the river Nile. The sacred clan-animals became the gods of the different towns. The whole country was now divided into two kingdoms: the kingdoms of Upper Egypt and Lower Egypt.

Riverside farmers

In the north, the Lower Nile valley had a warm, fairly wet climate, and here the people grazed cattle, sheep and goats on the broad meadows between the marshes and streams. Upper Egypt was very much drier, and it needed a lot of tremendously hard work to keep the desert from creeping on and on into the cultivated lands and destroying them. (Many of the fields that the ancient Egyptians once ploughed are now just sand.) The problem in Egypt was how to keep the fields watered; in Sumeria it was the other way round—canals had to be built to drain the water away. So in Egypt the yearly Nile floods

*A clan is a group of people descended from the same ancestor.

Egypt

Egypt, in ancient times, could be defended easily. To the north there was the sea, and to the north-east a desert over which any invaders would have to march for three days without water. Upper Egypt was bordered on both sides by barren cliffs and desert. In the south the Nubians (Egypt's southern African neighbours) could not get their boats past the waterfalls that we call Cataracts. At first the Egyptian boundary was at the First Cataract, and an armed fort guarded it from attack. Later in Egypt's history, the boundary was extended to the Second and Third Cataracts.

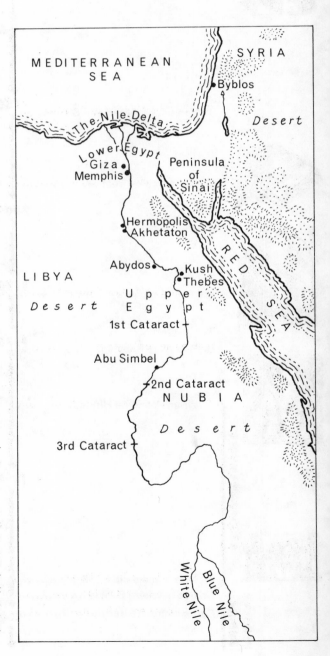

were welcomed with relief, for they brought fresh fertile soil to the land, and moisture for the spring planting.

There are two main branches of the Nile; the two rivers called the White and the Blue Nile meet at Khartoum in the Sudan. In July, August and September, the rains that fall near Lake Victoria swell the White Nile, and the snows on the Ethiopian mountains melt into the Blue Nile. The High Nile Festival, a time of great rejoicing, marked the beginning of the floods in ancient times. Then the farmers waited for the land to reappear, so that in November they could plant their crops in the rich black soil.

Besides grain, which grew plentifully, the farmers planted lentils and beans, onions, leeks and cucumbers. They used domestic animals to tread the seeds into the thick mud. The fields were separated from each other by little hard-mud walls, a foot or two high. They had to be rebuilt every November, and records were kept to show where each man's boundaries lay: here was the beginning of geometry—can you see why?

In the farm enclosures, farmers kept ducks, geese, hens and cows for fattening. Almost all the countrymen lived by farming. Some of them owned their own farms, but most were paid labourers. Even so, it was possible for everyone to live a reasonably happy (though hard-working) life during the peaceful periods of Egypt's long history.

Egypt becomes one kingdom

In about 3200 B.C., a powerful king united the two kingdoms, and became the sole ruler of Upper and Lower Egypt. We call this king Menes, though the deeds he is supposed to have done may really have been the work of several different kings. Menes belonged to the falcon clan, and the falcon became the symbol of kingship in Egypt for the next 3000 years. This falcon-god was called Horus.

Menes built Memphis as the capital of his new, united country. He dammed the Nile to control the yearly flooding, so that the water was distributed more evenly over the land, and for a longer period. Already Egypt was a land rich in farm products; in the wonderful work of goldsmiths and coppersmiths; in art and in culture. The state was well organized and well run.

Much later, the kings of Egypt were called 'Pharaoh' by the people; but nowadays we

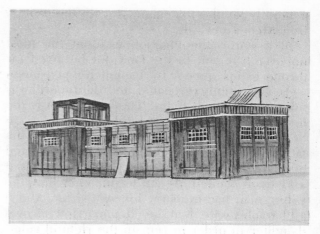

Egyptian house
Those who could afford to do so built themselves spacious houses of mud-brick and wood, with courtyards, pools and green gardens. For the next 3000 years, Egypt remained at this civilized level, in a way which the world has never seen since. Egyptian houses, temples, statues, paintings and tombs are among the most splendid ever created. Art and literature reached a very high standard.

Note that a nation does not have to have machines and electrical or atomic power to be civilized. At first the word just meant 'living in cities'.

The Narmer Palette
This is one of the oldest surviving pieces of carving from Dynastic Egypt. It shows Pharaoh Narmer (who may be the same as Menes) holding an enemy by the hair and striking him. This became a familiar attitude in later pictures of Pharaohs. The falcon sits near the king, and at the bottom lie dead enemy soldiers. Narmer here wears the White Crown of Upper Egypt. On the other side of the slate (not pictured here) he is wearing the Red Crown of Lower Egypt.

generally apply this name to all the rulers, from Menes onwards.

In a sense, the Pharaoh was not the most important person in the land, for he owed his throne to his queen. In ancient Egypt women were very highly respected, and all property was inherited through them. The Pharaoh was the husband of the queen, and did not rule because he himself had a right to the throne; he was the father of the next heiress, and *her* husband became the next Pharaoh. This meant that if a Pharaoh wanted his son to rule after him, the young man had to marry his own sister. And if a Pharaoh's wife died, he often married his own daughter in order to remain the rightful ruler.

Nevertheless, the Egyptian people honoured the Pharaoh, and not his wife, as the head of the country. They thought of him as a god whom they could actually touch and see. Besides having Horus as his own 'personal' god, he was to the Egyptians the living representation of the sun-god, Re, without whom there would be no life. When a Pharaoh died, they said that he joined the sun on its daily journey across the sky.

The Egyptians were a people who respected tradition, and throughout these 3000 years they did not change their way of life very much. So we can talk about their religion and their customs in a general way, and what we say will apply (with only minor variations) for any part of their 3000 years of civilization.

Priests and gods

The religion of the ancient Egyptians is difficult for us to understand—there seem to be so many different gods and goddesses. One reason for this is that when Menes united the clans, all their various gods had to have some part in the new religion and government. Later, other gods were 'imported' from foreign lands, and these were worshipped together with the old gods. The Egyptians were a very religious people, and their gods brought comfort and hope, and strength to endure the terrible years when the Nile did not flood properly, and there was famine. In countries south of Egypt, the kings were the 'rain-makers', who were supposed to be able to control the weather; in Egypt, where it hardly ever rained, the Pharaoh was the 'controller of the Nile'.

Next to the Pharaoh, the priests became the most important people in the land, not only because they talked to the gods, but also because

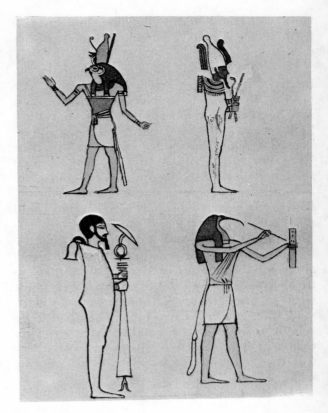

Gods of Egypt
There were hundreds of gods in Egypt, all with their functions and duties. Some of the most important are:

Horus; (top left) the falcon-headed god, was the Pharaoh's own god and is often seen wearing the Double Crown of Egypt.

Osiris; (top right) murdered by his brother, his body was cut up and scattered through the land. Isis, his sister-wife, collected the pieces together and buried them. Osiris was the god of the next world and the judge of souls.

Ptah; (bottom left) was a powerful god often shown wearing a Pharaoh's beard. He was the protector of craftsmen.

Thoth; (bottom right) the ibis-headed god of wisdom, learning, medicine, magic and all the skills practised by the priests.

Anubis; the jackal watched over all the ritual concerned with the dead.

they could predict flood or famine. As in Sumeria, they in fact did this by observation—that is they noticed how the stars and planets behaved, they noticed how the river flooded every year at about the same time (when the stars were in the same place in the sky), and they used this knowledge to tell people when to sow their crops. The farmers, and even the more educated townspeople, thought the priests had learnt their wisdom directly from the gods.

It was from these wise men that the Pharaohs learnt how to govern the country. A Pharaoh's training was very thorough. He had lessons in reading and writing; he was taught to hunt, to throw the light spear called a javelin, and to fight with sword and shield; and he was instructed in the details of his religion. The Egyptians liked to think that their Pharaoh was as wise and as fit as possible. They said of one of them that he could 'shoot at a metal target of one palm's thickness and pierce it in such a way that his arrow would stick out on the other side'. And of another Pharaoh: 'There is nothing that he did not know, he was Thoth in everything.' (What do you think this meant?)

Writing

Egyptians were already familiar with writing in the days of Pharaoh Menes. They had simply copied the Sumerians' idea of drawing little pictures of whatever they wanted to record. But whereas the Sumerians simplified their picture-writing very early, the Egyptians continued to write in pictures for centuries.

Each little picture originally stood for one word, or for one idea. Scribes (professional writers or clerks) recorded the major events of a Pharaoh's reign, and even the daily lives of the noblemen. Sculptors and artists recorded their history on the walls of temples and tombs. The quotations in this chapter and in Chapter 5 come from these inscriptions.

Later the Egyptians did develop a simpler form of writing, though they still used many of the same pictures. Instead of writing a different picture for each word, they used pictures to represent sounds as well as ideas. It is as if in English we wrote the word *idol* by drawing pictures of an eye and a doll, like this:

Later still, many of the pictures stood for single letters, or combinations of letters, almost like our alphabet—so then they had pictures which were words, pictures which were sounds, and pictures which stood for letters, all in one piece of writing. This is what makes hieroglyphics, as these kinds of symbols are called, so difficult for us to read.

Papyrus

The papyrus plant had many uses in ancient Egypt. The stems were cut and bound together to make baskets and containers, and were even used in building the pleasure-boats, fishing-boats and ferries which sailed on the Nile. The stalks were also hammered into a pulp to make a kind of paper. (*Papyrus* comes from the old Greek name for the plant: from it we get our word 'paper'.)

The papyrus lakes of Egypt have disappeared now. The level of the surrounding land dropped, and the sea came in, killing the plants. Other lakes which existed in the days of the ancient kingdoms have since dried up.

Hieratic script

For more 'day-to-day' writing—lists, or letters, the Egyptians sometimes used a much simpler and more flowing form of writing called 'hieratic'.

Besides learning to write, the Egyptians learnt to count and to reckon. They were very good at this, as we can see when we look at the monuments and pyramids they built. Their mathematicians, without our knowledge of algebra or trigonometry, worked out angles and heights to a fraction of an inch.

Noblemen sent their children to school when they were about seven years old. They became the priests, the doctors, the scribes, and the tax-collectors of Egypt. To maintain a high standard, the children were made to work very hard. An Egyptian proverb said: 'A youngster's ear is on his back; he listens when he is beaten.'

Craftsmen, artists and peasants

The upper classes, then, were all literate (able to read and write). Just below them in the social scale came the craftsmen, most of whom were not literate. The sculptors carved enormous granite statues of the Pharaohs, their queens, and the gods; the goldsmiths, coppersmiths and gem-cutters made beautiful delicate jewellery for rich noblemen and their wives to wear, and cups, bowls and ornaments for their houses. Builders hardened mud-bricks in the sun, and built spacious houses and temples. Gardeners planted trees and dug ornamental pools in the noblemen's gardens. Carpenters carved wood, brought all the way from Lebanon in Syria, and made furniture, which they often inlaid with precious stones, or covered with sheets of thin gold.

Most of the Egyptians—the ordinary peasants—did not have any of these things. They worked in the fields, repaired canals, fed the animals, took their rations of food in payment, and went home at night to their crowded little mud huts.

Dynastic Egypt

Right at the end of Egypt's long civilization, a priest named Manetho was ordered by his Pharaoh to write down the history of the country from the very beginning. Manetho very reasonably divided the rulers up into families, and called each line of rulers of the same family a dynasty. We still use his divisions now, because modern scholars have found that they are remarkably accurate. Menes, according to this list, was the first king of the First Dynasty, and Manetho himself lived during the Thirty-first Dynasty. We also divide the 3000 years up into 'kingdoms'. We call the three periods of Egypt's greatness:

The Old Kingdom	about 2800–2180 B.C.
The Middle Kingdom	about 2130–1780 B.C.
The New Kingdom	1580–1080 B.C.

The gaps between the kingdoms were periods in which weak Pharaohs allowed the country to fall into disorder and civil war, and invading armies took control.

In the next chapter we will see how Egypt was a country concerned with its own affairs in the Old Kingdom, and how gradually the people came into contact with other civilizations and peoples beyond their borders.

Egyptian Dress

Egyptian clothing was made of linen so finely woven that it might have been silk. Both men and women wore simple garments. The Pharaoh, the nobles and the officials all wore a short belted skirt, folded and pleated, sometimes into a stiff triangular 'apron' in front. Later on the fashion was to wear the skirt longer. Men often wore a striped cloth on their heads.

On ceremonial occasions the Pharaoh wore the Double Crown on his head, and a false beard was strapped to his chin. When he was not wearing the Crown, he wore an ornament called a 'uraeus'. It was shaped like the heads of two snakes, the cobra and the viper.

Women wore a long garment reaching the ankles, pleated and folded according to the latest fashion. Both men and women wore wigs in public. Women used cosmetics, and outlined their eyes with powdered malachite—a form of copper-ore—as protection against too much sun, and against eye-disease.

Labourers and slaves sometimes wore a loincloth round the waist; but many of them were completely naked.

Chapter 5 The Three Kingdoms

The Old Kingdom c.2800—2180 B.C.

The Egyptians of later ages came to think of the Old Kingdom as the Golden Age, when Egypt was at her most glorious. The state was highly organized, and there were many officials working in the government offices. The country was divided up into 20 'nomes' or districts, and administered by officials called 'nomarchs', all of whom were under the control of the central government at Memphis. The nomarchs were responsible for seeing that the canals were kept in order, and that the people paid their taxes regularly.

Taxes were paid 'in kind', that is in goods not money, and tax-collectors had the difficult job of receiving cattle, grain, tools, carvings and flax from each wage-earner in every home. Money—that is, coins with a certain fixed value—had not yet been invented. Early trade in the Nile Valley was carried on by barter. People exchanged property with each other. Later, the Egyptians adopted a system whereby every article to be exchanged had a fixed 'price'. A spiral or twist of copper was used as a measure, or unit. Thus a cow might be worth 40 units, and would buy (say) 4 lengths of fine linen, each worth 10 units. The units *themselves* were not used for buying and selling. The Egyptians did not think of the much simpler plan of using them as money.

The Pyramids

Much of the wealth of the country went into the building of huge tombs for the Pharaohs. They were buried with all their property around them, for, like the Sumerians, the Egyptians believed that in the next world the Pharaoh would need his furniture and clothes, his servants and his food (though in Egyptian graves, the servants were represented by statues).

Zoser's step pyramid and the god Imhotep
The step-pyramid of the Third Dynasty Pharaoh Zoser was designed by a nobleman named Imhotep. He was the 'Chief of the Works of the King of Upper and Lower Egypt'. The Egyptians remembered Imhotep for centuries because of his skill in medicine, and his knowledge of literature. They even worshipped him as the god of medicine, and associated him with Thoth, god of wisdom. Pilgrims went to his burial place for thousands of years, bringing mummified ibises to his grave as gifts. Why did they bring ibises, and not any other creature?

Menes' grave was a flat square tomb called a 'mastaba'. Later rulers built other smaller squares on top of the mastaba, making a tall structure which we call a 'step-pyramid'. They look rather like ziggurats, but they were tombs, not temples.

The Pyramids at Giza, near Cairo, tombs of the Old Kingdom Pharaohs Khufu, Kaefre and Menkaure*, were the next development in tomb design. The steps of a mastaba were filled in to make a smooth slope, which was coated with white limestone. Most of the limestone has gone now, so we have no proper idea of the effect these shining white pyramids had on the people living 4000 years ago. They must have been dazzling in the harsh Egyptian sunlight.

The Pharaoh himself watched his tomb being built, and his people often had to labour for as long as 20 years to ensure that their god-king would 'live for ever'. It was important to *them*, because of his relationship with the sun-god. So every winter season, some of the labourers rowed boats carrying great blocks of granite up the river from quarries in the eastern hills; others dragged the blocks from the banks of the Nile to the site of the new pyramid. The mere size of the work is astonishing to us today. These men cut stones with knives that were made only of soft bronze, with harder inset cutting-edges; and the stones themselves were so hard that they have lasted until now without 'weathering'. They had no pulleys, or cranes for lifting, and no mechanical engines. They put all the huge stone blocks into place with the help of wooden rollers and levers only. Yet they built the pyramids so accurately that it would be hard for us (with all our machines) to better them.

Until the nineteenth century A.D., when the Americans began to construct 'skyscrapers', Khufu's pyramid was the highest building in the world. His son Khaefre built the famous Sphinx next to his pyramid; the face of the Sphinx is probably a portrait of the king.

Since the Pharaoh had absolute authority, he was able to command his subjects to work for him on the time-consuming task of building his pyramid. He was their god, and they could not complain. His councillors and officials were often members of his own family, and the Vizier (a sort of Prime Minister) was often his eldest son.

*They are sometimes called Cheops, Chephren and Mycerinus, because this is how the Greeks later spelt their names.

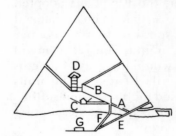

A Ascending gallery
B Grand gallery
C Queen's Chamber
D King's Chamber
E Descending gallery
F 'Well'-escape route
G Unfinished Chamber

The pyramids of Giza and the Sphinx
These are the pyramids we know so well today. But they are by no means the only ones still standing in Egypt. In ancient times there were pyramids stretching for 100 miles up the Nile. The picture at the top shows the Sphinx with the pyramids behind before the site was excavated in A.D. 1925. Below it, the full splendour of the Sphinx can be seen after the removal of thousands of tons of sand and earth.

A cross-section of Khufu's pyramid shows that it is not all hollow. The King's Chamber was shut off by workmen with huge granite blocks, pushed up into the gallery marked B. They then 'escaped' down the tunnels marked F and E, which they blocked up behind them.

Each nome was administered in much the same way, often by members of one family.

In the Old Kingdom, the whole of Egypt was working for the Pharaoh. To us, now, this seems an incredible way of life. But it certainly united the country and made it prosperous.

Once the state of Egypt had been organized, and was running smoothly, the Pharaohs began to look beyond their borders. In the north there were already small towns on the eastern shores of the Mediterranean. The land known as Lebanon was famous for its beautiful trees, and as early as the Second Dynasty (about 3000 B.C.) the townsmen of Byblos, on the coast, exported wood to Egypt. (Egypt had very little wood of her own.)

The copper on which Egypt's prosperity depended, and the precious stone called turquoise for ornaments, came from Sinai, across the Red Sea. This desert land was so hot and uncomfortable to live in, that the Egyptians used only slaves or criminals as their miners. Thousands of them died in the terrible heat, and there was always a demand for fresh slaves. Most of these unfortunate people came from the south and west. Egyptian slave-raiders crossed the borders into Nubia and Libya, and drove their African captives to the waiting ships on the Red Sea. Towards the end of the Old Kingdom, caravans were travelling deep into the heart of Africa, and may even have reached the Congo forest.

Then the Kingdom collapsed completely. The nomarchs became too powerful for the Pharaohs to control properly; royal authority became weaker, and finally the Kingdom came to an end, as each nomarch tried to gain more territory for himself. 'The land trembled ... all the people were in terror, the villages were in panic, fear entered into their limbs.'

Mummy

Pyramids, mummies, sun-worship and building in stone were all 'invented' just before the Old Kingdom began. A mummy (so named from an Arabic word meaning 'tar') is a dead body which has been so treated that it does not decay immediately.

The Egyptians soaked the bodies of their Pharaohs and important nobles in ointments, and bound them in linen, before putting them into their tombs. Many of these bodies have been found wonderfully preserved in the hot dry air of Upper Egyptian pyramids and rock-graves. The graves were on the western side of the river, towards the setting sun. New Kingdom Pharaohs and officials were buried in the Theban hills.

The Middle Kingdom c.2130–1780 B.C.

Surprisingly, Egypt survived 50 years of unrest and disturbances, and arose again, almost as splendid as before. The new Pharaohs of the Eleventh Dynasty built their capital at Thebes, in Upper Egypt; and because of this, Amun, the god of Thebes, became powerful. He was declared equal to Re, and all Middle Kingdom Pharaohs now worshipped Amun-Re, even though in the Twelfth Dynasty the court returned to Memphis once more. The priests of Amun

were delighted, for their wealth and prosperity were greatly increased.

The noblemen of the land were more important than they had been in the Old Kingdom. They built themselves elaborately decorated tombs, in which painters drew pictures showing the way they lived. It is because of these pictures — many of which can still be seen in Egypt — that we have such a good idea of the lives of the ancient Egyptians. During this period, the Pharaohs were buried in very modest pyramids, often built only of mud-brick.

Pharaohs and noblemen of the Middle Kingdom prided themselves on being kind and tolerant. It was a duty of the rich to feed the poor, and tomb-inscriptions like this are common:

'I grew corn, I loved Neper the grain god. In every valley the Nile greeted me. None hungered or thirsted during my reign.'

That was written in a Pharaoh's tomb: we can also read how noblemen comforted widows and looked after orphans, and how judges were upright in their decisions, and free from dishonesty. At the time of the Middle Kingdom, people believed that there was a life after death only for those who had been good on earth.

Now that less of the Pharaohs' time was occupied with pyramid-building, they could instead find out what was happening in the rest of the world. 'Travel' in ancient times either meant trading expeditions, or it meant armed invasion. The Middle Kingdom Pharaohs tried both. Their trading caravans travelled far into Nubia in search of gold; and their 'Byblos ships'* sailed across the Mediterranean to Crete for pottery and to Syria for wood and cloth, and to Punt for spices and plants, wild animals and ivory. Nobody knows exactly where Punt was. It may have been a name for many different ports in the Indian Ocean and the Red Sea, or it may have been a name for the coast of Somaliland.

As often happens, along with increased trade went a desire to gain more control over other countries. A Pharaoh of the Twelfth Dynasty, Senusret III, ordered his nomarchs to raise an army for him. It probably consisted of about 20,000 men. He armed them with bows and arrows, spears, clubs and shields, and personally led them by boat across the Mediterranean to present-day Palestine. When they returned, after claiming their conquests for Egypt, they left envoys† behind to represent the Pharaoh. Other troops were sent south during this dynasty, far into Nubia. They set up fortresses along the trade routes, and left a permanent guard of soldiers to protect them. Only genuine African traders were now allowed north of the First Cataract. To the west of Egypt, soldiers were constantly on the look-out for raiding Libyans.

*The people of Byblos built sea-going ships for the Egyptians, in exchange for farm produce and metal goods.

†Representatives or special officers sent to a foreign country on behalf of the ruler.

Kushites
Round about the time of the Eleventh and Twelfth Dynasties (Middle Kingdom) a new people arrived in Upper Nubia, south of the Second Cataract. The Kushites were very much influenced by the Egyptians. When they managed to turn the Egyptians out of their lands, they built their own capital, Napata. They copied the Egyptian architecture and worshipped Egyptian gods. At the end of Egypt's history, Kushite kings ruled Upper Egypt as well as Kush.

Whenever they could, they turned them out of the oases in the desert, or captured them and made them work in the copper mines.

All the spoils* of these campaigns were brought back to Egypt. Some were given as tribute to the gods, and so the priestly possessions grew even larger. Nomads living beyond the borders of Egypt heard of this marvellous kingdom, where there was so much wealth. It sounded to them like 'a land of plenty'. In times of drought and famine they crossed the terrible deserts as refugees, asking only to be allowed to live peacefully, and graze their flocks on the rich meadows of Egypt. These people were Semites from Palestine and North Arabia, and because of their arrival, many Semitic words enriched the Egyptian language.

The Hyksos kings
By about 1800 B.C., many of these Asian and Arabian refugees had come into Egypt to settle. Soon they were powerful enough to take over for themselves some of the rich lands of the Nile delta. Then more Asians poured in from the north-east, armed with iron weapons, and driving iron chariots drawn by horses. This was the very first time horses and wheeled vehicles had been used in Egypt, although the Sumerians

*Spoils are the possessions taken from a defeated enemy.

had had them for over a thousand years. We call these Asiatic invaders the 'Hyksos'. They took over the whole of Lower Egypt, and although native Pharaohs continued to rule in the south, they had no real power. We do not know very much about the 200 years of Hyksos control, because they did not keep records, nor did they build tombs or temples inscribed with hieroglyphics. They ruled in Egypt at roughly the same time as the Babylonians were supreme in the lands of Mesopotamia.

The New Kingdom 1580–1080 B.C.

At last there arose a leader strong enough to drive out the Hyksos, and revive the old Egyptian ways and customs. The new Pharaohs recognized the importance of chariots and horses and bronze armour, and the weapons they now used to restore law and order were all copies of the Hyksos ones. When there was a firm government again, they marched into Palestine, Syria and Mesopotamia in an attempt to drive the hated Hyksos well away from their borders. Parts of all these countries came under Egyptian rule, and it is very likely that during part of its history Crete, and perhaps Cyprus also, had to pay homage to the Pharaoh. From now onwards Egypt had a regular army, in peace as well as in war. Nubia was colonized, and the Pharaoh appointed as his representatives there the 'royal sons of Kush'. These men were responsible for the administration of the south, and for organizing the great trade caravans.

The conquest of new lands meant that even more wealth flowed into Egypt. All the subject kings had to send yearly tribute to the Pharaoh. Sometimes also, the messengers of foreign lands brought costly presents, in order to persuade the Egyptians to trade with them. We hear that:

'...while he (the Pharaoh) was hunting elephants, envoys from Babylon brought him gifts of lapis-lazuli, and from the heart of Asia Minor the great king of the Hittites sent silver and precious stones'. (Lapis-lazuli is a deep blue semi-precious stone.)

Trade flourished; Nubians from the south brought gold and ivory, the hard wood called ebony, leopard skins and ostrich feathers to Thebes, and exchanged them for the superb work of the Egyptian craftsmen and artists. They also brought slaves to work in the copper-mines, and to become the household servants, dancers and musicians in rich Egyptian homes.

Egyptian ships once more sailed up the east coast of the Mediterranean to Byblos, and returned with cargoes of 'cedar of Lebanon'. Sea-going ships brought back from Crete and Greece barrels of olives and wine, and bales of cloth. Hatshepsut, a queen of the Eighteenth Dynasty, imported from Punt:

'...fresh myrrh trees, ebony and pure ivory, with green gold of Emu, with cinnamon wood, with two kinds of incense, eye-cosmetic, with apes, monkeys, dogs, and the skins of the southern panther.'

A ship of Queen Hatshepsut being laden with treasures from Punt

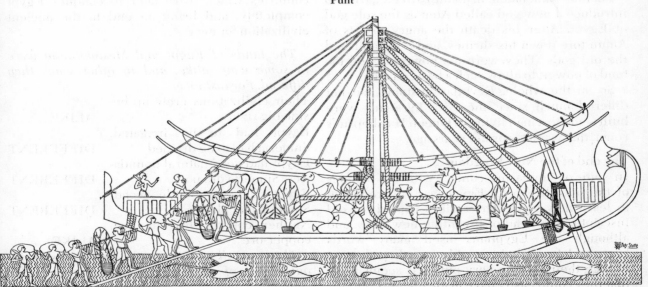

She wrote this inscription on the walls of her temple at Thebes, and planted the myrrh trees in the temple gardens.

Temples and rock-tombs

Huge sums of money were constantly being spent on the temples, and on paying priests to continue with prayers and offerings for the Pharaohs of the past. The burial customs changed in the New Kingdom, and labourers now cut great caves out of the rocks in the Theban hills. The walls were covered with inscriptions, and all the rooms were filled with furniture, clothing, food, flowers and statues. Then the cave-mouth was closed with rocks and plaster, and disguised to make it as unnoticeable as possible. Tomb-robbery was by now a great 'occupation' in Egypt, and watchmen were constantly on the look-out for thieves. Hardly any of the rich furnishings or jewels — or even the mummies themselves — were left untouched. There may of course still be graves that have not been found at all, but it is doubtful.

Rich people in Egypt during the New Kingdom lived in great luxury. They held parties, went for excursions on the river, were entertained by musicians and dancers, and hunted for wild animals or game-birds. There was plenty of food and drink for them, some of it imported. They had no wish to change their lives, and very little curiosity about peoples living outside Egypt. If a new god was introduced from abroad, they accepted him, but continued to worship the old gods as well.

Pharaoh Akhenaten, in about 1375 B.C., tried to introduce a new god called Aten as the sole god of Egypt. After his death the angry priests of Amun tore down his shrines, and re-established the old gods. They were too powerful, and too fond of power, to allow such a basic change.

So on the whole, Egyptian customs had not differed much since the Giza Pyramids were built — and to a man living in Queen Hatshepsut's reign, that was a thousand years ago.

The end of the New Kingdom

In spite of increasing contact with the peoples of the outside world, Egypt was still reluctant to learn new ways. The scribes copied out old inscriptions instead of inventing new ones, and although the Egyptians used many words borrowed from their neighbours, they did not change their writing very much. It seems to us that they could easily have made the next import-

Tutankhamun's mask
One tomb that robbers did not strip was that of a young Pharaoh named Tutankhamun, who reigned in about 1360 B.C. The tomb was found only 45 years ago, and in it were magnificent pieces of furniture, jewellery, pottery, statues and weapons. The Pharaoh's mummy was still undamaged. A mask of gold and lapis-lazuli covered his face, and his body was encased in a series of three golden coffins or caskets, one inside the other, carved in the shape of a man, and richly decorated. All this treasure was buried 'for ever', which tells us how very wealthy the country must have been. The contents of the tomb are now on show in the Cairo Museum.

ant step and invented an alphabet, but they never did so.

Even their attempts at colonizing other countries became half-hearted, and they were finally turned out of all the lands they had conquered. All real progress now took place in the new vigorous nations north and east of Egypt — countries which were later to conquer Egypt completely, and bring an end to the ancient civilization for ever.

The lands of Egypt and Mesopotamia were in some ways alike, and in other ways they differed. For instance:

Their civilizations grew up beside big rivers	ALIKE
Egypt had to be irrigated; Sumeria had to be drained	DIFFERENT
Egypt had good natural boundaries; Sumeria did not	DIFFERENT
Egypt had very little wood; Sumeria had plenty	DIFFERENT
Neither country had its own copper-ore	ALIKE

These are all geographical comparisons. Write out a list of similarities and differences in: religion, language, writing, politics, transport.

Chapter 6 Nations of the Near East

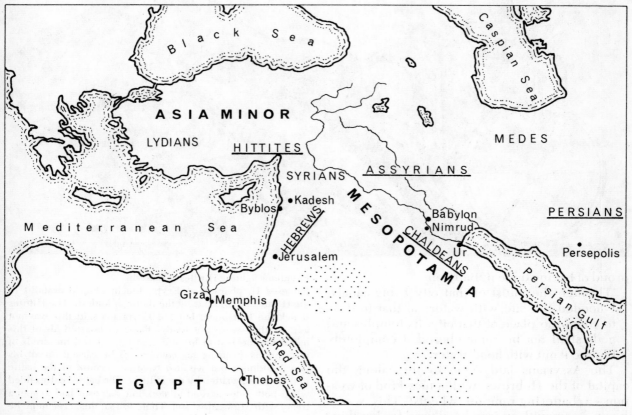

Map of the Ancient Near East
During the time of the New Kingdom in Egypt, the most powerful nations of the Near East were, in turn, the Hittites, the Assyrians, and the Persians. The Hebrews, as we shall see, were not warriors. They are important to us for a completely different reason.

THE HITTITES were a tough warrior nation. They were the first great western peoples to use horses—long before the Hyksos invasion of Egypt. Their soldiers poured into Babylon in about 1580 B.C., and 30 years later Egypt had to make a treaty with them.

THE ASSYRIANS were in many ways like the Babylonians, speaking a closely related language, and using the same cuneiform script for their writing. They too invaded Babylon, and broke the power of the Hittites. Their troops were well-disciplined, and for 700 years they were very much feared because of their great cruelty.

Sennacherib, who ruled the Assyrians from 705–681 B.C., was a terrible destroyer. Here is an ancient description of the damage he was

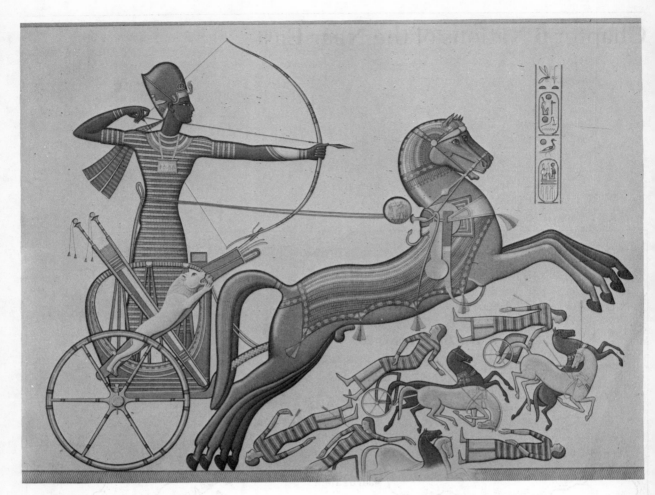

proud of having done in Babylon:

'Through the midst of that city I dug canals; I flooded the site with water: so that in days to come the place of that city, its temples and gods shall not be remembered, I completely blotted it out with flood-water.'

The Assyrians laid siege to Jerusalem, the capital of the Hebrews, with a new kind of weapon—a battering-ram on wheels. This was a heavy beam with an iron head used for breaking down walls or gates. In 667 B.C. they conquered Egypt, and divided the land into 22 districts under Assyrian governors. Right at the end of the great Assyrian empire there ruled a king named Assurbanipal. He came to the throne in 668 B.C. He was a well-educated and wise man, anxious that his country should live in peace. He collected all the old Sumerian texts he could find, and made a library which contained 22,000 tablets. Many of these tablets were found recently in the ruins of Assurbanipal's palace, and have since been studied by our scholars.

Egyptians fighting Hittites at Kadesh

Rameses II, pharaoh of Egypt, fought king Muwatallis of the Hittites in 1285 B.C., at the Battle of Kadesh. The Hittites struck the first blow, but the Egyptians said this was not fair, as they were not ready! Rameses boasted about this battle for the rest of his life, and he ordered hundreds of inscriptions, praising his courage, to be carved on all his new buildings; but we also have an account of the battle in cuneiform, written by the Hittites. The battle really ended when both sides agreed to stop, but Rameses had to sign a treaty with Muwatallis' son. Then, to seal the agreement, he married one of the Hittite princesses.

THE CHALDEANS retook Babylon, and rebuilt it. Then another people conquered both the Assyrians and the Chaldeans. They were THE PERSIANS, a people with a new religion called Zoroastrianism (after its founder Zoroaster), who swept across Asia Minor in five short years. Egypt and Babylonia were among the countries which became Persian provinces, or *satrapies*, ruled by governors called satraps.

The Persians 550–520 B.C.

Cyrus the Great, King of Persia, was perhaps the wisest of all Emperors. He found that the towns he conquered were in many ways more civilized than his own, so he allowed them to continue with their own customs. He did not interfere with their government, or with their religion. As long as the conquered nations were loyal to Persia, paid their taxes, and sent soldiers to fight in his armies, they could live as they liked. The Babylonians, the Egyptians, the Syrians and the Lidyans were no match for the expert Persian archers. All these countries had to pay tribute to the Persians—a people they all thought of as 'barbarians'.

The Chaldeans had built a mighty wall round three sides of the new Babylon, and the waters of the river Euphrates guarded the fourth side. But Cyrus, according to one story, dug a channel and diverted the river away from the city. His armies entered Babylon by crossing over the dry river-bed without a fight. In Babylon, Cyrus found hundreds of Hebrew slaves, sons and daughters of the prisoners taken when Nebuchadnezzar, Chaldean king of Babylon, captured Judah, 50 years earlier. Cyrus allowed them to go free, and some of them made the long journey back to Jerusalem.

Cyrus's son, Cambyses, had to make a treaty with the king of Arabia before he could take his soldiers over the burning desert to conquer the Egyptians. The Arabians, in return for peace in their own lands, supplied him with camels, to carry men and equipment and precious water. The Persian troops entered Egypt, and soon captured Memphis. The Egyptians had already managed to drive out the Assyrians, but now there was no strong Pharaoh to bind the country together, and keep out the new invaders.

But the new occupation was not entirely bad for Egypt. The Persians realized that a contented satrapy was better than a discontented one, so they worked hard to raise the standard of living in Egypt. Once more there was a healthy trade with Asia, and the neglected temples and statues and monuments were repaired.

Now that they had gained a large part of the ancient civilized world, the Persians started to learn from the peoples they had conquered. They adapted the old Sumerian cuneiform writing, and made from it a simplified syllabary* of

*A syllabary is a set of symbols representing syllables or parts of a word.

only 41 symbols—a great advance on the hundreds of symbols the Sumerian school-children had had to learn. We owe our knowledge of Sumerian literature to Assurbanipal the Assyrian, but we discovered how to interpret their writing because of the Persians. For King Darius I, who followed Cambyses, ordered a huge inscription to be cut in a rock. In order that everyone would be able to understand it, the sculptors engraved the inscription three times—in Persian, in Sumerian, and in another eastern

Zoroaster

We do not know very much about Zoroaster, the founder of the Persian religion. He probably lived in about 600 B.C. In this religion there were two gods, Ahura Mazda, all-good, lover of truth, and god of purity and light; and his opposite, Ahriman, who was the creator of evil. Zoroaster taught that all men should be on the side of good. Evil to him was to be conquered by fighting against it continuously.

Zoroaster hated the old Persian beliefs, which included the burning of animals to keep the gods contented. His religious ideas spread right across Asia from the Aegean Sea to India. In India today we have the last remaining worshippers of his god—they are the Parsees.

Persepolis
Cyrus's grandson, Darius I, brought together masons, carpenters, goldsmiths and iron-workers from Egypt, Babylon, Assyria and Greece to build his capital city, Persepolis.

He was immensely rich, and he produced gold coins for use in trading. (He had copied the idea of money from the Lydians.) He also started a banking system, and our word 'cheque' comes from Persia.

language called Susian. This triple inscription was deciphered in the nineteenth century A.D. Linguists (people expert in languages) who could read ancient Persian worked out the meaning of the parallel text in Sumerian. So now they had plenty of clues to help them translate the tablets they had found in the ruins of Assurbanipal's library.

Besides taking over cuneiform writing from the Sumerians, the Persians also used the Egyptian calendar, and their scholars learnt Egyptian astronomy and medicine. The artists copied Assyrian sculpture, and the builders built temples and columns like those of the Egyptians. The Persians were great 'borrowers', and their own capital city benefited from the centuries-old knowledge of earlier civilizations.

In order to reach their satrapies more easily, the Persians built excellent roads. One road stretched all the way from Egypt, through Babylon to India. On these roads there were staging-posts or stopping-places where messengers were given fresh horses and food.

In Dynastic Egypt, some of the Pharaohs tried to build a permanent canal between the Red Sea and the Nile. For lack of proper attention, it was always falling into disuse. Now the Persians rebuilt it, and widened it to allow two huge rowing galleys to pass each other. By using the canal, traders could reach Punt by boat without having a long walk overland to the Red Sea.

But an empire created so quickly depended very much on the quality of its leaders. The army consisted mainly of foreign soldiers, though the king himself had a bodyguard of Persians called 'The Immortals'. The foreign soldiers naturally felt more loyalty for their own countries than for Persia, and could only be kept obedient by strict discipline. Persia needed time, and a series of strong kings, for her new satrapies to settle down. But as we shall see in Chapter

8, only 40 years after the Persians captured Memphis, a new king tried to enlarge the empire by further conquests to the west. He wrongly believed that the Persians were too strong for any enemy to resist.

The Jewish People and their religion

We have already talked about a people called the Hebrews, who also lived in Asia Minor at this time. They are not remembered for their conquests, or their worldly power. They were

The Jewish Temple at Jerusalem

During the migration from Egypt the Jews used a kind of tent, called the Tabernacle, as their holy place. Later this tent became the model for the great Temple of King Solomon who built it about 950 B.C. King Nebuchadnezzar of Babylon destroyed it in 586 B.C.

After the Babylonian captivity has ended, in 539 B.C.,

the Second Temple was built. (The picture above is a reconstruction of it.) About 20 B.C. Herod, King of the Jews, rebuilt this temple on a larger and grander scale but it was destroyed when the soldiers of the Roman Emperor Titus captured the city in A.D. 70 and never rebuilt.

quite unlike the Hittites, the Assyrians, or the Persians, for they did not try to enlarge their territory, or enslave other peoples. Yet in the history of the world they have played a great part: they have left us a religion which is a living faith for millions of people today—and from which two other present-day world religions stemmed.

The Hebrews (or Israelites) were a small nomadic tribe who came to settle in southern Palestine. During the early part of their history, the Pharaohs enslaved them as labourers for building temples and statues; and they have a tradition that Moses led them out of this captivity. They wandered for 40 years with their flocks through Arabia and up towards Mesopotamia and Palestine. Moses was their leader all this time, and he made for them a new system or code of laws, and taught them the new religion, which we now call Judaism.

Out of the dozens of mountain spirits worshipped by the nomads of Arabia, Moses told them that Yahweh was their own special God. He wrote down the laws of Yahweh, which the Israelites called the Commandments, on stone tablets. Yahweh's first Commandment is:

Thou shalt have none other gods but me.
and the second:
Thou shalt not make to thyself any graven (carved) image...
Thou shalt not bow down to it, nor worship it.

All the other tribes used to worship before images and statues of their gods (we can read about the people who worshipped a golden calf in the Bible). But Moses wanted to give his people the idea of a god who had no shape, but was everywhere, and in their own hearts. Akhenaten, an Eighteenth Dynasty Pharaoh of Egypt, had had the idea of a single god, but even he used the image of the sun for this god.

At the end of his life Moses pointed out to the Israelites the rich plains of Canaan in Palestine, and told them that Yahweh had led them to the promised land. The Israelites settled in Palestine, and they lived side by side with the Canaanites, who already had towns and villages there. But the Israelites remained tent-dwellers until about 1000 B.C., when a warrior-king named David captured the Canaanite town of Jerusalem and made it the capital of a new uni-

ted country. The Israelites and the Canaanites became one people. King David ruled over the whole of present-day Palestine, and grew rich by trading with Egypt and Babylonia, and by allowing these countries to use his ports.

In 700 B.C. Israel fell to the Assyrians, and then Jerusalem itself was captured by the Chaldeans in 588 B.C. We have already seen how Cyrus, King of Persia, took Babylon, and allowed the Israelites to go home again. During the unsettled times when Assyrians and Chaldeans were overrunning the country, the only thing that kept the Israelites united was their faith in Yahweh. Many times some of them had returned to worshipping other gods, particularly the 'baals' of the Canaanites. But their prophets (people who had a religious conviction that they could save their country from destruction) demanded that the Israelites return to the worship of Yahweh. They condemned the rich landlords, and told the people that Yahweh was punishing them for their sins by allowing their enemies to triumph.

Judaism was a personal religion. That is to say, every man went on believing in the power of Yahweh, even when he was far from his own country. In other lands, a man who went to live away from home would adopt the gods of his new town. The Israelites did not do this. Some of their finest writings show that even in captivity they continued to believe in Yahweh. From that time right up to the present, the Jews (as they are now called) have been a scattered people, rather than a 'nation', united only in their faith. Since 1948 some of them have created a national state, Israel, including what used to be the old land of Canaan, and call themselves Israelis.

The Bible begins with an account of the beginning of the world. In this story, God made the world in six days, and rested on the seventh day. In remembrance of this, the Jews kept (and still keep) Saturday as a holy day, on which they do no work. The idea of a holy day was copied by people of other religions, and even by people with no religion at all. So today we have one day in the week on which shops and offices are closed, and religious services are held. For Christians, and many non-Christians, the day of rest is Sunday.

Chapter 7 Far Eastern Religions

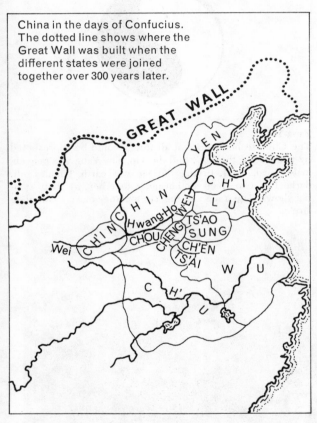

China in the days of Confucius. The dotted line shows where the Great Wall was built when the different states were joined together over 300 years later.

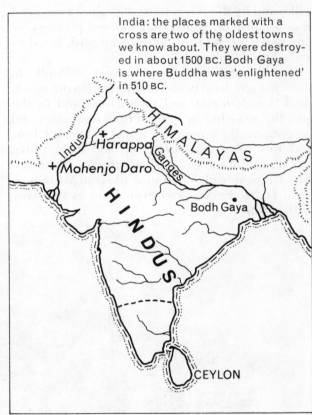

India: the places marked with a cross are two of the oldest towns we know about. They were destroyed in about 1500 BC. Bodh Gaya is where Buddha was 'enlightened' in 510 BC.

(1) CHINA

On the east coast of China, the first towns and villages were grouped along the river Hwang-Ho at about the time of Egypt's Middle Kingdom. (Look up the date of this on p. 26.) And although the Chinese did not build great temples or statues, as the Egyptians did, they already had all the basic characteristics of civilization which we have seen in North Africa and Mesopotamia.

The Chinese had their own system of writing, which by 1500 B.C. was so well developed that it must have been invented much earlier. They wrote down the names of their kings, and the lists of their crops, on pieces of bone, some of which have been found and read by our scholars. Chinese writing started as simple pictures, but was 'formalized' into a most elaborate system of 'characters' or symbols, which are used to this day. These characters are also really very complicated pictures.

Chinese wheelwrights (wheel makers) about 1700 B.C. built some of the earliest known wheels with spokes; and so their carts were lighter and

39

more comfortable than the Sumerian ones, with their heavy, solid wheels. The most commonly used animal for drawing carts, or even for riding, was the water-buffalo; though rulers and nobles used horses for their war-chariots. When a king died, his chariots and horses were buried with him in a deep pit, a custom which reminds us very much of the royal graves at Ur.

There was one other completely new discovery that the Chinese made—they found out how to spin the threads made by a certain kind of caterpillar called a silk-worm. They made clothes out of this spun thread, which we call 'silk', and by the 8th century B.C. they even used it as a fabric on which they painted pictures, or practised their beautiful writing with brushes and a kind of ink.

Travel outside China was very difficult—to the west are deserts and mountains, to the south, thick jungle-forest and mountains; and to the east the sea—but in spite of this, new ideas and inventions did sometimes travel between China and the west, particularly to and from India, the second of the two early eastern civilizations. The Chinese welcomed new ideas in astronomy from India, Persia, and even from as far away as Babylon.

Character

This is how the character for the word 'bright' probably developed:

The Chinese wrote first on bone, then they used bamboo strips. Later, they painted characters on silk panels.

Yang-Yin

The Chinese believed that all things could be represented by two forces, the Yang and the Yin. The Yang was heaven, male, hard, clear, bright; the Yin was earth, female, soft, dark. The two lived in harmony together, as their symbol shows. The Yang and the Yin together make a complete circle.

The Great Wall of China

Once China had been united, the emperor, Shih-Huang-Ti, built a 1,500 mile wall along the northern boundary, to keep out raiding nomads. It was built of earth and stone, with a roadway of bricks all along the top. At intervals there were watchtowers, where guards lit warning fires in times of danger.

Shih-Huang-Ti wanted his people to forget the past. He ordered all books, except those about medicine or agriculture, or divination, to be publicly burnt. Anyone who disobeyed was either burnt alive, or branded with a hot iron, and sent to work on the Great Wall.

The country was mainly agricultural, and the Chinese did not build great cities as other civilizations did. The nobles and lords built fortified castles, and their servants and tradesmen were grouped round the castles, outside the walls in a 'market' area. Everybody depended on everybody else, in a chain which led from the poorest slave or peasant, right up to the kings themselves. There was great respect for every kind of authority: a father was the master of his children, a lord had control over the lives of his servants, and the king had absolute power over all.

But the area over which a king ruled was limited. In time many states grew up in China, each with its own organization. For centuries the different states struggled against each other, and it was not until about 220 B.C. that China was united into one great empire.

Chinese religion and thought

The Chinese were a practical people, cheerful and hard-working. Their gods had always been the gods of nature: the soil, trees, mountains and streams. They used to regulate their daily lives by *divination* — that is, they tried to find out about the future. The Chinese method of divination was to write symbols on pieces of bone and then to break the bone to see where the cracks would come. They respected and revered the family, past, present and future. Each house had a little altar in one corner, and here the whole household prayed to the ancestors, whose names were written down and remembered for ever. The greatest sin a Chinese could commit was to dishonour his ancestors, by behaving in a manner they would have disapproved of. The family tradition thus had to continue so that each person who 'joined his ancestors' could be respected by his children and his children's children. So it was important to have children, and to bring them up to be well-behaved. Ancestor-worship was a good influence on behaviour, and it kept families together.

In ancient China, men loved to learn. The Chinese idea of a well-educated man was one who could write poetry, play music, paint, and talk intelligently. There were many schools where young men could go to listen to the words of wise teachers. Some of these teachers became famous, and their teachings have been remembered until the present day. One of them was a man named Kung-fu-tze, whom we call Confucius.

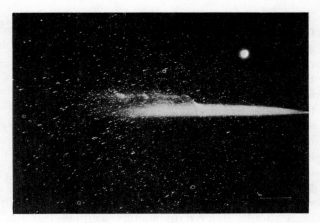

Halley's Comet
A few years before Shih-Huang-Ti's reign, the Chinese astronomers recorded the appearance of a great 'heavenly body'. We think this was the comet we now know as 'Halley's Comet'. In A.D. 1704 an English scientist named Edmund Halley discovered from old records that there is a comet which can be seen from our earth every 75 years. Its next appearance is due in 1985.

Confucius

The teachings of Confucius (552–479 B.C.)

Confucius was not a leader of religion, and he did not teach people about God, or a life after death. One of his pupils once asked him about this, and he replied, 'We have not yet learnt to know life. How can we know of death?' His teachings were about good government and social behaviour. The relationships between a man and his son, a ruler and his subjects, a husband and his wife, and an older and younger brother, should be the same; on the one hand kindness and thoughtfulness, and on the other, respect and obedience. Confucius believed that men should behave in society as they did in their own homes — the whole nation was one big family. 'Never do to others what you would not like them to do to you.' A good man, Confucius said, does not worry if his goodness is not noticed; he is more concerned with seeing goodness in other people.

Confucius thought that ceremonies and customs were important, and that the old Chinese traditions should be preserved. As a reward for honesty and right living, men might expect to have health and happiness in *this* life.

The Chinese listened to his words, and after his death his disciples (or followers) wrote them down. In time Confucianism became the state 'religion', and government servants had to pass examinations in the teachings of Kung-fu-tze before they could be promoted.

(2) INDIA

At about the time of Zoroaster in Persia (the sixth century B.C.), new ideas about religion, and the meaning of life, were forming in India as well as in China. People had reached a stage when they wanted to know why they were on earth at all, whether there was a life after death, and why they should behave well, rather than badly.

The ancestors of the Hindus had lived in India since about 1500 B.C. They had arrived as invaders from the north-west, travelling from central Asia through Afghanistan to north India. They had destroyed a people belonging to a much earlier civilization, based on the Indus Valley. They regarded themselves as better than the original inhabitants of India, many of whom still lived in villages and homesteads throughout the country, and this superiority gradually grew into the elaborate caste-system of the Hindus.

A caste was a group of people who all did the

Mencius

Mencius was a disciple of Confucius who carried on the teachings. This is one of his sayings: 'When Yi (a famous archer) taught people to shoot, he told them to pull the string on the bow its full length. The man who wants to cultivate himself must also develop himself to the full extent. A great carpenter teaches his apprentice to use squares and compasses. The man who wants to cultivate himself, must also have squares and compasses for his conduct.'

same traditional job, and who were linked together by marriage, and by custom. They were separated from people of other castes by strict rules, which forbade them even to eat with 'outsiders'. The top caste was that of the Brahmins or priests, and the lowest people of all had no caste — they were the 'untouchables'. In between were the warriors, merchants and farmers, servants and labourers. Nobody was allowed to marry outside his own caste; as a man was born, so he remained for the rest of his life.

By the sixth century B.C., Hinduism had developed into a very mixed religion. There were dozens of different gods and goddesses; there were legends of gods who were sometimes born as men; there were sacred cows; and there were cruel goddesses, whose mouths dripped blood. There was also a much more spiritual belief that the human soul, or Atman, could unite with the spirit of the universe, the Brahma. There are still so many different beliefs that Hinduism has been called 'the encyclopaedia of all religions'. Because of this wide variety of worship, Hindus are very tolerant of other religions.

Buddha (about 560–480 B.C.)

In northern India, near the Himalayas, around the middle of the sixth century B.C., there lived a Hindu king. In about 560 B.C., the king's wife bore him a son, who was called Siddhartha Gautama. One day, a holy man asked to see the child. The baby was carried to the holy man, and it put its feet on to his bowed head. The holy man immediately threw himself to the ground before the child, and when he saw this, the king did the same. The child's action was to them a sign that Siddhartha Gautama would become a religious teacher, greater than the holy man himself.

But the king wanted his son to become a great prince rather than a poor monk, so he asked the holy man, 'What shall my son see to make him retire from the world?' The holy man answered: 'The four signs—an old man, a sick man, a dead man, and a monk.'

So from that time onwards the king made sure that his son lived within the walls of the palace. The child was brought up in great luxury, and he never saw hunger, or sickness, or death. He grew up, married, and had a son of his own. Then one day, when he was 29 years old, he left the palace to see for himself what lay beyond its walls. And he saw 'the four signs'.

Now Hinduism taught that all people were tied to the Wheel of Life. When they died, they were born again, and so on for ever. The reward of a good life was a happy rebirth; and punish-

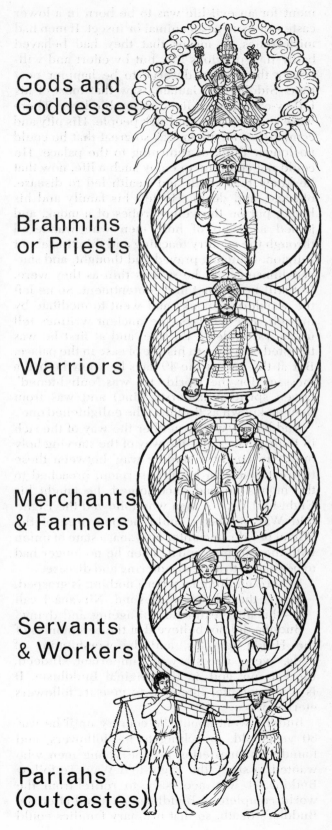

Gods and Goddesses

Brahmins or Priests

Warriors

Merchants & Farmers

Servants & Workers

Pariahs (outcastes)

The Caste System

A Hindu tries hard throughout his life to gain 'merit' (spiritual credit) for himself so that his next life on earth will be better. This is the only way to belong to a higher caste. It is impossible for him to improve his present position, but good behaviour might be rewarded in his next reincarnation (rebirth). Voluntary work, such as sweeping the temple grounds, giving food to beggars and to priests, gains a man merit.

ment for an evil life was to be born in a lower caste—or even as an animal or insect. If men had misfortunes, it meant that they had behaved badly in a previous life, but by effort and will-power they could deserve to be happier next time. Siddhartha Gautama saw that most of his fellow-countrymen lived miserable lives. There were so many poor and sick people. His pity and compassion for them was so great that he could no longer think of returning to the palace. He could not continue to enjoy such a life, now that he knew that youth and health led to disease, old age, and death. He left his family and his home, put on the yellow robes of a monk, and joined a group of holy men who wandered through the country teaching and thinking about religion. Gautama prayed and thought, and starved himself until he was as thin as they were. But still he did not find contentment. So he left the wandering monks and went to meditate by himself. For 49 days, the ancient writings tell us, he sat under a Bo tree, and at first he was tempted to return to his life of ease in the palace. But at the end of the 49 days he knew he had a message for the world. He was 'enlightened', (given spiritual understanding) and was from then on known as Buddha, 'the enlightened one'.

Buddha's way was neither the way of the rich in their palaces, nor the way of the starving holy men. He taught a 'middle way' between these two extremes. In his first sermon, preached to the monks he had once joined, he taught his Eight-fold Way. A man who followed the Eight-fold Way perfectly could become free of the Wheel of Life, and enter Nirvana, a state of union with the supreme spirit. Then he no longer had to be reborn to a life of suffering and disease.

'Where no thing is, where nothing is grasped, this is the Isle of No-Beyond, Nirvana I call it—the utter extinction of ageing and dying.'

Buddha did not believe that the ceremonies of the Hindu temples, and the worshipping of gods, were necessary or important. Indeed, there is no 'god' in the original Buddhism. It is a way of life, intended to give its followers eternal peace.

Buddha went about the country until he was 80 years old, preaching to his followers, and founding monasteries for the young men who wanted to study the Eight-fold Way. To follow Buddha, it was necessary to retire from the world completely. Buddhism changed after the Buddha's death, so that ordinary families could

Statue of Buddha

There are statues of the Buddha in all parts of the eastern world. Some show him standing, others sitting in the typical cross-legged position shown above. Many of these statues are beautifully carved and coated with gold. Buddha's Eight-fold Way consisted of:

Right Knowledge,	Right means of Livelihood
Right Intention,	Right Effort
Right Speech,	Right Mindfulness
Right Conduct	Right Concentration.

also live their lives according to the Eight-fold Way, but without Buddha's other rules about men not marrying, and not working for money.

Missionaries carried the Way to China, Tibet, Ceylon, Burma, Java, Mongolia, Japan and Korea, and each of these countries changed the original teaching a little, so that it fitted in with their own ideas of how to live. The Chinese added Buddhism to Confucianism, and most of them followed both Ways.

But it seems that none of these peoples liked to have only a 'Way'. They wanted a religion, with temples and gods and goddesses. So by 200 B.C., there were statues of Buddha in Buddhist temples, and even a whole host of 'Bodhisattvas' or saints, who were worshipped as disciples of Buddha. They worshipped the Amitabha Buddha, a kind and merciful god who lived in the 'Pure Land' of heaven; and a goddess named Kuan Yin, who guided the good to everlasting life. So even the idea of Nirvana changed in these other countries. By 600 A.D., both Buddhism and Confucianism were very different from the teachings of their founders. In India itself, where Buddha had lived, his 'Way' grew so like Hinduism again that it has now almost died out.

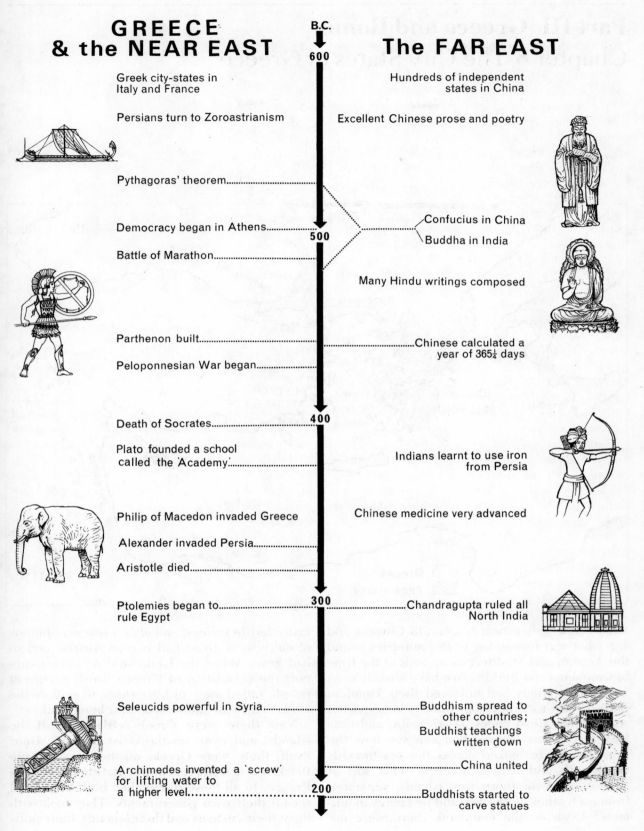

GREECE & the NEAR EAST

B.C.
600

The FAR EAST

Greek city-states in Italy and France

Hundreds of independent states in China

Persians turn to Zoroastrianism

Excellent Chinese prose and poetry

Pythagoras' theorem.................................

Confucius in China

Democracy began in Athens........... **500**

Buddha in India

Battle of Marathon............................

Many Hindu writings composed

Parthenon built.......................................Chinese calculated a year of 365¼ days

Peloponnesian War began......................

Death of Socrates............................. **400**

Plato founded a school called the 'Academy'......................

Indians learnt to use iron from Persia

Philip of Macedon invaded Greece

Chinese medicine very advanced

Alexander invaded Persia.....................

Aristotle died.......................................

Ptolemies began to............................. **300** ....Chandragupta ruled all rule Egypt   North India

Seleucids powerful in Syria...................Buddhism spread to other countries; Buddhist teachings written down

....China united

Archimedes invented a 'screw' for lifting water to a higher level................................. **200** ....Buddhists started to carve statues

45

Part III Greece and Rome
Chapter 8 The City States of Greece

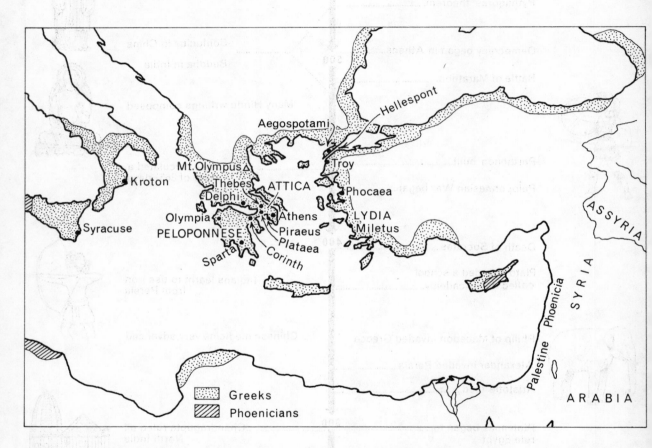

Let us now go westwards again to Europe, and see what was happening in the countries round the Aegean and Mediterranean Seas at the time of Confucius and Buddha. We have already seen how the Persians had enlarged their kingdom until by 520 B.C. they controlled a large part of Asia Minor. Read pages 34–37 again, and then look at the map above. You can see how the Persian empire looked across the sea towards the islands and bays of Greece. What sort of people lived on those tiny islands, separated from each other by the sea, and by craggy mountains? Even on the mainland, there were not

many fertile valleys, and after a few generations of cultivation, trees had become scarce, and so had grass. When the land could no longer support the population of Greece, small parties of people sailed away in little ships, to explore the lands to the east and west of their homeland.

Now there were Greek settlers on all the islands, and even on the coast of Asia Minor itself; there were Greeks on the shores of the Black Sea, and in present-day Italy and southern France. In all these places they built towns and set up their own governments. They took with them their customs and their legends, their skills and their traditions. They still thought of themselves as Greeks, even though their only connection with their homeland was through trade.

Greece, then, was not so much a nation, as a collection of city-states, each ruling itself, and each in turn rising to prosperity. Thebes*, Corinth, Miletus, Syracuse, Athens and Sparta were all at one time important centres, and the two we chiefly remember now are Athens and Sparta.

The emigration† of Greeks to new colonies caused a lively trade to grow up, and soon the sea-faring states (and in particular Athens) were among the most important traders in the Mediterranean and even the Black Sea. They copied the new silver coins which the Lydians had invented, and with this new currency they bought goods to enrich their cities.

Athens, with its port at Piraeus, was a powerful state with a fine navy. Part of the population of Athens was always away at sea, carrying oil and wine to distant lands, and bringing to Athens the grain which she could not grow herself. The soil of Greece was more suited to growing olives and grapes than wheat, and people everywhere rely on a starchy food like wheat, or rice, or maize, for making their 'staple' diet of porridge or bread.

The Greeks and the Persians at War

Cyrus, king of Persia, fought a great battle with Croesus, King of Lydia, in Asia Minor. Now Croesus at that time was overlord of the Greek states in Asia, in an area that the Greeks called 'Ionia'. Croesus lost the battle, and his empire, including Ionia, was taken by the Persians. The Ionians hated their new masters, and they rebelled against them, which caused the Persians to punish them severely.

When the Athenians heard that their fellow-countrymen were being persecuted by the Persians, they sent ships across the sea, and then marched overland with the Ionians, and burnt the Persian city of Sardis. Cyrus's son, Darius I, was furious that such a small city-state as Athens should defy the might of Persia. His own people were all his slaves; they could be beheaded, or have their property taken from them, whenever he said the word. Now he was determined to force his rule on the Greeks too.

*There are two towns called Thebes. Where is the other one?

†To emigrate is to leave one's own country to settle in another. To immigrate is to come to a foreign country to settle.

Greek pottery
The Greeks made beautiful pottery jars to hold wine and olive oil for export. They were sometimes decorated with geometric designs, and sometimes with pictures of gods, people and animals. Whatever they did, the Greeks tried to do well. The vase, pictured above, shows Aphrodite, the goddess of love and beauty.

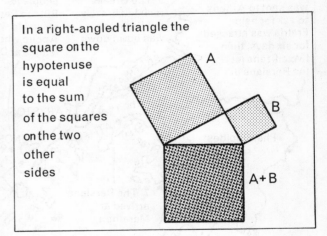

In a right-angled triangle the square on the hypotenuse is equal to the sum of the squares on the two other sides

A

B

A+B

Pythagoras's Theorem
Every schoolboy or girl has heard of Pythagoras's theorem, illustrated here. Pythagoras lived in the sixth century B.C., and in about 530 he settled in Kroton, in southern Italy. He founded a brotherhood, which studied numbers, science, astronomy and music. Pythagoras believed that numbers were the purest of ideas, in which everything else could be expressed. His influence on the later Greeks was very great; it was not always a good influence, because they thought he was *totally* right, and did not develop his theories. Later generations of mathematicians were held back by this belief in the finished perfection of Pythagoras's ideas.

He sent messengers to all the city-states, asking for tribute of earth and water, as a sign that they were willing to become Persia's allies. Many states hurriedly did as Darius asked, but it is said that the Athenians threw the messengers into a pit, and the Spartans pushed them down a well–telling them to collect their own earth and water!

Now there lived in Persia a man who had once been a leader in Athens. His name was Hippias, and he had been banished by the Athenians in 507 B.C. Hippias was an old man by this time (it was the year 490), but he still wanted to rule Athens. So he helped the Persian forces to find a good landing place, within easy reach of Athens, yet far enough away to be unguarded. On the map below you can see the route the Persians took.

When the Athenians heard that the Persians were landing at Marathon, a general named Miltiades ordered the young men to collect food for themselves, and march northwards to meet the enemy. If possible, he wanted to save Athens from being burnt and plundered as Eretria and Karystos had been. (See the map below.) They came to the plain of Marathon, and camped at the southern end, and here they were joined by men from the nearby small city of Plataea.

The Persians, as they began to line up in battle formation, with their best and strongest soldiers in the middle, suddenly saw an amazing sight: the little Athenian army was actually running straight towards them. The Persians thought the Greeks had gone mad, and they hastily got out their spears and shields and advanced to meet the running soldiers. Miltiades had put *his* strongest soldiers at the sides of the battle-line, and these men ran round the Persian army to left and right, and the Persians found themselves engaged in hand-to-hand fighting on all sides at

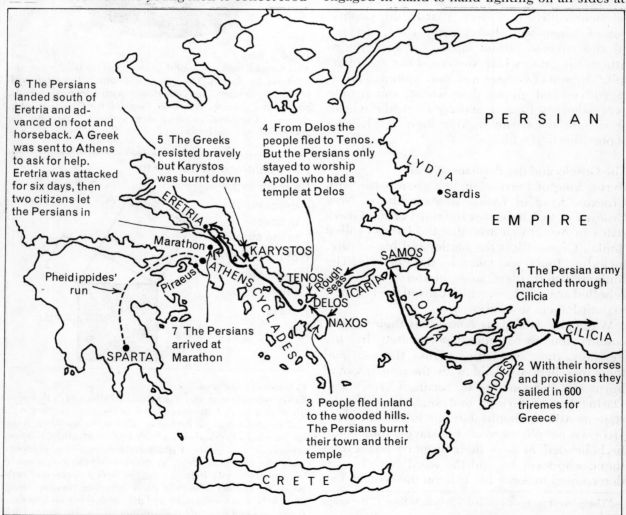

6 The Persians landed south of Eretria and advanced on foot and horseback. A Greek was sent to Athens to ask for help. Eretria was attacked for six days, then two citizens let the Persians in

5 The Greeks resisted bravely but Karystos was burnt down

4 From Delos the people fled to Tenos. But the Persians only stayed to worship Apollo who had a temple at Delos

PERSIAN

LYDIA

•Sardis

EMPIRE

ERETRIA

Marathon

KARYSTOS

SAMOS

Pheidippides' run

Piraeus

ATHENS

TENOS

Rough seas

ICARIA

1 The Persian army marched through Cilicia

CYCLADES

DELOS

NAXOS

CILICIA

7 The Persians arrived at Marathon

SPARTA

RHODES

2 With their horses and provisions they sailed in 600 triremes for Greece

3 People fled inland to the wooded hills. The Persians burnt their town and their temple

C R E T E

How the Persians reached Marathon in the summer of 490 B.C.

1. Find these places in an atlas, or on a globe. How far did the Persians travel from their capital, Persepolis?

2. What is a 'Marathon race' today?

3. Imagine you were living on the island of Naxos when the Persian fleet was sighted. Tell the story of the next few hours.

once. By running towards the Persians, the Athenians had not allowed them time to let loose their usual deadly flight of arrows, and they were not nearly so good at fighting with swords. So the Persians panicked, and tried to retreat to their ships. But over 6000 of them were killed on the beaches or drowned in the sea. Herodotus, a Greek historian who recorded the Persian Wars, says that the Spartans were unable to join the Athenians until too late. Their lives were guided by the moon and the stars, and by custom they could not march until the moon was full.

After the horrible defeat at Marathon, the Persians sailed round to the Athenian port of Piraeus; but the Athenians, even though they were tired out by their hard fight on the beaches, had already returned there on foot, and were lined up on a hill overlooking the port. The Persian commander decided that one battle

against this determined people was enough, and he ordered his fleet to return home. Now all Greece was ready to defend the land from invasion by the Persian king. Ten years later, it was Sparta's turn to win glory in battle.

The Pass of Thermopylae
King Darius died, and his son Xerxes succeeded him. Xerxes was a cruel, vain man, who thought he could win any country for himself, so long as he had enough men. His soldiers, like those of Darius, came from all parts of his huge empire, and Herodotus says he even had Libyan and Ethiopian troops,

'. . . clothed in the skins of leopards and lions, and with long bows made of the stem of the palm-leaf . . . They carried spears, the head of which was the sharpened horn of an antelope; and in addition they had knotted clubs. When

Bridging the Hellespont
The biggest problem for Xerxes was how to get his army across the Hellespont (see map on p. 46). He decided to build a bridge of boats across the water. Xerxes' first attempt failed, because a wind arose and blew the boats away. Herodotus says:
'Xerxes was full of wrath [anger], and straightway gave orders that the Hellespont should receive 300 lashes . . . . While the sea was thus punished by his orders, he likewise commanded that the overseers [foremen] of the work

should lose their heads.'

The second attempt succeeded. For each bridge his engineers tied over 400 boats together, with strong cables, and moored them with huge anchors. They laid planks across to form a road, and covered them with grass and brushwood. Then they built walls along each side, so that the horses and baggage animals could not see the water and be frightened. One bridge was used for the army; the other for the baggage animals and supplies. It took a whole week for the army to cross.

they went into battle they painted their bodies, half with chalk, half with vermilion [a brilliant red].'

This huge band of men, possibly about 300,000 altogether, with their horses and camels, their tents, baggage-animals, and food supplies, and their slaves carrying their armour, marched to fight the Greeks. It was the Athenians whom Xerxes especially wanted to punish; his army marched northwards through Thrace, and then followed the coastline towards Athens.

It was now August, 480 B.C., and the Olympic Games were being held. Nothing was allowed to stop the Games, so there was no proper Greek army ready to meet the Persians. In Sparta there was a religious festival, and so there also the main army could not move. But Leonidas, a king of Sparta, marched north in spite of the festival, with a picked band of soldiers called the 'Three Hundred' and many helots, or slaves. On the way other Greek soldiers joined this little band, and so the first people to meet the Persians were these few thousand men. Leonidas hoped that they would be able to hold the Persians in check until the Games and festival were over, to allow the other Greek armies time to come to their aid.

Leonidas picked a good place for his defence. Between the mountains and the sea there was a narrow pass called Thermopylae. Here the Phocians, in whose country it was, had built a wall to keep out raiders from the mountains. Leonidas and his men strengthened the wall, and waited in the pass for the Persians to arrive.

Xerxes, riding in a chariot behind the main army, was told that the pass ahead was blocked by Greeks. He decided to pitch camp, quite certain that the Greeks would run away when they saw how big his army was. He waited for five days. He laughed when he heard that the Spartans were practising gymnastic exercises, and combing their long hair. He was scornful when a Greek in his army told him this showed that the Spartans meant business; they always dressed their hair before a serious battle. Xerxes imagined that his men would deal with the Spartans in a few hours, and then he could march south to take the whole of Greece. On the sixth day, when it was clear that the Spartans would not run away, Xerxes ordered one of his army divisions to go forward and force their way through the Pass.

But Leonidas had chosen his battle-ground

The Olympic Games
Most of the city-states held yearly athletic meetings. There were also 'national' athletic meetings, in which Greeks from all over the country and the islands competed. The Olympic Games, held every four years, were the most famous. Everybody who could leave his work went to watch the athletes from his own town. During the Games, all quarrels and even wars were forgotten. The Greeks were completely absorbed in racing their horses and chariots, running, jumping, wrestling and throwing the discus. The winners were given a crown of olive leaves, and sometimes pottery jars of olive oil.

wisely. The Pass was so narrow that only a few of the enemy could approach at a time. Soon the entrance was piled high with enemy dead. When the Greeks wrote the history of this battle, they said that the Persian troops panicked, and would have run from the furiously fighting Spartans, but their officers were always ready with their long whips, and they desperately fought on. Xerxes now realized that the Spartans were tougher than he had thought. On the second day of the battle he sent in his own Persian guards, the Immortals*, but even these experienced troops could not make the Spartans yield. Perhaps the Spartans might have managed to hold the Pass until help arrived, but for a Greek traitor. This man led some of the Persian troops by a mountain route, which came out to the south of Thermopylae. Someone ran and told Leonidas that he was going to be attacked from both sides at once, and he immediately commanded most of his forces to march southwards, to escape from the trap. He and his Three Hundred alone waited for the new attack.

*There were 1,000 Immortals. They were so named because if one man was killed, another immediately took his place.

As the Persians poured into the Pass from both sides, one by one the Greeks were killed. Leonidas was one of the first to die. The others fought to the bitter end, with broken spears, with stones and even with their bare hands, and they killed thousands of the invaders. But by nightfall there was not a single Spartan left alive, and the narrow Pass was choked with dead men. Xerxes marched towards Athens.

Meanwhile, in Athens, the leader Themistocles hastily sent all the women and children and old people out of the city, over the water to Salamis and Aegina. When Xerxes arrived, Athens was a town almost without people. But the Acropolis*, where the temples were, was guarded, and the priests and soldiers fought fiercely (but in vain) to save them from being burnt. While their town was blazing, Themistocles and the sailors were preparing their fleet five miles away at Piraeus.

Once he had won Athens, Xerxes turned his attention to Salamis. It was now autumn, and soon the weather would be too bad for fighting. The Persian navy sailed towards the island, and when the Greeks saw how many ships there were, many of them wanted to give up, and make peace with this mighty king who had such a vast army and navy. But Themistocles had already met the navy in battle once, while the Spartans were holding Thermopylae. His little

*See p. 53.

ships had managed to do quite a lot of damage to the Persian fleet, and his men were eager to fight again. So Themistocles grouped his ships in the narrow channel between Athens and Salamis, and waited until they were surrounded by enemy ships. Xerxes also waited. He saw the Athenian navy caught, as he thought, like a mouse in the jaws of a cat. He ordered his throne to be brought on to the shore, so that he could sit and watch the cat close its teeth.

The Athenians attacked first. There were so many Persian ships that they got in each other's way. They were so large that the wind caught them and blew them so that their broad sides were facing the bows of the little Athenian ships. The Greeks used their own ships, which were armoured with battering-rams, to rip open the sides of the Persian warships. The Persians suffered terrible damage; Xerxes could hardly believe his eyes as the channel filled with wreckage.

The result was a complete victory for the Athenian navy, and Xerxes had to go home. Most of his army went with him, struggling back along roads that were now beginning to be covered with snow. In the spring, the Greeks really united to drive the Persians away for good, and they won two land battles on Greek soil. Xerxes never managed to conquer Greece, and in the end he gave up trying.

Greek Galley of 500 B.C.
Greek ships were narrow with shallow hulls (bodies) which allowed them to sail close to the rocky coastlines. If the winds were favourable they could be sailed from one island to the next, but in calm weather they were rowed by about 170 oarsmen. The oarsmen were arranged in three banks, probably on two levels. Ships with only two banks of oarsmen were called biremes, those with three rows – triremes (above).

Chapter 9 Athens and Sparta in the Fifth Century B.C.

After the Persian Wars were over, Athens entered its 'Golden Age'. The Athenians were very fond of talking and thinking. They liked to ask 'why?' about the world they lived in, and they tried to find out what the world was made of, what shape it was, and why it existed at all. One man said that all living things were based on water, another thought the material of life was a colourless liquid; and yet another said there were four basic elements*, earth, fire, air and water. A Greek scientist developed the first theory of atoms. They knew the earth was round (though many people did not believe this), they measured its size, and they even calculated its distance from the moon and the sun. Men called 'sophists' taught the young men how to think, and how to apply their brains to problems in mathematics, astronomy, medicine and philosophy — the love of wisdom. In the summer in Athens, men used to gather in the streets to talk about these matters, and to discuss geometry, or poetry, or the laws in their new government, which was called a 'democracy'.

Government by democracy was a new idea. It began in 507 B.C., when a leader called Cleisthenes 'took the people into partnership'. Democracy was a completely different way of government from anything the world had ever known before. We have already seen how in the earlier civilizations the king was the head of state, and the absolute ruler. In all these civilizations, from Egypt to China, it is often only the king whose name is now known to us. Greece was the first place in history in which ordinary common people were listened to, and whose names are remembered today. This is not only because the Greeks are nearer to us in time; the

A young Greek boy at school
The boy is being taught to read. On the right sits the pedagogue, an old slave who looks after the boy when at school.

Persians, and many other nations, were still ruled absolutely by a king, and we do not know very much about their common people's thoughts or ideas.

In Athens all adult males were automatically members of an Assembly, which voted for a Council to deal with day-to-day problems, and a Court to judge law cases. Nobody could seize power for himself, for once a year the Assembly was allowed to vote against anybody who seemed to have too much ambition. They wrote his name on a broken piece of pottery called an *ostrakon*, and if 6000 or more members of the Assembly voted against the same man, he was banished for ten years. After that, he could return and could claim his property once again.

Other states in Greece were ruled by kings called 'tyrants'. Our present word 'tyrant'

*Elements are the simplest parts into which something can be divided. Water is not really an element; it is made of two elements, hydrogen and oxygen. Nor, of course, are earth or fire or air.

means a bad, oppressive ruler, but Greek tyrants were not always bad. Some states were half-way to becoming democracies, and they were called 'oligarchies'. They were ruled by a few rich citizens. Athens itself had all these types of government at one time or another. (Hippias had been a tyrant of Athens.) The Athenians experimented with types of government just as they experimented with all other ideas.

A favourite Greek saying was 'Know thyself', and men were taught to think about their own motives, and to be honest with themselves. They were encouraged to strive for perfection, in their minds and in their bodies. Every male Athenian practised in the gymnasium every day, and they were scornful of those who would not strip naked and wrestle, or run, or throw the javelin.

Boys were taken to school by slaves called 'pedagogues'. Their teachers taught them to read, and to write with a pointed instrument called a stylus on a tablet covered with soft wax. They learnt to recite poetry, and to speak well in public. Music-masters taught them to play on the pipes or on the lute. The pedagogues, who sat and waited until the lessons were over, listened as well, and they sometimes became just as well-educated as their young masters.

The boys went home for their meals, which were prepared by their mothers and the household slaves. They ate simple dishes of goat's cheese, olives, honey and bread, and drank home-made wine. Their houses were built of sun-dried brick round a central courtyard. There was no proper water-supply, and the slaves were kept busy filling jars from springs and wells.

When they grew up, Athenian men were not often at home: they were too busy listening to the sophists, attending the Assembly or the gymnasium, or taking part in games and religious festivals. (There were so many slaves that there was no need for the freemen to work very hard.)

Beauty was all around the Athenians. On the highest part of Athens, the Acropolis, stood the Parthenon, a temple built to the goddess of Athens, Athena. Her statue inside was 40 feet high, and covered with gold. Round the Parthenon were other graceful temples with gleaming white columns and gabled (pointed) roofs. Athenians working in their fields and vineyards beyond the walls could see them shining in the sun.

Greek religion and their gods

Religion was a part of everyday living. It was the bond which held the scattered city-states together. The gods and goddesses were all thought of as having the same characteristics as ordinary men and women, but they had greater power and they lived forever. Their home was on Mount Olympus.

Each city-state had a sacred place, usually the highest part of the town, set aside for temples. These are some of the gods they worshipped:

Zeus; ruled Mount Olympus as king of the gods and lord of the weather. The Olympic Games were held in his honour.

Pallas Athena; goddess who watched over all civilized life.

Apollo; worshipped at Delphi where as the god of prophecy, he had a famous oracle. He was the son of Zeus. He looked after musicians and archers and was a lover of truth.

Aphrodite; (pictured above) was the goddess of love and beauty.

Poseidon; god of the sea, was very important to sailors and fishermen. When he became angry he caused storms.

Dionysus; god of wine, could make people both happy and miserable. He brought the vine to Greece. His yearly festival was a public holiday when everyone enjoyed himself.

Pericles 490–429 B.C.

Pericles, one of the greatest statesmen of Athens, was a young boy during the Persian Wars. He was one of the people sent out of Athens to Salamis. When the wars were over, Pericles grew up in a city which was being rebuilt in every way. He was proud to be an Athenian. He very much approved of the Athenian sense of liberty, where a man was allowed to develop his own personality. He liked the way in which they were taught to be 'all-rounders', so that even the humblest citizens were able to play the lyre, recite poetry, act in plays, and take part in politics — as well as being first-class craftsmen by trade. Everybody did everything to the best of his ability. Pericles once said:

'Some people call the man who takes no part in public affairs unambitious. We Athenians call him useless.'

The only people who did not take part in the government were foreigners (often other Greeks), slaves, and women. Foreigners were tolerated,

Pericles

Play acting

The audience sat on stone seats in an outdoor theatre. The actors were on the stage in the middle. There was usually a chorus in these plays; it commented on the action, and told the audience the background of the story.

Actors wore masks to show what sort of part they were playing. The comedians wore smiling masks, and the players of tragedy wore masks with turned-down mouths. Today you may sometimes see these masks outside theatres: they are copied from old Greek masks.

People went to the theatre for the whole day. The plays were put on one after the other, and prizes were given for the ones people enjoyed most.

54

but were not allowed to vote; slaves had no rights at all; and although women were often the heroines of plays, and Athena was a much-respected goddess, in real life women were expected to keep in the background. Pericles himself said:

'The greatest glory of a woman is to be least talked about by men, whether they are praising or criticizing...'

The Theatre in Greece

In poetry and play-writing the Greeks had no equal. Every year the authors of plays competed to see whose play should be performed at the annual festival. Many of these plays still survive, and are sometimes performed today. They often tell stories that the Greeks knew well—stories about gods and goddesses, and the mortals they watched over. Many of them were tragedies, showing how men were really at the mercy of the gods, of their fellow-men, and even of their own thoughts and actions. The Greeks did not always want 'happy endings' for their plays. They knew that life was hard and people were often unhappy. People do not always have the fate they deserve. The Greeks were quite realistic about this, and their ideas of right and wrong went far deeper than those of many people in civilized lands today.

But Greek theatre was not all tragic. There were gay comedies as well. The Greeks were able to laugh at themselves, and were never afraid of the truth, even if it was undignified

The Trojan Horse

The stories of the gods and heroes of old were written down by Homer in about 750 B.C. Most of the stories were traditional tales, handed down for generations. Some of them are really faint memories of things that actually happened during the much earlier Mycenean civilization in Greece. The most famous story is about a ten-year war fought by the Greeks against Troy, a city near the Hellespont. The Greeks left a huge wooden horse outside the Trojan walls, and the townspeople dragged it into the town. That night a door opened in the body of the horse, and Greek soldiers climbed out and captured the town. Most of this story is legend; but we do know that Troy existed, and that it was destroyed. The Mycenean cities were over-run by less civilized Greek invaders from the north in about 1100 B.C. Refugees fled to the islands and to Athens. The Athenians were their descendants; the Spartans were the descendants of the invaders. By the time of Homer, only myths and legends of the Myceneans remained.

---

and made people look silly. So they watched plays which mocked the leaders of the Assembly, the sophists, the doctors, the high-born land-owners, and the ordinary workmen.

Everybody went to the theatre, and everybody argued about the plays afterwards, often far into the night. The writers of plays were greatly honoured, and a poet in fifth-century Athens was 'a light and winged and holy thing'.

Sparta

One state in Greece was entirely different from the rest. Sparta, to the west of Athens in the land called Peloponnesus, had two kings, and was ruled as a military state. The kings were more like generals, for they commanded the army, while the affairs of the kingdom were controlled by councillors. Leonidas, who died at Thermopylae, was a Spartan king.

Whereas Athens turned to the sea and kept a large navy, Sparta had no port, and the whole state was one large army. The Spartans lived and died as soldiers, and Spartan mothers used to tell their sons as they went into battle: 'Come back with your shield, or on it!' In other words, they must win or die.

This strange way of life was brought about because Sparta had even more slaves than the Athenians did. Early in their history the Spartans had conquered the neighbouring hill-peoples, and instead of allowing them to keep their own government, they enslaved the whole population. The slaves were known as 'helots'. The Spartans had to keep themselves armed and alert, because they were greatly outnumbered by the helots, and they were always afraid of rebellion. Sometimes groups of helots *did* try to revolt against their masters, but the Spartans had an efficient 'secret police' which usually managed to murder such plotters before they could act.

In order to keep Sparta like a military machine, the rulers banned all trade with foreigners, and even with other Greeks. Their houses were so bare that the beautiful foreign silks would have been out of place. They ate black bread and soup made of black beans, and ignored the more tasty olives and grapes eaten by the rest of the Greeks. Even the idea of coins was banned, so that no Spartan could buy from anybody in another state. Among themselves they used clumsy pieces of iron money, which were useless outside Sparta.

When a Spartan baby was born, its mother and father had to show it to a council of elders. Healthy babies were allowed to live, but weak babies were left out on the mountainsides to die. (Other Greek states also exposed weak children in this way.) When Spartan boys were seven years old, they were taken from their mothers, and joined the other young men in a barracks where they began their military training. They stayed there until they were grown up, and were not allowed to live in their own houses again until they were 30 years old.

Spartans were famous all over Greece for their skill in games and fighting, and also for their singing. When a young man was ready to fight for his country, he was given a suit of heavy

Spartan soldier
The Spartans were also known as 'Laconians'. They were famous for their dry, unemotional way of speaking. At Thermopylae they were told that the arrows of the Persians were so numerous that they would darken the sun. 'So much the better,' a Spartan replied, 'for we shall be able to fight in the shade.'

bronze armour, a red tunic, and a helmet decorated with dyed horsehair. The best and strongest soldiers formed the main bodyguard of Three Hundred—an honour which all Spartan men wished for. The Three Hundred were the envy of their companions, but even they had no freedom as we know it. Their whole lives were strictly disciplined, and even their wives were chosen for them, for they too had to be athletes, and strong enough to have healthy sons who would also become soldiers.

This military way of life, and their lack of beautiful temples or statues, made the Spartans totally different from the easy-going Athenians, with their love of perfection and their stress on fitness for its own sake. Yet both were Greek-speaking peoples, and as we have already seen, they sometimes united when an enemy threatened their lands.

Chapter 10 How Greek Fought Greek

As long as Athens remained a small self-contained city-state, all was well. But at the end of the Persian Wars, the Athenians formed an alliance with the Ionian city-states in Asia Minor. They made an agreement that these states should provide money or ships for a fleet that could protect all Greece from invasion. A politician named Aristides worked out how much money each state should give. The money was kept on the island of Delos, and the ships sailed off to join the Athenian fleet. From the name of the island, the federated states were known as the Delian League.

Unfortunately, after a time it was obvious that Athens was gaining more benefit from the League than any other state. The Athenians had now moved the money to Athens, and they were accused of using it to build the temples on the Acropolis. The other members of the League also objected because Athens was sending soldiers to live in their cities; they were removing the local politicians, and forcing the Ionians to obey Athenian laws. Altogether Athens was behaving as though the states of the Delian League were her own private empire.

Sparta was alarmed by this, because she was afraid that Athens would soon be the leader of the whole of Greece. It was certainly clear that by now Greece ought to have a united policy against Persia. But Sparta was not willing for that policy to be controlled by Athens. So, after Athens had threatened two of Sparta's allies, the Spartans decided that they must stop their rival. The long war that followed very much weakened the civilization Athens had built up. It also led, in the end, to the downfall of Sparta.

The war is called the Peloponnesian War after the Peloponnesian League, the group of states allied to Sparta. Most of them were in that part of Greece that is called the Peloponnesus.

Phoenicians trading

The main rivals to the Greek traders in the Mediterranean were the Phoenicians. These extremely successful merchant-seamen lived in towns on the eastern shores of the Mediterranean. Their ships carried embroidered linen sails, and were hung with purple and blue curtains. Purple dye (made from a kind of shell-fish) was their main export, but they also went from port to port buying and selling cargoes of horses, ivory and ebony (from Syria), tapestry and cloth (from Assyria); corn, honey and oil (from Palestine), and spices and gold (from Arabia). They sailed west and north, till they came to the tin-mines of Britain and Spain. Tin was in great demand in the Mediterranean countries, for mixing with copper to make bronze.

The Peloponnesian War 431–404 B.C.

The Greek city-states took sides in the war, and for 27 years Greek fought Greek. Every spring, when the snows had melted, the armies of Sparta, and the Athenian navy, set out to damage each other's lands. It was not a 'total war'; the ordinary life of Athens continued much as before, with poets and playwrights commenting on the political situation, and even making fun of the whole thing. But there were times when nobody could forget the horrors of war. When the Spartans marched far south into Attica, all the country people fled to Athens. The city was crowded with refugees, sleeping in the streets, in the markets, and even in the temples. It is not surprising that under these conditions food became short, and disease broke out. In the summer of 430, the plague was so bad that hundreds of Athenians died every day. Pericles himself caught it, and was so weakened that he died the following year.

Both sides were often cruel and merciless. The Athenians murdered all the men on an island that fought for Sparta, and took the women and children as slaves. When the people of the city

Reconstruction of Acropolis

of Syracuse in Sicily, who were allies of Sparta, captured an Athenian army, they put the prisoners to work in stone-quarries. Few of them survived, because the conditions were so terrible.

So the bitter quarrel went on. Sometimes city-states changed sides, sometimes even generals went over to the enemy. The end was complete defeat for the Athenians. King Agis of Sparta seized a small town only 14 miles from Athens, and was able to stop any help, or even food, from reaching the Athenians from the north. Worse news was to follow, for the Spartans made a treaty with Persia. They received money from a Persian prince and built their first navy. Now the Athenians were no longer masters of the sea. Under their leader Lysander, the Spartans surprised and captured an Athenian fleet, and sailed south towards Attica. They stopped grain ships reaching Athens from Ionia or the Black Sea. When the news of the naval disaster reached Athens, 'on that night, no man slept'. A few months later, Athens surrendered to the Spartans.

The 'Thirty Tyrants' and the fall of Sparta

The Spartans took away Athens' empire, tore down the city walls, and sailed away with her fleet. They set up a government of 30 men of their own choosing. Many Athenians were murdered, or had their property taken from them. The vine and olive orchards were nearly all destroyed, and these trees take many years to grow. Nobody had any money, and many slaves were therefore sold abroad so that people could buy food. In the year that followed, there was so much misrule in Athens that the people rose in protest. The Spartans had hoped to unite Greece under their leadership, but they did not know how to govern men who had always loved personal liberty. They themselves were too much like machines to rule wisely, and in only 35 years Athens was once again the spiritual centre of Greece.

One reason for the decline of Sparta was that suddenly the Spartans had money; the defeated states had to pay tribute to her. These people had never owned anything at all, and now they saw the advantage of wealth. Some became very rich, but they did not know how to deal with their money. Those who remained poor envied them, and there was great discontent in Sparta.

In the conquered states, the Spartan soldiers and politicians were hated and feared. They did nothing to bring the states back to prosperity, and soon there were rebellions all over Greece. Thebes in particular rose against the Spartans, and in 362 B.C. defeated them. Sparta had been held together by its military rule, and the new way of life caused the state to collapse.

A new kind of society now grew up in Greece. The army, the government, the theatre, and even the market-place began to be taken over by professionals. Soldiers were no longer recruited only in times of danger; there were now professional soldiers who were paid to fight. (When there were no wars in Greece, they sometimes went to Asia and fought for the Persians instead.) There were professional politicians in charge of state affairs. In the play-houses, people went to see a particular actor, rather than a particular play. (In the old days all the actors were amateurs, and the crowd did not know their names.) And there were now shops which sold bread and wove cloth, so that the housewives no longer had to give these jobs to slaves in their own homes. The city was becoming much more 'commercial', and in this new society people were more in-

a	A alpha	b	B beta	g	Γ gamma	d	Δ delta
e	E epsilon	z	Z zeta	e	H eta	th	Θ theta
i	I iota	c,k	K kappa	l	Λ lambda	m	M mu
n	N nu	x	Ξ xi	o	O omicron	p	Π pi
r,rh	P rho	s	Σ sigma	t	T tau	y,u	Υ upsilon
ph	Φ phi	ch	X chi	ps	Ψ psi	o	Ω omega

Writing

The Greeks took over the Phoenicians' way of writing, and they altered it to suit their own language. Our word *alphabet* comes from *alpha* and *beta*, the Greek names for A and B. The Greek for D is *delta*, from which we get *our* word delta, meaning a place where rivers join to make a triangle with the sea. (Look at the Nile Delta on p. 22.) We use some Greek letters as symbols in mathematics. The Greeks themselves still use the old alphabet.

clined to value money. Riches, and not mental and physical excellence, were now the new goal.

Socrates, 469–399 B.C.

But there were people who spoke against this worldly attitude, and the greatest critic was a philosopher named Socrates. He himself was a poor man, who had once been a stone-mason. But he left his job in order to find out about life, about himself, and about goodness. He was 66 years old when the wars with Sparta ended.

The way Socrates looked for goodness was by questioning everything, and thus making his friends (and himself) think more deeply than they had before. For instance, if someone said that loyalty was a good thing, Socrates would ask him questions like: 'What do we mean by loyalty? Is it *always* good? Is it a good thing to be loyal to a bad king? Does not a man have the right to his own opinion–and can he not therefore be *disloyal* in this situation?' And then the conversation would probably turn to whether a man could follow his own conscience, or whether he should obey his king, or his government, blindly.

Many of Socrates' listeners loved this kind of argument. It was different from the methods of the sophists, who just lectured to a silent audience. Socrates had a band of devoted followers, but he also made enemies. Politicians and other public men did not like to be beaten in argument by this old man, with his cloak in rags and with no sandals on his feet. It is a very human weakness that we all like to hold on to our beliefs, just because they are ours—even when they are shown to be wrong, or partly wrong. Some people did not realize that Socrates was genuinely searching for the truth, and not trying to trick them by clever argument.

Athens was only just beginning to restore order and confidence after the wars with Sparta, and the politicians felt that Socrates was destroying the beliefs and ideas that the city needed. It was the wrong time to make people uneasy about their ways of thinking, and unsure about their religion. Socrates, they felt, was a bad influence on the young men of the town. So they brought a charge against him of teaching young men to think and act wrongly, and of introducing strange gods.

At his trial, Socrates could have brought his wife and children to plead for him, but he did not. He could have asked to be exiled, and the request would probably have been granted. Instead he made a speech which only angered the Court. 'I am a sort of gadfly*,' he said, 'and the State is a great and noble horse which is slow to move, and requires to be stirred to life.' He told them they ought to give him free meals for the rest of his life, because they would never have anyone like him in their city again. Then he said perhaps they should fine him, and he named a tiny sum of money. But the majority of the citizens of Athens voted against him, and he was condemned to death by poison.

Socrates never wrote down his thoughts or conversations, but later his young friend Plato recorded everything he could remember. He shows Socrates to be an interesting and lively man, whose ideas are as true today as they were when he thought of them 2000 years ago.

*Gadfly is a general name for various kinds of flies that bite animals.

Socrates

Socrates once said about a politician who was angry with him: 'Well, I don't suppose either of us knows anything beautiful or good, but I am better off than he is—for he knows nothing, and thinks that he knows; I neither know nor think that I know!'

The playwright Aristophanes wrote a comedy called 'The Clouds' in 423 B.C. It is about a simple man who has been ruined by his son's passion for chariot-racing. He takes his son to Socrates, in order that he may learn how to win his law-suits. In the play Socrates is paid to teach people how to win arguments by trickery. He did not teach for money in real life, neither did he cheat in argument. But unfortunately the Athenians believed in Aristophanes' view.

Look up in your dictionary the modern meanings of:

sophistry	spartan
pedagogue	laconic
tyrant	academy

Chapter 11 Alexander the Great

Now a completely new people became powerful in Greece. At the northern end of the Aegean Sea lay the country of Macedonia. The Macedonians were a mixed race, partly Greek but also partly descended from northern tribesmen. The Greeks thought of them as near-barbarians. In about 350 B.C., the Macedonians had a well-trained army, mainly of foot-soldiers armed with very long spears called pikes. They marched in a close formation called a phalanx, with their pikes pointing forwards towards the enemy, and their right arms protected by the next man's shield.

During the Persian Wars, Macedonia had fought *against* Greece, and the Greeks were very suspicious of this mixed race that lived so close to them. Philip, who was king of Macedon from 359–336 B.C. (50 years after the death of Socrates), was an ambitious man, determined to make his country powerful. He invaded Thrace, and seized for himself some rich gold mines. With his new wealth he provided Macedonia with an even bigger and better army. He invaded Thessaly, and marched far south into Greece.

Demosthenes, one of Athens' leaders, protested against this invasion, and said to the Athenians:

'See, Athenians, the height to which the fellow's insolence has soared: he makes noisy threats and talks big ... he cannot rest content with what he has conquered: he is always taking in more, everywhere casting his net round us, while we sit idle and do nothing. When, Athenians, will you take the necessary action? What are you waiting for?'

But another Athenian named Isocrates wanted peace with the Macedonians. He appealed to Philip to unite Greece against the Persians. So Athens was divided into two parties, one for war and the other for peace.

The Macedonians invade Europe, Asia and Africa

Philip and his army marched right down to Boeotia, just north of Attica, and he defeated a mixed force of Athenians and Thebans. He was now in command of almost the whole of Greece, but before he could organize this new empire, he was murdered by his own palace officials.

Demosthenes was delighted to hear of Philip's death. He thought that the Macedonians would now go back to their own country, and that Philip's son Alexander was too young to be a nuisance. But Alexander was 20 and far from being a child. He had been taught by a remarkable Greek tutor named Aristotle. From him he learnt the ancient tales of Homer, and the traditions of the Greeks. Though only half-Greek himself, Alexander had great respect for Greek culture*, and saw himself as a descendant of the heroes of old. He immediately marched south to remind the Greeks that they were now part of *his* empire. Thebes rebelled, but the treatment the Thebans received from Alexander's army (6000 people were killed, and 8000 sold as slaves) horrified the other city-states. They decided that it was far safer to remain quiet under their new conqueror.

Then Alexander took a large army across the Hellespont into the Persian Empire. The King of Persia, whose name was Darius III, was lord of all the old countries of Assyria, Babylonia and Egypt, and he was very rich. Alexander, in spite of his Thracian gold mines, was comparatively poor. He was determined to win some of the wealth of Persia, and almost immediately he succeeded.

Darius's army was not nearly as well disciplined as Alexander's. His soldiers were mostly

*By culture we here mean a particular form of civilization and its characteristic products, intellectual, social, religious, artistic, etc.

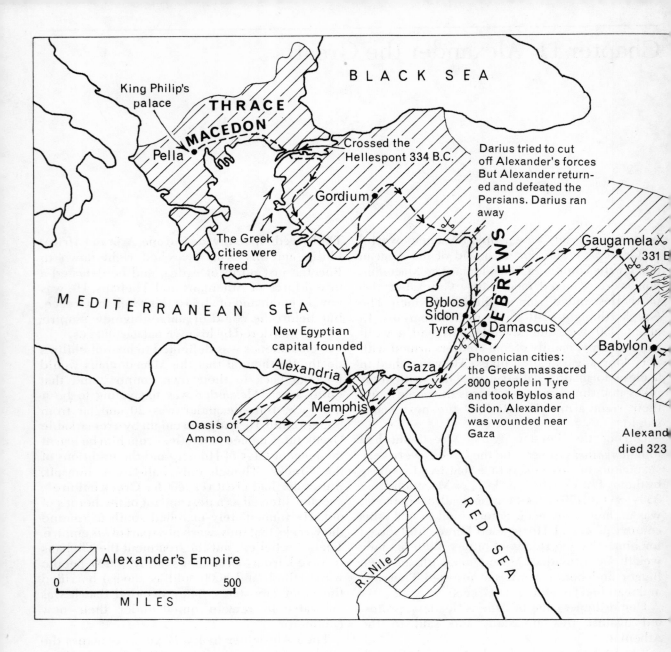

The map shows:

BLACK SEA

THRACE

King Philip's palace

MACEDON

Pella

Crossed the Hellespont 334 B.C.

Gordium

Darius tried to cut off Alexander's forces But Alexander returned and defeated the Persians. Darius ran away

The Greek cities were freed

Gaugamela
331 B

MEDITERRANEAN SEA

HEBREWS

Byblos
Sidon
Tyre
Damascus

Babylon

New Egyptian capital founded

Alexandria

Gaza

Phoenician cities: the Greeks massacred 8000 people in Tyre and took Byblos and Sidon. Alexander was wounded near Gaza

Alexand
died 323

Memphis

Oasis of Ammon

RED SEA

R. Nile

Alexander's Empire

0   500

MILES

mercenaries (hired soldiers), many of them from Greece. They were badly organized, and they had no personal loyalty to the king. They were quite likely to desert if they were not paid well. Darius's navy was not completely Persian either. Most of his ships and sailors were taken from the ports of Phoenicia and Ionia. Alexander quickly showed how superior his forces were: he defeated a Persian army soon after landing in Asia and then marched south to cut off the ports. He was so pleased with his victories that he sent home 300 suits of Persian armour, with the message:

'Alexander, son of Philip, and the Greeks (except the Spartans) have won these from the barbarians of Asia.'

After marching across Asia Minor, Alexander met a Persian army commanded by Darius himself, and again he defeated the Persians. Darius fled to the east, farther into Asia, while Alexander turned south into Syria where he captured the ancient Phoenician city of Tyre. Then he decided to cross the desert into North Africa. At the Nile delta he founded the town of Alexandria, and was proclaimed Pharaoh of Egypt. He was welcomed

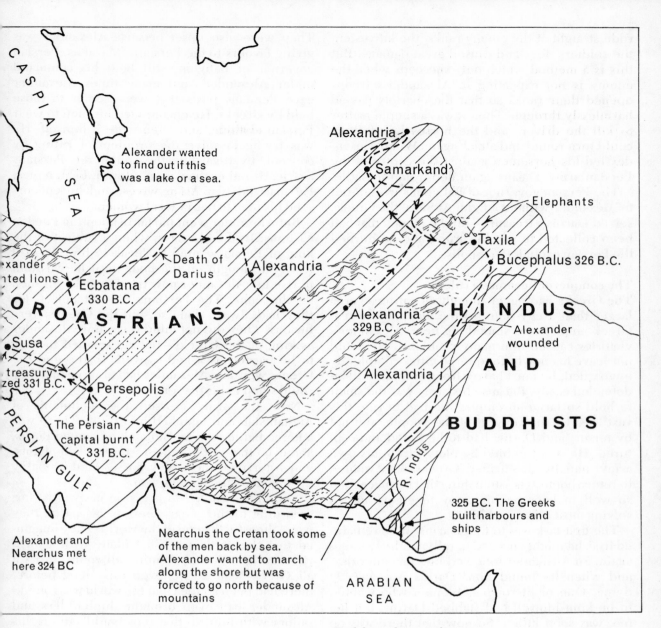

Alexander wanted to find out if this was a lake or a sea.

Alexandria

Samarkand

Elephants

Alexander hunted lions

Ecbatana 330 B.C.

Death of Darius

Alexandria

Taxila

Bucephalus 326 B.C.

Susa

treasury seized 331 B.C.

Persepolis

Alexandria 329 B.C.

HINDUS

Alexander wounded

AND

Alexandria

BUDDHISTS

The Persian capital burnt 331 B.C.

R. Indus

325 BC. The Greeks built harbours and ships

Alexander and Nearchus met here 324 BC

Nearchus the Cretan took some of the men back by sea. Alexander wanted to march along the shore but was forced to go north because of mountains

ARABIAN SEA

ZOROASTRIANS

CASPIAN SEA

PERSIAN GULF

---

with rejoicing, for the Egyptians were tired of the harsh and brutal way in which the Persian satraps had treated them. But Alexander did not stay long in Egypt. He was afraid that the Persians in Asia might again seize the cities of Phoenicia and Ionia. He returned to fight once more with Darius.

At Gaugamela in Mesopotamia the Macedonians met the last and largest Persian army. The Persians now introduced into their army chariots with long knives fixed to the wheels. When the drivers whipped up the horses and

Find these places on the map:

Gordium; Here Alexander was shown an ancient chariot lashed to a pole with a knot that an oracle had said could be untied only by the man who would one day rule all Asia. Alexander merely cut the knot in half with his sword.

Oasis of Ammon; Alexander went into the desert to consult a famous Egyptian oracle. (Oracles were supposed to forecast the future.) How far did he have to travel to do this?

Damascus; At this ancient city Alexander captured Darius's war chest containing all the money for paying his soldiers.

Alexandria; Five towns with this name are shown here. Are any of them still called Alexandria?

Susa; Was the treasury seized by Alexander while he was on his way to or from India?

rode straight at the enemy ranks, the knives cut the soldiers' legs and caused great damage. But this is a method which only succeeds when the enemy is not expecting it. Alexander's troops opened their ranks so that the chariots passed harmlessly through. Then it was a simple matter to kill the drivers and the horses before they could turn round and attack again. When Alexander led his horsemen against the centre of the Persian army, Darius again fled from the battle.

The Persian governor of Babylon surrendered to Alexander without a fight. At Susa, the Greeks seized Darius's treasure — all the money that had been collected to pay his army; and he burned the Persian capital, Persepolis.

The conqueror becomes a ruler

The Greeks had never thought of ruling an area larger than a city-state, so the making of a real Greek empire was something new. Alexander's victories caused him many problems. He could not leave his newly conquered cities completely unguarded; he must have a frontier that could be defended easily. Because his army was too small to hold so large an empire, he had to rule this vast area by the consent of the people, and not by terror; and Darius had to be found and captured. He was troubled by plots within his own army, and by dissatisfied Greeks who wanted to return home. It is astonishing that he succeeded so well in keeping his army together, and in solving most of the problems.

The first task was to find Darius. If he remained free, he might succeed in rallying the Persians again. So Alexander followed him day after day, and when he found him, Darius was already dying. One of his own noblemen who wanted to be king himself had stabbed Darius, but he, too, was soon killed. So now that there was no Persian king, Alexander made himself ruler.

Still he went on towards the east. His campaigns for the next few years were part-conquests and part-exploration. He built 16 new cities, all called Alexandria, where the streets were laid out in a grid-pattern (with roads crossing each other at right angles), and the buildings were Greek in style. (Most of these 'Alexandrias' are now called by different names.) Wherever he went he introduced Greek ideas, and built temples to Greek gods. Year after year the army marched with him. The men were often ill with dysentery and malaria, and they were afraid that they might never return home.

They were also upset because Alexander was giving favours to the Persians. Mazaeus, Persian governor of Babylon, still held his command under Alexander; and many times Alexander gave Persians posts that were senior to those held by Greeks. He encouraged his men to wear Persian clothing, and often wore it himself. He was trying to solve the problem of ruling by consent, by regarding the conquered Persians as friends rather than as an inferior, beaten race. He married two Asian wives, and he encouraged his men to marry local women.

But Alexander went too far in adopting Persian customs. In the old days, when a subject of the king of Persia wanted to speak to him, he had to lie full-length on the floor until he was told to rise up. Alexander now tried to make his men do the same. The Persians did not object, for they had always done so, but the Greeks were furious. They did not mind regarding Alexander as king of the Greeks — but he seemed to want to be treated as a god as well. In the end the Greeks won, and Alexander had to agree that they could stand in his presence.

Now the army crossed the mountains of Afghanistan and marched into India. There was a fierce battle with an Indian king named Porus, and even though the Indian army used elephants, which terrified the Greek horses (and probably the men too), the Greeks won.

Alexander wanted to press on eastwards, for, according to the geographers in his party, they were almost at the end of the world. They imagined that the earth was a flat plate, with a huge river called 'Ocean' running all round it. (Not all Greek scholars believed this — long before, there had been an idea that the world was round.) Alexander had even brought shipbuilders and sailors with him, so that they could sail on this Ocean. But the army was now too far from home. The soldiers heard rumours of deserts and jungles, and thousands more elephants between them and the sea, and they refused to go any further. Moreover, the monsoon had come, and the solid ground was now a mass of wet mud.

Alexander was furious with his army, and even said he would go on alone. But he consulted his oracle, and the signs were against such a journey. So reluctantly he turned back. When at last he reached Babylon again, he had been away ten years. In Persia there was now great confusion, and even though Alexander was exhausted from his wanderings, he could not rest. There were

quarrels to be settled, temples to be rebuilt, laws to be made, and the whole empire had to be organized. Alexander tried his utmost to persuade Greeks and Persians to live together in harmony and friendship. He decided to live in Babylon for a while. Babylon, which had once been so beautiful, was neglected and overgrown. The canals had been smashed by the Persians, and the surrounding country had gone back to swampy marshland. Slowly Alexander's workmen restored the buildings and drained the land.

Alexander's decision to live in this damp, mosquito-ridden city was fatal for him, and it lost the Greeks an empire. In June 323 B.C., when he was only 33 years old, he died in Babylon from malaria.

What happened afterwards

Alexander had no successor strong enough to carry on his work, and his great empire collapsed after he died. It was divided into six parts, each ruled by one of Alexander's generals. The two areas which flourished most were Syria and

Alexander's Army in Asia

The Issus mosaic at Pompeii shows the young Alexander (on the left) leading the charge against the Persian king, Darius, at Issus.

There were 35,000 foot-soldiers in Alexander's army and 5000 horsemen. The army also took with them siege towers on wheels, rams for breaking down town walls, catapults for hurling spears and stones, and materials for building bridges. Besides soldiers there were architects, builders, geographers, historians and biologists. Alexander sent specimens of new plants back to his old tutor, Aristotle.

Egypt. General Ptolemy became Pharaoh, and there were Pharaohs of the same name in Egypt for nearly 300 years. Syria was ruled by a family descended from General Seleucus, and were known as the Seleucids.

The Greek language, customs and culture lived on in many of the places Alexander conquered. The first Buddhist statues, imported into India from Afghanistan, are shown in Greek clothes and with Greek faces. The new towns had Greek architects, and their buildings were unmistakably Greek. Alexander had opened up a vast area of the world for Greek colonists, who continued to trade with the Mediterranean and Aegean countries. New farms in India, Turkestan and Persia grew wheat to sell in Greece and Italy; and for the first time the Mediterranean world was able to import citrus fruit, such as oranges and lemons; apricots, buffaloes, geese and cotton.

In Egypt, Alexandria became the new capital, and one of the most important cities in the world. Not far from the new marble palace of the Ptolemies, there was a famous university. Its scholars became known all over the European and Asian world: Euclid, who taught mathematics, Zenodorus, who produced the first Greek grammar; Erasistratus who studied medicine, and Eratosthenes the geographer. There were 700,000 books in the university library.

Silks from China, cotton goods from India, gold and silver from Persia, carpets from Turkey, and tin from Britain were all sold in the market-place of Alexandria. But Alexandria was really the only town in Egypt which maintained a high standard of civilization. The Ptolemies did not always rule the country wisely, and in later years they turned it into a nationalized state. Land-owners were compelled to till their land for the state, and were forbidden to work elsewhere. They received orders about what crops to grow, and how many animals to keep. They had to sell their produce to the state at fixed prices, and free competitive trading was forbidden by law. The people of Egypt became mere slaves in their own country, with their thoughts only on how they could survive another day. The glory of Egypt had at last departed.

Pharos

The Pharos of Alexandria was a lighthouse built in 284 B.C. by the first Ptolemy. It was 150 metres (480 feet) high and is one of the Seven Wonders of the Ancient World.

The other six wonders of the Ancient World are: (1) The pyramids of Giza, Egypt; (2) The Hanging Gardens of Semiramis, Babylon, Iraq; (3) The tomb of King Mausolus of Caria, Halicarnassus, Turkey; (4) The Temple of Diana, Ephesus, Turkey; (5) The Statue of Apollo, or Colossus of Rhodes; (6) The statue of Zeus, Olympia, Greece.

How many of these still stand? How many can you find mentioned in this book?

66

Chapter 12 The Rise of Rome

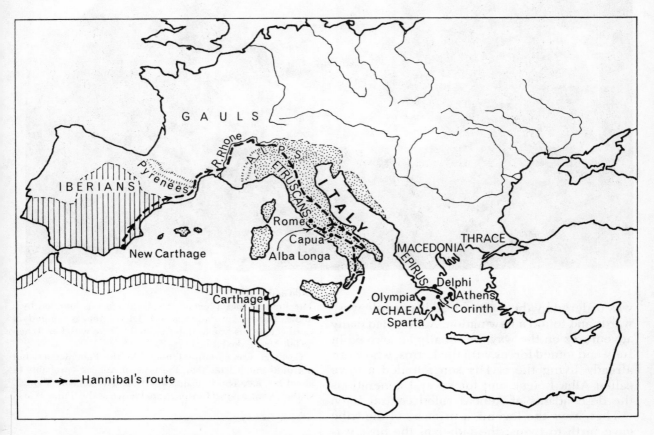

We have seen how the Greeks colonized the islands and the mainland round the 'toe' of Italy. But since all their trade was with the Greek islands and the Mediterranean ports, they did not disturb the other tribes who lived in the central and northern parts of present-day Italy.

The most advanced peoples of Italy at this time were the Etruscans, who had reached a high degree of civilization. They may have come originally from Lydia in Asia, and their art, their clothes, and their religion all show influence from the East. The Etruscans made statues of stone and bronze, painted pictures on their walls, and built temples and tombs. They could read and write, and they traded with the Celts who lived north of the Alps.

Romulus and Remus

Besides the Etruscans there were many smaller tribes in Italy. There was one small community that was part of a group called 'Latins', and they lived near the river Tiber. Their chief town was called Rome, and we now know them as 'Romans'.

Much later in their history, the Romans invented legends about their origins. They said that in far-off times a prince of Troy named Aeneas

Dido and Aeneas
The Romans had a legend that Carthage was founded by a
noble Phoenician lady named Dido. Aeneas landed at
Carthage on his way to Italy, and fell in love with her. When
he left Africa, she killed herself.

Carthage was certainly founded by the Phoenicians—but
not until much later than the time of Aeneas—probably in
about 800 B.C. The Romans called the Phoenicians 'Punici',
so their wars against Carthage are known as the 'Punic Wars'.

---

was ordered by the gods to lead his people westwards and found a new nation. Aeneas had many
adventures on the way, but finally he arrived in
Italy and joined forces with the Latins, who were
already living there. His son founded a town
called Alba Longa, and for several generations
the descendants of Aeneas ruled central Italy.

Then, says the legend, a princess of the tribe
gave birth to twins; the father of the boys was
supposed to be the god Mars. The king demanded
that the boys, who were called Romulus and
Remus, should be left to die on the banks of the
Tiber. There they were found by a she-wolf,
who took them to her lair, and brought them up
with her own cubs.

Later Romulus and Remus grew up in the care
of a shepherd, and when they were men they
became leaders of the tribe. Then there arose the
question of which of them should be king. They
decided to rely on heavenly help, and to search
the sky for a sign. Remus looked up and saw six
vultures, and immediately his friends said he

should be king; but now Romulus saw 12 vultures, and *his* followers proclaimed *him* king.
Then followed a long argument—'Romulus saw
twice as many vultures!' 'Yes, but Remus saw
the vultures first!'—and there was a battle in
which Remus was killed. So Romulus ruled the
city, and called it Rome. The date was now about
750 B.C. At the same time in Greece, Homer was
writing down the tribal stories and legends, and
the Olympic Games were held for the first time
in 776 B.C. From about this date, Roman history
ceases to be only legend, and becomes more
reliable.

Rome becomes a Republic

The Romans began to form a city-state, gradually making their territory larger as they took over lands from their neighbours. From about 640 to 500 B.C., Rome seems to have been ruled by Etruscan kings, who taught the Romans their civilization. Rome began to look like a prosperous town, with temples, market-places and palaces. The Romans had a constitution, and an army recruited by the rich noblemen. They wore armour and carried shields and spears very like those of the Greeks.

But in time the Romans decided that they did not want to be ruled by Etruscans. King Tarquin, who was nicknamed 'the Proud', had expanded the state, and built new towns in outlying provinces. But he was not popular, and when he was away from Rome with his army, the people deposed, that is, dethroned him. They swore that never again should a king rule in Rome, and instead decided to have two magistrates who would hold office for a year only.

Rome had two kinds of citizens. The first group were called patricians. They were wealthy landowners, who had a vote in the Assembly, and who held all the high positions in the government and the courts. The rest of the people were called plebeians. They had no vote, and could not hold office. A plebeian was not allowed to marry a patrician, and so could never change his status—his position or rank. This inequality caused great trouble in the early days of the republic. Both classes had to pay taxes, and the plebs formed the largest part of the army, so they saw no reason why they should not have equal rights with the patricians. It was the army which finally changed the situation. On their return from a campaign, they organized a 'sit-down strike' outside Rome, and refused to return to battle. The patrician Assembly had to give in, and they allowed the plebs to send two (later ten) men called 'tribunes' to the Assembly. This was the beginning of greater power for the plebs, and soon mixed marriages were allowed, and the plebs even had their own Assembly.

Many of the patricians were dismayed at the way in which the lower-class citizens were gaining power. They believed that the rule of the country should be in the hands of the rich and well-born, who had time to become professional politicians. The struggle for power continued, the patricians losing ground all the time; in 289 B.C. the plebs could even pass laws without asking permission from the Senate (the patricians' 'Upper House').

Pyrrhus

Meanwhile the armies of Rome were striking out in every direction, pushing the frontiers of the Roman Republic farther north, east and south. Rome was now the leading city of Italy, and all the other tribes, including the powerful Etruscans, had been subdued. The Greeks who lived in sea-ports in the south of Italy became alarmed, and they sent to Greece for help. An army arrived, led by a Greek called Pyrrhus. The Greeks managed to get hold of a number of war-elephants from India, and Pyrrhus brought some of them to Italy. At first they caused complete confusion among the Roman troops, but although Pyrrhus won two battles, and marched nearly as far as Rome, the Romans would not make peace. After fighting another, drawn, battle he had lost so many men that he went back to Greece, and the Greeks of southern Italy had to submit to Rome.

The Romans united Italy under their government by building roads throughout the country, and by seeing that all the various tribes obeyed

Pyrrhus

Pyrrhus was the king of a Greek state about 80 miles from Italy by sea. Although Pyrrhus won his battles in Italy, they had cost him so much in men and supplies that he returned home, saying, 'Another such victory and I am lost!' We use the term 'Pyrrhic victory' even now, to describe a contest won at too high a price.

the same Roman laws. Soon everybody was speaking the Roman language, Latin. Roman rule was not harsh, and the new roads brought great improvement in trade, so the conquered tribes settled down well, and there were few uprisings. The Romans used foreign soldiers in their armies, and this brought a sense of unity among the young men who fought side by side for a common purpose.

The Punic Wars

Across the water, on the North African shore, stood a busy port and town called Carthage. For centuries the people of Carthage had been among the most important traders and merchant-seamen of the western Mediterranean, and they even rounded Spain and sailed north to the barbarian islands of Britain. (There they exchanged cloth and wine for quantities of tin.) Their only trade rivals were the Greek colonists in Italy and France, but by 500 B.C. the Carthaginians had shown that they were the masters of the sea. Now these Carthaginians watched as Rome also began to trade by sea, and worse, to cross to Sicily, which the Carthaginians regarded as their own trading base. War broke out between the two powers.

The Romans had not yet built a proper fleet of ships, and so they were at a disadvantage. But one day they found a Carthaginian ship driven aground, on the shore, and they made 100 copies of it. They trained their soldiers to row by sitting them on wooden benches on the shore, but this makeshift* training did not make very good sailors! The Carthaginians could easily win a sea-battle; so the Romans turned sea-battles into land-battles by equipping each ship with a *corvus*. This was a kind of bridge with an iron spike at the end, which they let down with a crash on to the deck of an enemy ship. The spike held the corvus in place, and armed Romans dashed across to fight hand-to-hand with the Carthaginians.

The Romans won the First Punic War, after the two navies had spent over 20 years chasing one another round Sicily and the toe of Italy. The Romans took the islands of Corsica, Sardinia, and Sicily.

Hannibal the Carthaginian

The Carthaginians tried to make an empire in Spain, and they built towns and trading posts all along the south coast. In the spring of 218 B.C., a Carthaginian leader named Hannibal went on the attack against Rome once more. He decided on a most daring plan; he would attack by land, from the north. He started from his Spanish port, New Carthage, with a large army; besides the Carthaginians themselves there were Iberians and Celts from Spain, and well-trained African troops, including tough Numidian horsemen. There were also thousands of baggage-animals, horses, mules and donkeys, and even 37 elephants with their Syrian or Indian riders. Elephants were no longer an unusual sight in the armies of Europe and Asia.

By the time Hannibal had crossed the Pyrenees mountains, his army had been reduced in numbers. Many men had been killed in battles with hostile tribesmen, some had been left behind because they were sick or wounded, and thousands had deserted. They had already marched for three months, and they were tired of the everlasting tramp in unfamiliar land. They had to beg, steal or fight for their food, or live off the charity of the herdsmen and cultivators whose homes and villages they passed on the way. It was growing late in the year, and the weather was turning colder. Hannibal had to use all his influence and charm to make his mixed army continue at all. Fortunately not all the tribes they met were unfriendly, and one tribe even gave them warm clothing and shoes and helped them to repair their weapons.

At last the ragged army reached the Alps— those immense mountains which stretch across the north of Italy, and in which there are peaks up to 14,000 or 15,000 feet high. This test of their courage and endurance was a greater ordeal than even Hannibal imagined it would be. Twice in the narrow passes between the mountains, wild tribesmen rushed at them to plunder their baggage. Mules and horses fell over the cliffs into the valleys below, and many of their precious bundles of food and clothing were lost. There was very little to eat in the high slopes, and men and animals alike starved. Most of the elephants died, and the hungry soldiers cut up their flesh and roasted it on their cooking fires.

By now their clothes and shoes were in rags, and they were dirty, hungry and exhausted. The wind tore at their bodies, and the rain and snow soaked them to the skin. Many were sick and had to be left to die. Then suddenly, the front

---

*A makeshift is a substitute for the real thing.

of the army reached the top of the pass, and saw below the wide plain of north Italy. They had been marching and fighting for five months, and at last their goal was in sight.

Hannibal made a speech to his men at the top of the pass, telling them that the worst was now over. But he was wrong. The way down was narrow and steep. The first men in the long line trod on soft snow, but by the time the last stragglers passed along that way, the snow had all been removed by the feet of other men, and they had to walk on slippery ice. But at last the survivors of that terrible journey were down in the plain, and after spending winter in camp, the long march south began.

The Second Punic War

The Romans heard of Hannibal's arrival, and they sent one of their consuls to stop the invader's advance. His name was Scipio, and he had just come from Spain, where he had missed Hannibal by only three days. (Hannibal was already safely across the Pyrenees.) The Roman legions were much more disciplined than the wild Celts whom Hannibal had been fighting in northern Spain and France. The Romans were confident of winning this battle, as they had won so many before. But they had never met a man like Hannibal. After a brief and bloody battle, Scipio had to

Hannibal's elephants

Nobody is certain whether Hannibal's elephants came from India or from Africa. When they were crossing the river Rhône, between the Pyrenees and the Alps, they built huge rafts for the elephants; fortunately, once they had stepped on to them, the elephants were too terrified to move. It must have been almost impossible to find enough food for them on the 1500 mile march to Italy. They slowed up the army in the Alps, because their drivers were continually having to find paths wide enough for them to walk on.

retreat. His defeat was mainly due to the Numidian horsemen, who galloped quickly into battle, armed with spears. They were away again before the Romans could harm them; and soon they were ready to attack in a completely different part of the battle-field.

This first victory encouraged the Carthaginians. They followed it with two more great battles, which they won by Hannibal's brilliant planning. In both cases the Roman army was led into an ambush; hidden Carthaginian troops attacked them suddenly and unexpectedly, and most of the dead on the field were Roman soldiers.

A strange situation now developed; the Romans did not want to have any more battles with the Carthaginians, because their losses had been so large. So they had to allow Hannibal to stay in Italy, merely following his army about and occasionally capturing or killing small parties of men who left the main army in search of food. Hannibal took the city of Capua, which he made his headquarters, and he actually stayed in Italy with all his soldiers for 14 years.

During all this time there was only one more important battle. This was at Cannae when, it is said, 80,000 men were killed in one day. This is an astonishing figure; but with no medicines or pain-killing drugs, the fate of all badly wounded men was almost always death. Many begged their friends or their enemies to kill them, and so stop their agony. Both sides were horrified at the slaughter. The Roman army was almost completely destroyed and it was one of the worst defeats the Romans ever suffered.

But Hannibal never took Rome—it was too well built and guarded—and Rome would not make peace. His brother Hasdrubal tried to join him with a second army—using Hannibal's route over the Alps. But he was killed in north Italy by the Romans, and his head was cut off and sent to Hannibal's camp. Hannibal now knew that he would never conquer the Romans in their own land.

Another Roman army was commanded by Scipio's son, a military genius who came to be known later as Scipio Africanus. He went across the sea to Spain, and besieged all the Carthaginian towns there. He captured all of them except Cadiz. Then Scipio Africanus turned south, and landed in Africa near Hannibal's own capital, Carthage.

Hannibal had to leave Italy and go home to defend his country, and in a fierce battle he was finally defeated. Scipio had learnt his strategy* from studying Hannibal's own methods. He had managed to persuade the Numidian prince to come over on to his side, and this time it was the Carthaginians who were plagued by the swift and deadly horsemen. When the Cartha-

Scipio Africanus

*Strategy means the art of planning a campaign in the best way. The word for using troops in the best way in a single battle is 'tactics'.

ginian elephants charged, the Romans were ready for them, and the Roman lines opened to let them harmlessly through, just as Darius's chariots had passed through Alexander's lines, 130 years before.

The Romans had won the Second Punic War. Hannibal escaped, and spent the rest of his life as a refugee in Asia. All the Carthaginian warships were set on fire, and her territories overseas given to Rome.

That is nearly the end of the story of the Carthaginians. They might have continued as a small trading nation, but the Romans could not forgive Carthage. They decided to wipe out the city completely. In 146 B.C., after a terrible siege, a Roman army destroyed Carthage. It is said that the Romans ploughed salt into all their lands, so that the survivors could never again till the soil of their homeland.

Chapter 13 The Roman Republic

If a Roman wanted to take public office, he first became a *quaestor*, or junior officer. He then became an *aedile*, and supervised public works, such as building, irrigation and tax-collecting; if he was a successful *aedile*, he might become a judge or *praetor*. Consuls, who were the two annually elected chief magistrates of Rome, were elected from among the *praetors*; and a man who had been made consul many times might become a *proconsul* or governor of a province – the top rung of the ladder.

The post of governor came into being when Rome started to claim other countries outside Italy as 'provinces'. Sicily, Sardinia, Corsica, parts of Spain and North Africa were ruled by Rome after the Punic Wars, and during the next 50 years the Romans conquered Syria, Palestine and Macedonia, and made them into Roman provinces as well. The *lingua franca* (common language) of the Roman world was not Latin but Greek. Many people in the new provinces had learnt Greek already, because of Alexander's conquests. Even the Romans themselves often spoke Greek – especially those living in the seaports of Italy, where they met Greek-speaking seamen. At first the Romans were not good at writing literature, or making statues, or painting, so they copied Greek literature, religion, art and architecture. They were a much more serious-minded people than the Greeks. Their art and literature both show this. They were down-to-earth and practical, and more concerned with day-to-day living than with philosophy and theory.

The Romans had got rid of their kings, and tried to rule their country as a republic, but this form of government never really worked successfully for them. There was too much difference between rich and poor people. Rich landowners bought up all the land and worked their large

Roman Army

The Roman army was divided into centuries, cohorts and legions. A century contained 100 men (sometimes only 80), six centuries made a cohort, and a legion had ten cohorts. The commander of a century was called a centurion.

In battle, a legion had three fighting lines. The front line went into battle first, there was a supporting line behind them, and in the rear a reserve line. The cavalry (horsemen) protected the left and right wings.

In the Greek phalanx, the whole army was fighting right from the start of the battle. The Roman idea of having a reserve line was an improvement, because these men were fresh and rested when their turn came to fight.

When they were not fighting, the legionaries had to drill, and march for miles with heavy packs on their backs. 'Their drills were bloodless battles; their battles bloody drills,' one writer said. If a legion mutinied or ran away from danger, every tenth man was killed.

farms with slave-labour. There were thousands of slaves in Italy now, brought in after the foreign wars. This meant that thousands of peasants were now landless and unemployed, and they flocked to Rome to look for work. In the town, businessmen built large blocks of flats to accommodate all these people. The houses were badly built, and sometimes they collapsed and killed dozens of families. Rome was very overcrowded, and a law was passed to stop carts and other wheeled vehicles from coming into the town during the daytime. So all the transporting of farm produce into the city had to be done by night. There was never a moment when the city was quiet.

The unemployed 'freemen' could not find work in the city, for the slaves were doing it all for no wages. The only way they could earn a living was to join the army.

In the old days the farmers provided soldiers from among their labourers for the army; wars were usually fought between planting the crops and harvesting them, so that the army could be disbanded in time for the men to go back to the land. But now that the soldiers depended on the army for their living, they were no longer eager to be released. So, although the army was disbanded after every campaign, most soldiers immediately signed on for another year's fighting, and retired into winter-quarters (lodgings) at the country's expense.

If there was no war, then there was nothing at all for the unemployed to do. A Roman historian said: 'The men who fight and die for Italy have nothing but air and light .... They are called the masters of the world, yet they have no clod (lump) of earth to call their own.' Various reformers tried to give land back to these people, and the country came to the brink of civil war because the landowners (many of whom were Senators) would not agree. The struggle was still between two classes of people, but the division was now slightly different. Because of earlier reforms, many people from families which had once been plebs, were now wealthy. The reforms had not really changed anything except the names of the two classes, for there was still an upper class (now called *optimares*), and the ordinary people (*populares*).

Besides the struggles between these two classes, there were rivalries between the Senators themselves. Sulla, one of the consuls for the year 88 B.C., was strong enough to make himself a dictator. He was cruel and merciless, and he

Togas
All Roman men wore togas made of woollen cloth, reaching the ankles. Senators wore a purple stripe on their togas, while an emperor might have a completely purple toga. Ordinary people were not allowed to wear purple clothes.

killed 6000 men who were the supporters of a Senator who had opposed him. They were executed just outside the Senate House while the members were in council. The Senators were shocked, but they could do nothing about it. Sulla told them to pay attention to his speech and not listen to the noise outside. 'Some naughty people,' he said, 'are being punished at my orders.' The Republic was no longer working properly, and though the Senate did not then know it, this form of government was about to end in Rome. But before it ended, there was a long civil war, and much Roman blood was shed.

74

Julius Caesar, 108–44 B.C.

Julius Caesar, one of the Romans most widely known about today, was born in about 108 B.C. He began his public career with the post of *quaestor* in Spain. And although this was a very junior appointment, it is said that he made his fortune while in office. He was a shrewd man, and ambitious. He realized that without spending money he could not rise to power, and he used his new fortune to bribe his way into high appointments. He paid for expensive gladiatorial* shows and chariot races, in order to win the support of the people. In 64 B.C. he was given the highest priestly rank in the land—the position known as *Pontifex Maximus*, the Chief Priest. The *Pontifex* was elected for life.

In 59 B.C. Caesar became a consul. He was heavily in debt, and he realized that he must somehow have financial support. He decided to join forces with two important men in the Senate, Pompey and Crassus. Pompey had led the army to war against the Syrians, and had made Palestine a province of Rome; Crassus was a rich land-owner. They were called the 'Triumvirate', the 'three-man-Government', and they held power even over the Senate.

The Gallic Wars

In 58 B.C. trouble broke out in Gaul. The Helvetii, a tribe who lived in western Switzerland, were constantly being attacked by German tribes from the north, and they decided to leave their homes and migrate westwards into present-day France. Caesar was now Governor of the provinces of Cisalpine Gaul and Illyricum (North Italy and the coast of modern Yugoslavia). He immediately marched into Gaul in order to stop the Helvetii from crossing the river Rhône; in the battle that followed thousands of the Helvetii were killed, and their provisions captured. It was a senseless war, because the Helvetii were not a threat to the Romans. Caesar probably fought in order to gain more money for himself, and more power and fame in Rome.

Before he went back to North Italy, Caesar joined forces with the local Gauls to stop the German tribes, living east of the river Rhine, from invading their country. The German king, Ariovistus, had already been officially titled 'king and friend of the Roman people', so the Romans

*Gladiators were men who fought with swords or other weapons against other gladiators or wild animals to entertain the Roman crowd in the 'circuses'.

Religion

Most of the Roman gods were adopted from the Greeks, but their names were changed. Zeus, king of the gods, became Jupiter*. Aphrodite became Venus and Poseidon, god of the sea, became Neptune. Dionysus, god of wine, was Bacchus to the Romans.

Besides these 'imported' gods, the Romans worshipped some much earlier gods of their own. Two especially important ones occupied a place in every home. They were the *lares* and *penates*, the household gods who looked after the family. The picture above shows members of a family making sacrifices to Lar. Most homes had a Larium where small sacrifices to Lar could be make to ensure the well-being and happiness of their family life.

*This is a case where the name has not been completely changed. Zeus became 'Deus Pater' or 'Father God' to the Romans, and that soon become Jupiter.

should not have made war on him. But Ariovistus foolishly led his army across the Rhine, knowing that Caesar would oppose him. He was utterly defeated by the Roman legions, and Caesar wrote: 'Two campaigns were thus finished in a single summer.'

Up till now, there had been no thought of extending the Roman lands to the north. But during the years between 58 B.C. and 49 B.C., Caesar and his legions carried out what Caesar described as 'the conquest and pacification*

*To 'pacify' means to make peaceful.

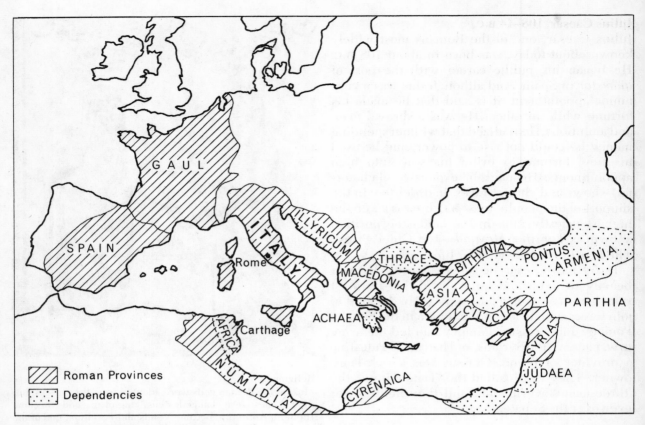

The Roman Republic at the time of Caesar's death.

of Gaul'. In fact his legions fought without pity against a brave and determined people, and because the Romans were better equipped and better disciplined, in those nine years they killed so many Gauls that it was impossible for the survivors to be anything else but 'peaceful'. Some tribes were almost completely wiped out defending their own homes.

The Gauls became so afraid of the Romans that they joined together to try to conquer the legions. One of the most confusing the bewildering things to them was Caesar's habit of doing the unexpected. When a Gallic king named Vercingetorix raised his flag as a signal of revolt, Caesar was over 100 miles away; yet he marched his legions day and night through snow, and reached Vercingetorix's capital long before the Gauls expected him. Caesar kept his legions alert and 'on their toes' by never telling them his plans in advance. He would suddenly order them to practise drill, or to march 20 miles in full armour just as they were settling down to a meal. They had to be prepared to go anywhere, at any time. No soldier was ever unfit through lack of exercise, even when he was far from the

battle-line, or in winter-quarters. But though Caesar was strict, he was also just. His men were proud to be under his command. He called them 'comrades', and they knew that he would never make them bear sufferings and hardships that he himself could not endure.

By destroying so much of his enemies' land, and by killing all their soldiers, Caesar actually made the war more difficult for the Romans. For the other tribes became desperate, and this made them tougher and less likely to surrender. But even Vercingetorix was in the end forced to give in, because his people were starving in a besieged town called Alesia. They had even got to a point of considering eating the old people and the babies in the town, when Vercingetorix finally surrendered. Now Caesar held the whole of Gaul for Rome. In Rome itself, the delighted Senate declared a public thanksgiving that lasted for 20 days.

Meanwhile Crassus had been killed while at war in Asia, and the Triumvirate was broken up. Caesar and Pompey were now rivals for power rather than partners. During Caesar's absence, Pompey had become very powerful among the

76

optimares who controlled the Senate. Caesar, however, was the idol of the *populares*. The Senate ordered Caesar to disband his army, but Caesar refused, and in 49 B.C. he marched south with his legions across the river Rubicon, into Italy. It was against the law to enter Italy with an army, and the Romans realized that Caesar meant to gain control of Rome by force. Pompey hurriedly left the city, and escaped with his legions to Greece.

Caesar was in many ways a rash man, and many times in his career he put himself and his men in great danger because of lack of planning. A modern historian has remarked that more than half of Caesar's campaigns were taken up with getting out of difficult situations that he should not have got into in the first place! It was only because he was so confident of his own powers, and was able to give confidence to his men, that they followed him at all.

The people of Rome expected Caesar to be as merciless as Sulla had been, and they trembled to think of the executions, and the seizing of property ahead. They had heard about Caesar's bloodthirsty methods in Gaul. But Caesar realized that a civil war (a war between the citizens of the same country), should be conducted differently, and he tried to win the people over to his side by mild and generous behaviour. But he knew that he would always be in danger while Pompey was alive, so he followed him with his army into Greece. Pompey was finally defeated at Pharsalus, in Thessaly, and he escaped, leaving behind most of his army. He went to Egypt and asked if he might live there.

Caesar in Egypt

In Egypt, Ptolemy XIV, the Pharaoh, was at war with his sister Cleopatra, who wanted the throne for herself. Ptolemy was afraid to let a Roman general into his country, so instead of receiving Pompey with friendship, he had him murdered. When Caesar arrived in pursuit of Pompey, he was handed his rival's embalmed* head.

Without realizing it, Ptolemy had brought great trouble for himself, for Caesar met and fell in love with Cleopatra, and took her side against the Pharaoh. Caesar stayed in Egypt for nearly a year, during which time Ptolemy was drowned in a battle, when his barge capsized (turned over) on the river Nile. His warships were burnt by Caesar in Alexandria harbour, and his younger

*To embalm is to preserve a dead body from decaying.

Britain

In 55 B.C. and again the following year, Caesar took an army to Britain. The hostile islanders, many of them refugees from Gaul, fought fiercely against the legions. They used chariots to take them into battle, then the warriors leapt out and fought on foot. The charioteers took their vehicles away and had them ready to help in a quick retreat, or in moving the warriors to another part of the battle. Caesar did not have enough troops with him to conquer Britain. In the first century A.D. Romans invaded and conquered England and part of Scotland.

The picture above is a reconstruction of the barracks at a typical Roman fort in Britain in the first century A.D.

brother, Ptolemy XV, was made joint ruler with Cleopatra.

When at last Caesar returned to Rome, he was powerful enough to make himself dictator for ten years. But he did not stay long in Italy, for there were still many supporters of Pompey overseas, and he had to fight first in Libya and then in Spain before the civil war finally ended.

At last Caesar had achieved his aims—he was the sole ruler of Rome. He held the greatest feasts and gladiatorial shows that the city had ever known. In one day 400 lions were hunted to death in the arena, and two enormous armies of criminals and war captives were made to fight each other to the death, in order to excite and entertain the Roman people. Caesar even ordered that a great area of land should be flooded, so that a sham naval battle could be fought. Many of the citizens of Rome were thrilled by these extraordinary entertainments; others were horrified. There were four Triumphs in four days: to celebrate the victories in Gaul, Egypt, Syria and North Africa. Many chiefs and kings were led through Rome in chains, including Vercingetorix, who was publicly executed; and Cleopatra's sister Arsinoë, who was later released.

Caesar had his statue placed with the statues of the gods at the public games, inscribed 'to the unconquerable god'. He gave his friends new posts in the Senate; and since the *populares* had always been on his side, many of the new Senators were centurions, scribes, and even Gauls. He forbade the people to spend too much money on luxuries, while he himself wore purple garments and sat on a gold throne in the Senate House. He was king of Rome in all but name, and some of the Senators decided that he should actually be called 'King of Rome'. But two of the Senators, Cassius and Brutus, feared Caesar's power, and they knew that the other Senators would never vote against Caesar. So they plotted to kill Caesar before the Senate met to discuss the question of kingship.

The meeting was planned for the 15 March, 44 B.C. Caesar had already been warned by a fortune-teller to 'beware the Ides of March', but Brutus persuaded him to go to the meeting, even if only to dismiss the waiting Senators. On the steps of the Senate House, Caesar met the fortune-teller, and said to him scornfully, 'You see, the Ides of March have come', and the man replied, 'Yes, but they have not yet gone.' Less than an hour later, Caesar lay dead. As he sat listening to the Senators' petitions, a number of people pressed forward, took out hidden daggers, and stabbed him to death. When Caesar saw that Brutus, whom he had loved, was among the murderers, he said, 'You, too, my son?'

If you have a copy of Shakespeare's play Julius Caesar *in your library, read Act III.*

We still use some abbreviations from Latin in everyday English. For instance:

i.e.	id est	that is to say
p.m.	post meridiem	afternoon
A.D.	anno Domini	in the year of our Lord
etc.	et cetera	and the rest/others
p.s.	post scriptum	something that is 'written after'
N.B.	nota bene	'note well'
e.g.	exempli gratia	for (the sake of) example

Cleopatra and Mark Antony
Although the Ptolemies were Greeks and not Egyptians, they followed the customs of the old Egyptian Pharaohs. So Cleopatra had to marry her brother Ptolemy XIV. On his death, she married the younger brother, who became Ptolemy XV. Caesar married her in an Egyptian ceremony, and they had a son, Caesarion, who was later murdered in Rome. By this marriage the Egyptians recognized that a Roman dynasty had now taken over from the Greek one. After Caesar's death, Cleopatra married another Roman, Mark Antony, and they ruled together from Alexandria. But Octavian, later called Augustus, first emperor of Rome, defeated the Egyptian forces, and both Mark Antony and Cleopatra committed suicide. The coin above was made during the reign of Mark Antony and Cleopatra. It shows Cleopatra on one side, Mark Antony on the other.

The Julian Calendar
Julius Caesar reformed the calendar and named the seventh month 'July' after his own name. The Roman mosaic above depicts July and August. September, October, November and December originally meant 7th, 8th, 9th and 10th month, after the Latin words *septum, octa, novem,* and *decem.* When Caesar re-arranged the months they kept their names but are now the 9th, 10th, 11th and 12th months of the year. The 'Ides' fell either on the 13th or 15th of each month. The Julian Calendar was in use until A.D. 1582.

Chapter 14 The Roman Empire

Julius Caesar's successor was his great-nephew, Octavian. Octavian had complete power in Rome, and called himself 'Augustus' or 'supreme'. Although he refused to be crowned, or accept any other title, he was in fact the first Roman emperor, and his reign began 300 years of peace in the Empire (though there were short uprisings from time to time). We call this the time of the *pax romana* or 'Roman peace'.

One of Augustus's first acts was to build a temple to his predecessor Julius Caesar, which encouraged the people to think of Caesar as a martyr, and a god. From this time onwards the emperors were all, in varying degrees, worshipped as gods, and their pictures appeared on the standards which the legions took into battle. Soon there were priests for the new emperor-worship, and people in the provinces who did not bow down before the emperor's shrine were severely punished. So although the 'provincials' (people who lived in the provinces) were free to worship their own gods, there was now a worship which was shared by all the people of the empire. The Roman gods, except for Jupiter and the *lares* and *penates*, were almost completely replaced by the new living god-emperor.

Augustus was not a vain man, and he probably did not for a moment believe that he was really divine. But he recognized that Rome, and the newly-conquered countries, needed a symbol that all the widely different peoples could look up to. It was no longer possible for this vast Empire to be ruled by a succession of yearly consuls, all of whom had different ideas about how to govern. Augustus kept the Senate, and let it make laws. But he himself had the real power.

Augustus was not at all like an Asian ruler—he did not need rich clothes, splendid palaces, and daily banquets to hold the respect of the

Virgil

The poet Virgil lived during the reign of Augustus. His greatest work is the *Aeneid*, a poem in 12 books, telling of the founding of the Latin race by Aeneas the Trojan. Aeneas tells the story of his wanderings to Dido in Carthage (see p. 68). At one point in his magical journey, Aeneas goes down to the Underworld and meets future heroes. One of these is Augustus, whom he calls 'the leader often promised, Augustus Caesar of divine descent; he shall establish a golden age in the countryside once ruled by Saturn.'

Virgil's books were so popular that they were used in schools even in his own lifetime.

people. In fact he wore only home-spun togas and leather sandals, and ate quite simple meals. He was always ready to hear the requests of his people, and he allowed residents of all Italy to become citizens of Rome. He kept in touch with the Empire by appointing 30 governors, each with his own province. He built roads and aqueducts*, temples and circuses in the provinces, and encouraged the provincials to live as the citizens of Rome did.

Had Augustus called himself king, and tried to get rid of the Senate, he would probably have been assassinated as Julius Caesar had been. But he cleverly combined dictatorship with rule by the Senate, and everybody was satisfied. He took on a difficult job, and handled it well and firmly. His last words were: 'Have I played my part in the comedy of life creditably enough?' Later generations agreed that he had, and spoke of him as the best emperor that had ever ruled over them. He had managed to stop the constant quarrels in Rome, and he prepared the way for the great *pax romana* in Europe, Asia and North Africa.

The Pax Romana

During the next 300 years, not all the emperors were as keen to 'play their part' as carefully and conscientiously as Augustus had. But in spite of this the Empire grew, and the conquered territories settled down, mainly because of excellent government in the provinces. Even Gaul, which had suffered so much from Julius Caesar's armies, began to flourish again in a new way, as people built new towns and villages on the Roman plan. Men from the provinces were sometimes called up into the Roman army as auxiliaries ('helping' troops), and they marched and fought with the legions as non-citizen units. The auxiliaries could become Roman citizens, with a grant of land, after 25 years' service, and many of them were happy to do so.

The Empire was now greater than the individual emperors. A Roman general once told the Gauls that they should bear the rule of a bad emperor in much the same way as they endured years of flood or drought; there were sure to be better times ahead. Roman law, and the ability of Roman officials, kept the Empire in peace in spite of troubles in Rome itself. Two of the best-known 'bad' (possibly even mad) emperors were Caligula and Nero. Caligula is said to have given his horse a marble stall and purple blankets, and made it a consul; and he forced rich men to leave their money to the state. Nero killed his own mother and his half-brother. During his reign Rome was burnt in an accidental fire, and rumour said that Nero had lit the fire himself, and had stood watching the flames, while playing

*Aqueducts are channels carrying water, usually *over* the land or across valleys, by being built on arches.

a lyre, a small kind of harp. After the fire Nero blamed the Christians for starting it, and he ordered them to be torn to pieces by lions in the arena where the gladiatorial shows were held. During A.D. 68 and 69, there were four emperors in Rome, one after the other. Two of them were murdered, and the third committed suicide. The fourth was Vespasian, one of the great emperors, who managed to put an end to the civil unrest.

Even the successful and 'good' emperors allowed a great deal of cruelty to go on in the Empire. The games and gladiatorial contests, where thousands of men were tortured and killed each year to entertain the Roman crowds, were often attended by the emperors themselves. It is not surprising that the Roman soldiers who were so used to seeing bloody entertainments in the arenas at home, were often brutal to their prisoners. But this was an age of cruelty, and their enemies, the Gauls, the Britons, and the German tribes, were just as cruel themselves. The remarkable thing is that after a battle, the conquerors and the conquered lived side by side at peace, working for the good of the community as a whole. Perhaps the gladiatorial shows and chariot-races, which were now held in all the major towns of the Empire, were a way of 'letting off steam' in times of peace. The Roman settlers in these towns had no feeling of superiority over the native inhabitants; Roman citizens married native wives, and they and their children lived in Roman-built towns under Roman law. This mixing up of peoples was the Roman strength; they could never have kept their Empire for so long if they had not allowed the conquered peoples to be equal under the law. Instead of feeling inferior and bitter, the provincials gradually acquired a new pride in themselves and their settled way of life.

Britain

By the second century A.D., the northern limit of the Empire was the great wall built by the emperor Hadrian across the width of Britain. On the wall, legionaries from Gaul and Spain, Britain itself, Syria and Italy, kept watch for attacks from Caledonia as Scotland was then called. Britain had been left alone for nearly 100 years after Julius Caesar's visits. Then, under the emperor Claudius, the legions sailed once again across the English Channel and marched inland, building roads and bridges, temples and towns. Some of the British tribes were friendly, others

hostile. The Britons in Wales fought fiercely in their mountain fortresses and strongholds; the people of Caledonia were never subdued. The Iceni, a tribe living in present-day Norfolk, revolted, and led by their queen Boudicca (or Boadicea), they marched south and burnt three new Roman-British towns, killing all the inhabitants with great ferocity. We have a description of this wild British queen, written by a Roman historian:

'She was very tall, in appearance terrifying, in the glance of her eye most fierce, and her voice was harsh. A great mass of the tawniest (yellow-brown) hair fell to her hips. Around her neck she wore a large golden necklace; and she wore a tunic of many colours over which a thick cloak was fastened with a brooch.'

She rode a war-chariot into battle; when she was at last defeated she poisoned herself.

For 40 years three Roman legions were kept busy in Britain, building forts, checking raiders, and putting down rebellions. And after the invasion was over, Britain, from Hadrian's Wall to the south coast, enjoyed Roman peace and prosperity. The Roman Governor of Britain was considered a great man, second only to the Governor of Syria.

Hadrian's Wall

Hadrian built a great wall from the river Tyne to the Solway, in order to help the legions defend Roman Britain against the northern tribes. Parts of the wall still exist today. It was over 112 kilometres (70 miles) long, protected by a ditch and a mud ramp. There were forts all along the wall, and on the southern side small markets grew up, with shops and taverns where the local people sold their goods to the soldiers stationed in the forts. Along the top of the wall, sentries walked to and fro between their own fort and the next, always on the lookout for the painted barbarians of the mountains. Was this wall anything like the Great Wall of China?

The trade routes of the Empire

In the east, most of Alexander's empire fell to the Romans. They built forts to guard their boundaries, and stationed soldiers from other parts of the Empire to control the new provinces. Although travelling was still a very slow business, soldiers and administrators often served hundreds of miles from their home towns. For the first time the ordinary common people began to see for themselves how other countries managed their affairs. Whole families left Italy and settled in 'colonies' in other parts of the Roman world. The emperors themselves often went to the provinces to review the troops; Claudius visited Britain, and Vespasian knew it well; and Trajan, an emperor whose birthplace was Spain, visited Alexander's palace in Babylon.

The Romans were not the only travellers: teachers and doctors, artists and sculptors, left their homes in Syria and Turkey, Greece and North Africa, and went to practise their skills in the flourishing towns of Italy. There was a great exchange of peoples, and there was also an increase in trade. Tin, gold, sheepskins and corn came from Britain by sea, and on the backs of donkeys along the straight Roman roads: camels and donkeys plodded day after day along the old Persian highways, bringing silks and precious stones from China and India, silver, crystal (a very clear kind of quartz) and salt from northern Asia, and corn from Russia. The Romans even bought spices which had been grown in Ceylon, but they did not go there themselves.

All the time the Romans had to be careful not to take too much from the provinces. They needed corn to feed the people of Rome, but if they went on demanding it even in time of famine, trouble followed.

On the Sea of Marmora, just south-west of the Black Sea, Byzantium grew in importance because of its central position for trade between east and west. There were so many trading ships sailing across the Black Sea that soon pirates became common, and the Romans had to keep a fleet of 40 ships to protect their cargo boats.

The ruins of Pompeii

In A.D. 79, the volcano Vesuvius (in the background of the picture) erupted and lava and ash completely buried two Roman cities. A Roman writer named Pliny watched the eruption from far off. He said it looked like 'a pine tree, for it shot up a great height . . . into several branches.' The eruption continued for three days, during which stones and ash were hurled across the countryside.

One of the buried cities, Pompeii, has been dug up by archaeologists, and beneath the layers of ash and lava were found buildings, furniture, and even fossilized remains of people and animals. Pompeii was a wealthy city, and most of the inhabitants could read and write. From the remains that have been uncovered we can see how a typical Roman city was organized.

North Africa and Egypt

Trade with North Africa was even more important to Rome than trade with the east. The whole coast of North Africa was settled by farmers, whose corn crops went to feed the rest of the Empire. Egypt provided a great deal of the income of Rome, and the Roman emperors always took care to manage the country well. Every year corn and gold left Egypt for Italy by ship; these rich imports of gold meant that the townspeople of Rome did not have to pay high taxes; and in some reigns they were actually given free food and lodging, while the slaves did all the work.

In Egypt, Alexandria was still a great centre of learning, and as in other parts of the Empire, many of the inhabitants spoke Greek. There was a large Jewish population there, and they carried on a flourishing trade with the east. They used a caravan route from the Nile Valley to the Red Sea, to bring to Alexandria the silks and spices of China and India.

In Rome, and in the other cities of Italy, builders imported African marble, and painted African scenes on their walls. The Romans were fascinated* by the tales of strange animals and dark-skinned people, which they heard from those who had travelled to Roman towns in Algeria, Libya and Egypt. It was an exciting time for those with enquiring minds. There were so many new things to see and to learn about. The provincial people, whose culture had already been influenced by the Greeks, gained from

*To be fascinated is to be so interested that one might be under a magic spell.

Trajan's Column

Trajan, the first non-Italian emperor, built a new Forum in Rome in about A.D. 100. As architect, he chose a Greek who lived in Damascus, in the Roman province of Syria. The Forum held shops and offices, and two libraries, one for Greek books, and the other for Latin books. On a column between the two libraries, a spiral frieze (an ornamental band) was carved with scenes from Trajan's campaigns in Dacia, north of the Danube.

their contacts with the rest of the world. Philosophers and historians, mathematicians and astronomers went to the university at Alexandria; among them were some of the greatest thinkers the world has known. Scholars exchanged ideas, and built up a great library so that those who followed them might carry on where they had left off. Some of the ideas and theories of these men, living during the *pax romana*, were not improved upon until recent times.

Many provincials were now allowed to apply for Roman citizenship, and some even became emperors. Trajan and Hadrian, both excellent emperors, were Spaniards, and Septimius Severus was an African from Leptis Magna. There was a great feeling of unity in the Empire, and even the Greeks said, 'An attack on Rome is an attack on us.' The great genius of the Romans was that they were able to govern so many different countries, yet allow each one to keep its own customs, language and religion. Cyrus of Persia and Alexander of Macedonia had tried to do this too, but they did not have the thousands of quiet, efficient, able administrators that the Romans had, nor their ability to blend together the conqueror and the conquered.

83

Chapter 15 Life in the Empire

The Roman and Greek characters were quite different. A Roman preferred action, while to a Greek the most important thing was thinking. The Greeks regarded the Romans as barbarians when they first met them, because when the Romans conquered a civilized city, they destroyed the works of art—merely because they did not recognize that they were beautiful. The Romans, on the other hand, thought the Greeks were pleasure-loving and idle, and could not understand their liking for talk and discussion. One Roman consul told a group of Sophists that if they came to his court-house, he would settle their arguments for them: he did not understand that most of their discussions were about things that can have *no* final answer!

All Romans knew something of the laws of their country, and a lawyer was highly respected. In the days of the Empire he received fees for his services, but during the Republic he had to rely on presents from his clients, the people who used his services. A wrongdoer was granted a public trial, and his lawyer helped him to prepare his speech of defence. The accuser also had a lawyer as an adviser. There was no such thing as having 'the state' as the accuser as we do today for criminal trials; all lawsuits* were entered into by private persons, the one accusing the other—even for crimes like murder. Trials were often won by the lawyer who made the best speeches, and a man could become famous for the way in which he was able to win a trial.

Although the Romans seem to us now to have had little imagination, they were trustworthy and honest, law-abiding and just. The provincials respected them, and learnt to live by their laws.

A Roman family was ruled by the father. He had complete control over his sons until they

*To take action against somebody in a court of law is 'to sue'; an action in a court of law is a lawsuit.

Roman dress

In the privacy of his own home, a Roman 'freeman' felt more comfortable without his toga, and appeared in the tunic, which normally he wrote underneath. But if he went into the street so dressed, he was likely to be mistaken for a workman or even a slave, who is pictured above.

A Roman freeman's wife also wore a tunic, as in the picture, and a belted gown reaching down to the ankles. When she went out she wore a hood. Both men and women wore sandals tied with leather laces in the house, and stronger leather shoes out of doors. Peasants and slaves were either barefooted or wore clogs or sandals in the street. The Roman freemen disapproved of a man who wore sandals in the street, or a woman who was not dressed in the latest fashion.

were 16 years old, and over his daughters until they married. All the decisions were made by him, although his wife was allowed to own property, and to have some influence over the upbringing of her children. The parents, if they were well off, would almost certainly find a Greek tutor for their children, and would encourage them to read and write in Greek as well as Latin. The girls as well as the boys learnt to read and write, and to know something of history, geography, mathematics and astronomy. They studied law, and learnt long passages from the law books by heart. The Greeks, you remember, used to get together over a meal to discuss philosophy, poetry, or religion. The Roman idea of good conversation was less intellectual and more gossipy, or more practical: they were inclined to talk scandal, or argue about the qualities of a new consul, or exchange the latest news of an uprising in Jerusalem. They could not see the point in endless discussion about abstract theoretical things.

Educated Romans often went to Greece and to Egypt as tourists, and they marvelled at the Parthenon and the Pyramids, just as modern tourists do. By the time of Augustus, the Pyramids were already nearly 3000 years old. The Ptolemy Pharaohs had restored many of the old temples, and they too attracted Roman travellers. We even know the names of some of these tourists, for they carved them on the temple walls!

All the big towns of the Empire, Londinium, Caesaraugusta, Lutetia, Byzantium, Neapolis, Tingis*, and many many others—copied the pattern of Rome. Wealthy Roman citizens, whether they were by birth British, or Celts from Gaul, or Syrians or Libyans, built houses just like those in Rome, with floors decorated with mosaics (pictures made with small coloured stones), courtyards with fountains, and wall recesses for the *lares* and *penates*. They ate, where possible, the same kinds of food, and they drank wine imported from the vineyards of Gaul and Italy. Their common culture became a common bond.

In Rome itself, in some periods it was said that the rich got sick from eating, and the poor from not eating. Certainly the rich ate huge meals with great enjoyment. They often invited friends in for the evening meal, which was the main time for eating. They lay on long couches

*Find these towns on a modern map. They are now called London, Saragossa, Paris, Istanbul, Naples and Tangier.

Roman writing

By the time of the Republic, the letters of the alphabet had become almost the same as the capital letters we use today. We call the alphabet used in this book 'Roman'. The Latin inscription above, carved on stone, is part of a commemoration to a priest named CLAUDIO SOSSIANO SEVERIANO.

For ordinary writing, the Romans used wooden tablets coated with wax, on which they scratched the words with a pointed metal 'stylus'. When writing documents, letters or books, they used either papyrus or parchment made from sheepskin. Books were often written on one long sheet of papyrus, then rolled up: but sometimes they were cut and the pages sewn or stuck together, rather like modern books. They wrote with goose-feather pens and black ink. There were bookshops in the Forum where slaves sat all day copying popular books for sale.

I	III	V	VII	IX	XI	XXX
1	3	5	7	9	11	30

L	XC	C	D	M
50	90	100	500	1000

Roman numerals

Even now we sometimes use these Roman numerals to number chapters in a book, or the hours on a clock face, or as dates on a monument. The Romans had no nought, and without it, modern mathematics is not possible.

In the Roman system, if you wrote a lower number before a higher one, such as X before C—XC, the result was 'one hundred *minus* ten', or 90. The date '1977' would be written like this: MCMLXXVII

85

round the dining table, while slaves served them large helpings of eggs and fish, the small squirrel-like animals called dormice cooked in honey, poultry and small roasted birds, game and fruit. The poor in the cities were lucky to get a ration of bread and a handful of olives, washed down with a cup of sour wine. To stop them from rioting, and to keep them fed and occupied, some emperors allowed them free bread and put on free circus-shows. The upper classes were always afraid that the discontent of the unemployed, living in their smelly, unventilated and crowded apartment houses, would cause them to rise against the rich and bring civil war again to Rome.

Every year there were feast days on which everybody, rich and poor alike, stopped work and joined in the general rejoicing. In December, all Romans celebrated the Saturnalia, feast of the god Saturn, at which people gave each other presents, and a mock-king was crowned as ruler of the feast. The slaves had the day free, and their masters waited on them at dinner. On other feast days there were public games and circuses, and chariot races.

Home of a wealthy Roman

A Roman house in a wealthy district was built as two squares joined together. One square was called the 'atrium' and the other the 'peristyle'. The atrium was the place where the gentleman of the house had his offices, and perhaps a library. In the centre of the atrium was an unroofed space, within which there was a pool called the 'impluvium'. Small dark bedrooms opened off the atrium. There were no outside windows; in towns, shops were often built against the walls of a rich man's house.

The Roman family spent much of their time in the peristyle where, as you can see in the picture, there was a central garden surrounded by columns with statues, fountains and birdbaths. The dining-room and more bedrooms opened off the peristyle.

The builders of the Empire

All over the Empire, the Romans built roads. They were so well constructed, that many of them are still used today. They were built, where possible, completely straight. Where there were rivers, the Roman engineers built bridges or fords; where a hill crossed the route, they built tunnels, or cut away the banks. Each road had foundations about five feet deep, and they were made with whatever long-lasting materials were at hand. Usually there were heavy rocks for the foundations, then earth and rubble—broken bricks and stone. Near the towns, the top layer of the roads was made of stone blocks. (The word 'street' comes from the Latin for 'paved road'.) Elsewhere the surface might be gravel, flint, or even a type of cement. There was a drain at each side of the road, and kerbstones edging the road stopped the surface from sliding into the ditches. There were milestones along the way, usually marked with the name of the emperor during whose rule the road had been built. The legions marched along these roads, often with straggling lines of prisoners; baggage animals were led along them, and carts piled with trade goods rattled by from one end of the Empire to the other.

As well as roads, the Romans built aqueducts to carry water to the towns from the nearest river. The aqueducts were built as a series of arches, with a water-channel at the top. They had a continuous gradual downward slope towards the town, so that the water flowed at a steady rate all the time.

The Romans loved to bathe in public baths, and everywhere they went they constructed these huge buildings. They went to the baths to talk to their friends, as well as to clean themselves. There were rooms in which they could exercise with weights, or oil their bodies with scented oil or have them rubbed and massaged by slaves; there were hot baths, steam baths, cold showers, and changing rooms. The water was heated by a furnace, and the heat was also spread by pipes under the floor of the baths. Wealthy Romans often had private baths in their houses, and heated their rooms by hot air circulated underneath the floors. Some of the public baths were built of a type of cement, which was poured over a huge wooden framework.

Roman road—the Via Appia at Rome

A Greek once wrote admiringly of the Romans: 'You have measured out the world, bridged rivers, cut roads through mountains, filled the wastelands with staging posts .... Be all the gods and their children called upon to grant that this Empire and this city flourish for ever ....'

As time went by, it no longer mattered that 'citizens of Rome' had never actually been to the parent city. Even the emperors themselves did not always live there, but divided their time

Roman baths at Bath, in S.W. England

between the various towns in the provinces. Septimius Severus, the emperor from Leptis Magna, was born in North Africa, but died at York in northern England, in A.D. 211. Most of his advisers came from Asia and Africa, and he allowed foreign languages to be used instead of Latin in official Roman papers.

To a Roman citizen living when the Empire was at its height, it must have seemed that the world would go on forever in the same way. But over in the north-east, across the mountains and plains of Asia, vast numbers of men, whom the Romans called 'barbarians,' were slowly moving westwards. In the years to come, the Empire had increasing trouble with these nomadic tribes.

Commodus, who was emperor from A.D. 180–192, was more interested in gladiatorial shows and circuses than in defending the Danube frontier. In Rome itself at this time, half the population lived on free food and had free entertainment, while most of the other half were slaves. The Romans at home could not see that they must work to keep their Empire; they were fed at public expense—what more could they want? But Rome was using more money than it earned, and this situation could not last. When Commodus tried to increase taxation in his provinces, there were revolts and riots. He was finally killed by one of his own guards, and for the next 100 years the army had real control, and elected their own emperors. Civil wars between rival generals were common, and the Huns, Goths and Visigoths took advantage of these troubles to invade the borders of the Empire.

The last emperor to rule from Rome was Constantine. His mother was British, and he was born in York. His army marched into Italy from Britain and Gaul, and defeated other claimants to the throne. It is said that on his way to Rome he saw a vision in the sky—a cross, with the words HOC SIGNO VINCE—'by this sign, conquer'. Whatever the truth of this, he did make Christianity (the religion whose symbol is the cross) the official state religion of the Roman Empire.

Constantine could see that there was no point in maintaining Rome as the capital of the Empire. He himself lived at Nicomedia, a port on the Sea of Marmora, and in A.D. 330 he transferred the administrative capital to Byzantium, one of Alexander the Great's cities. The name of the city was changed to Constantinople. (It is now Istanbul.)

Constantinople was then much more 'central' than Rome. It was truly the meeting point of east and west. It had long been a place where merchants exchanged their goods, and it was built in an ideal position, on a thin strip of land jutting into the sea. It had a good climate, and there was plenty of good farming land nearby. Here Constantine could build afresh the old spirit of discipline and training that had once made Rome itself great. The old capital became no more than a provincial town, though for a time there was an 'emperor of the West' who lived there.

But the attacks of the barbarian peoples from the east increased in strength. Most of these peoples belonged to the German tribes of the Franks, Goths, Saxons and Vandals. The legions fought valiantly to hold the Empire's long frontiers. For over 200 years they had succeeded, often after hard fighting, in defeating the invaders, but at last, in A.D. 407, the barbarians crossed the river Rhine into the Empire, plundering and destroying as they went, and this time they were too strong for the legions to drive them out. The Roman frontier had been broken for ever. Other tribes followed, and soon all of western Europe—Britain, Gaul, Spain, North Africa and even Italy—was lost to the Empire.

Constantine had been wise to move his capital; and Constantinople remained a centre of civilization long after the barbarians had overrun the western half of the Roman Empire. The period that followed is known as 'the Dark Ages'. But here and there, some of the wisdom and knowledge gained by the Greeks and Romans was remembered. Most of the people who kept the old learning alive were Christians, living in small monasteries as far apart as Ireland and Syria, Iceland and Ethiopia. On the remnants of the old civilizations, the world was to build new nations with new ideas and ideals.

Greek schoolboys learnt the stories of Homer by heart; Roman schoolboys learnt the Law.
Write down the differences between the Greeks and Romans in:
government;
their attitude to foreigners;
the geography of their countries;
their fighting formations;
public entertainments;

Part IV Christianity and Islam
Chapter 16 Jesus of Nazareth

Palestine, on the eastern shores of the Mediterranean, was only a small part of the Roman Empire, but it was a very troublesome part. The Jews of Palestine did not like Roman rule. They already had to pay taxes to their own Temple, and now the Romans were demanding still more taxes to help pay for the administration of the Empire. Worse still, the Romans said that the Jews should worship the statue of their emperor.

Most of the other Roman provinces did not mind adding the Roman emperor to their long list of gods; but the Jews, who only had one God, Yahweh, objected strongly. They said they could not obey, because of their first and second Commandments (see page 38). And what was more, the earthly leader of the Jews, they said, was the High Priest of Jerusalem, not the emperor of a foreign power. There was a great deal of unrest in Palestine, and many uprisings, which the Romans repeatedly stopped by armed force.

In this troubled country, there was born a boy who was named Jesus. He was the son of Mary, a Jewish girl married to a carpenter of Nazareth, called Joseph. Joseph was said to be a descendant of King David. The story of Jesus is written down in the four Gospels, which are part of the New Testament in the Bible. Two of the Gospels start with the story of Jesus's birth. They tell how Joseph and Mary his wife travelled to Bethlehem, to take part in a census, or counting of people, ordered by the Romans. The little town was so crowded that there was no room for them to lodge at any inn, and they had to sleep in a stable. During this time, Jesus was born.

We do not know much about the childhood of Jesus. But St Luke tells us how his parents took him to Jerusalem when he was about 12 years old, for the Feast of the Passover. As Joseph and Mary were returning home, they missed Jesus, and had to go back to look for him. They found

John the Baptist
Although Palestine belonged to the Roman province of Syria, part of it (Galilee) was actually ruled for Rome by a king named Herod, who was half-Jewish.

Herod was allowed to have power in his part of Palestine as long as it was obedient to Rome, so he was eager to keep the peace. His own wealth and position depended on it. He saw how popular John the Baptist was, and he became afraid that the fiery preacher might lead the people to defy Rome. So he had him imprisoned and beheaded.

him in the Temple, listening spellbound to the priests' words. During this early part of his life, he surely must have learnt all he could about the Jewish faith, and thought about God, and man's relationship to God.

Jesus had a cousin named John, who was almost the same age as he was. When they were both about 30 years old, John was already a well-known holy man in Palestine. There were many wandering preachers in those days, and they often lived as John did, wearing camel-hair cloaks and eating wild berries and honey. John impressed the people of Palestine by his teaching, and crowds gathered round him when he started to baptize people in the river Jordan. They waded into the river, and John poured water on to their heads, as a sign that they were sorry for their sins, and would try to do better in future. John was known as 'the Baptist' because of his method of bringing people to repentance.

One day Jesus went to the river to be baptized by John. St Matthew says that when Jesus came out of the river, the Spirit of God came down from heaven like a dove, and a voice said, 'This is my beloved Son, in whom I am well pleased.'

Jesus helped John to baptize the people for several months, then he began a new kind of teaching. With a group of disciples he went about the land of Galilee talking to people about God as their Father, and healing the sick. Thousands of people followed him, and believed that he was the Messiah—that is, a leader for whom they had been waiting for generations. ('Messiah' means 'the Lord's Anointed one'. The word 'Christ' comes from the Greek word for 'Messiah'.)

The popular Jewish idea of a Messiah was of a man who would rid them of the Romans, and lead the Jews to glory by creating a splendid new kingdom. Obviously, to defeat the might of Rome, such a Messiah would have to be a strong and clever general, and he would need far more soldiers than little Palestine could produce. But in any case, Jesus was not at all like this. He did not believe in defying Rome. He taught that people should make peace with God the Father in their own hearts, and not bother so much about the irritations of everyday living. His Kingdom was 'not of this world'. It was within each person's own self, if he only cared to look for it.

Jesus was a most compassionate man, for he pitied the distress of others and desired to help them. He told people that God was a God of love, not of vengeance, as some of the old Jewish tales of God had made Him out to be. In almost every story in the Gospels, we read of the mercy and love of God. People began to feel that they could be happy and 'blessed' without being rich, or well-born.

Jesus healed many people in a way which is beyond our knowledge: for instance, people who had such diseases as a crippled hand, a twisted back, leprosy, fits and madness, are said by the Gospel-writers to have been cured by a touch of his hand. On one occasion Jesus even restored

The Gospel writers

'Gospel' originally meant 'good news'. Many people during the two centuries following Jesus's death wrote down the good news contained in his teaching; of these writings, four are part of the New Testament of the Bible.

St Mark was the first Gospel-writer of the four, and he probably wrote his book in Rome, having heard the story from Jesus's disciple, Peter. St Matthew added more incidents to Mark's writings, and his Gospel is fuller and more detailed. St Luke was probably a Gentile, and a healer. He seems to have used some stories that Mark and Matthew did not know about. St Luke's Gospel may have been told to the writer by John, one of Jesus's disciples, when he was a very old man.

The Gospel of St John was once supposed to have been written by this same John, the disciple. But some modern scholars think that this is doubtful. It was written later than the other three Gospels.

The illustration is of a painting from a seventeenth century Ethiopian manuscript of St Luke and St John.

a man to life. We know that he did not do these things 'for show', because he told his patients that they should be quiet about how they were healed; he said it was their own faith that led to their cure. God had restored their health because of their faith in Jesus.

Much of Jesus's teaching was by parable—that is, by means of a story which taught a lesson. This was a popular Jewish way of teaching, but Jesus went further than most Jewish preachers. He did not believe that people should merely 'follow the Law' by keeping the rules about what they could eat, or by doing no work on the Sabbath (Saturday). Many Jews thought that by offering the right sacrifices, and praying at the right times, and giving money to the poor, they were doing God's will. Jesus thought these acts were meaningless unless they were sincerely carried out. A poor fisherman might easily please God more than a rich priest who prayed all day. There are many instances in the Gospels where Jesus said things which surprised the crowd because they were fresh and new. He did not attempt to change Jewish laws and traditions: only to interpret them in a new and more joyous way. He summed up the Ten Commandments of Moses in these two new rules:

Love the Lord your God with all your heart, with all your soul, with all your mind, and with all your strength;

Love your neighbour as yourself.

Jesus did not deliberately start a new religion. He was only concerned with making the Jewish faith more alive. But his teachings did in fact lead to the religion we now call Christianity.

The priests were furious because Jesus criticized them, and because he allowed people to do things which *they* thought were against Jewish religious law. They tried to trap him by asking him difficult questions about whether it was lawful to pay tribute to the emperor of Rome; or whether his disciples should rub ears of corn together to make flour on the Sabbath. (They called this 'work'.) Jesus's replies were always calm and reasonable; the priests could not make him say anything that was irreverent to God, or even disloyal to Rome.

Jesus spent three years teaching the people in this way. Peter, one of the disciples, was the first to say that they thought Jesus must be the Messiah they were all looking for. The priests also waited for a Messiah, but they were outraged when they realized that Jesus might claim this title. They felt that their power

Judas betraying Christ in the Garden of Gethsemane
Judas was one of the twelve disciples of Jesus. We do not know why he betrayed Jesus. The Gospels say he received 30 pieces of silver for this action, but this amount would not seem enough to betray his master if it were just for greed. Perhaps this was only part-payment. After Jesus's death, Judas hanged himself, probably in remorse.

The Jewish Passover Feast
The Feast of the Passover was held every year at a special time; all male Jews were required to travel to Jerusalem for the ceremonies. There were ritual animal sacrifices in the Temple, and at the end of the day groups of people ate a meal together. The feast was held in memory of an event which occurred when the Israelites were slaves in Egypt: they saved themselves from death by smearing lambs' blood on their house doors. According to the Old Testament of the Bible, the Angel of Death then 'passed over' these houses.

Jews were not allowed to eat bread made with yeast during the Passover. This was in memory of their flight from Egypt, when there was no time to bake proper bread.

was threatened by this carpenter's son, and they easily persuaded the Roman procurator, Pontius Pilate, that Jesus's popularity might lead to a revolt. (A procurator was rather like a Provincial Commissioner.) Pilate knew that if the Jews had a popular leader who claimed to be the Messiah, the result might well be a bloody war. This he wanted to avoid—and so did the priests, and so did Herod. Jesus's mission was completely misunderstood by all these people, for he also passionately wanted peace—the peace of God in men's hearts as well as peace in Palestine, and peace in all the world.

This total misunderstanding led to great tragedy. Only three years after he began his teaching, Jesus rode into Jerusalem on a donkey, for the Feast of the Passover, and the people waved palm branches as he went by. Later, he went into a garden called Gethsemane to pray. Jesus knew the authorities were against him, and that he did not have long to live. Judas, one of his own disciples, but a traitor, led armed guards to him, and kissed him on the cheek, so as to point him out to the soldiers. Jesus was led away for trial before the Jewish court. We do not know all the details of this trial, but after it was over the priests gave Jesus back to the Romans, saying that he had called himself the King of the Jews. The Romans killed Jesus by the method they used for non-Roman citizens—crucifixion. But in spite of this horrible and degrading* death, Jesus was not forgotten. His words and ideas live on today, kept alive by Christians all over the world. The early Christians found passages in the Jewish holy books to support their belief that Jesus, 'of the House of David', was the Messiah for whom they had been waiting. Many prophecies in the Old Testament seemed to fit in with events in the life of Jesus.

Christians everywhere celebrate two great festivals, Christmas, in honour of Jesus's birth, and Easter. On the Firday before Easter Sunday, they commemorate his death on the cross, and on the following Sunday (Easter Day), his miraculous resurrection, or rising again, from the dead. It is told in the Gospels that after three days Jesus's tomb was found empty, and for several weeks afterwards he was seen by many people. They say he walked and talked and ate with them, and then, St Luke wrote, 'He ascended into heaven.'

---

*Degrading—bringing dishonour.

The Early Christians

Jesus had often talked about a 'second coming', when he would return and establish an everlasting kingdom of peace. The disciples thought this would occur in their lifetime, and after Jesus's death many of them went out to preach this to the people. Some of his followers gave away all their goods, as Jesus had told them to, and lived a wandering life of poverty. In the Acts of the Apostles (in the New Testament of the Bible), we read how later missionaries left Palestine and preached about Jesus to the 'Gentiles'—that is, to non-Jews. They had great success among Greek-speaking peoples who believed in the idea of 'One God', but who could not become Jews because they did not want to follow the whole of the Jewish religious law. We have seen how Jesus had wanted to improve the old Jewish faith for the *Jews*; but it was the non-Jews who were more readily converted, that is, changed their beliefs, after his death. The Christian religion in the end became a completely Gentile faith.

The first Christians in Rome were persecuted and hated, because they were misunderstood. The Romans were generally tolerant of other people's religions: there is no record of any other

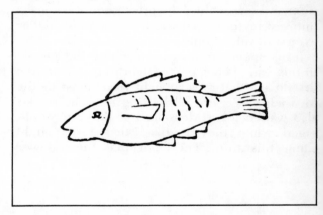

The sign of the fish
Early Christians were like a kind of universal club. They celebrated their own feasts (the 'Last Supper' instead of the Passover, for instance), and they tried to act according to their new faith. This was never easy, for almost everywhere they went, they were surrounded by Roman citizens, who worshipped many different gods.

The Christians had a sign by which they could recognize other Christians. It was a rough drawing of a fish. The Greek for 'fish' is 'ichthus', and the letters I CH TH U S could also stand for the initial letters of the Greek words for 'Jesus Christ, God, Son and Saviour'. The sign of the cross, now the universal Christian symbol, was not used in the early days of Christianity.

religious belief being forbidden. But, like the Jews, Christians refused to recognize the Roman emperor as a god, and so they were persecuted officially for this reason. And because of the persecution, they met in secret; the secret meetings led to all sorts of tales of sinful practices, and the Roman people thought they were plotting against the state.

Jesus had shown that even the poorest people, slaves, and even women—all of whom were kept out of many religions—could become Christians, and so many of the Roman Christians were very humble people. Hundreds of them were killed because of their faith, and some endured terrible deaths in the Roman arenas to provide entertainment for the crowd. But even this helped Christianity to spread, for the Roman spectators were very impressed by the Christians' courage as they stood facing the charging lions. They felt that a religion that inspired such bravery, even in women and children, must be worth following. Soon even some of the emperors agreed to allow people to follow this new religion, and it spread throughout the Empire. Antioch in Syria, Alexandria, and Rome itself, became the three great Christian centres of the world.

The Christian Church is organized

The four Gospels were written in Greek, so that all these different Christian communities might read the words of Jesus, and it was only later, in about A.D. 200, that Latin began to be used in churches. By then the Christians had developed an organization in which there were local churches headed by bishops. The bishops were under the authority of an archbishop, and by 700 they all acknowledged the Bishop of Rome (the Pope or Father) as Head of the whole Church.

For a time the Christians at Constantinople (now capital of the eastern Roman Empire) also acknowledged the Pope in Rome, but quarrels broke out between east and west, and then eastern and western Christianity developed separately. The split led to the Churches we now call Roman Catholic on the one hand; and Greek and Russian Orthodox on the other.

Wherever they went, the new Christian missionaries of the west tried to win people to their religion by persuasion. In England, for instance, an early Christian writer says:

'The heathen temples of these people need not be destroyed, only the idols which are to be found in them . . . . If the temples are well

Peter and John healing the lame man outside the Temple
Jesus said to his disciple Peter; 'You are Peter, the Rock; and on this rock I will build my church.' [Peter comes from the Greek word *petros*, meaning rock.] After Jesus's death Peter carried on his work in Palestine. The priests forbade him to continue preaching in the name of Jesus; but after being punished by them, Peter continued to lead the new church. He taught the Gentiles in Asia Minor, and then went to Rome where it is believed he was crucified.

built, it is a good idea to detach them from the service of the devil, and to adapt them for the worship of the true God.'

The old pagan festivals were changed bit by bit, until they became Christian ceremonies. (Christmas took the place of the old Roman 'Saturnalia', and other new year festivals; Easter was once a spring festival to celebrate the return of the corn.) The same Christian writer says that teaching Christianity was like climbing a mountain; nobody would run to the top, but would advance slowly, step by step.

After the collapse of the western Roman Empire, in some remote places there were only a few Christians left, and they retired to monasteries and guarded the precious manuscripts which recorded their faith. In other parts, the 'barbarian' invaders of the Roman Empire had already been converted to Christianity themselves, and there grew up Christian kingdoms in which rough warriors tried to follow the ideas of the peace-loving Jesus.

Chapter 17 Christianity Spreads

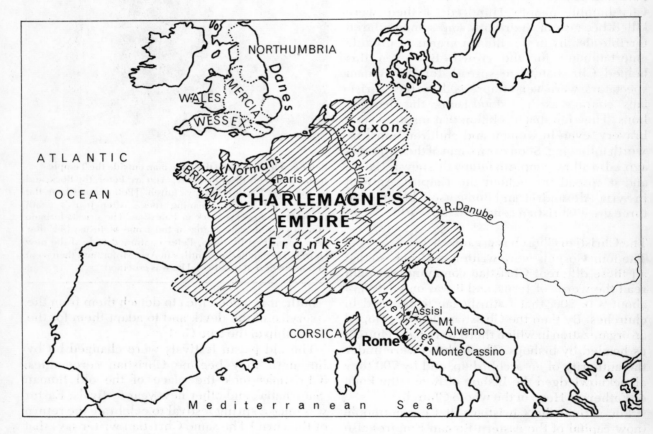

The 'barbarian' invaders of Europe soon settled down in their new homes. There grew up many new kingdoms, some of which were converted to Christianity. Before they heard of this new religion, some of the peoples of Europe had believed in all kinds of 'nature' gods. None of their beliefs could explain what happened after death, and they were attracted by a religion which taught about a future heaven. One warlord in England persuaded his king to adopt Christianity by saying, 'Sometimes on a cold winter's night a bird flies through a window of the hall, into the warmth and light. It pauses a

moment, then flies out again through a second window. Our life is like that. For a moment we are in the light and warmth. Then we return to the cold darkness. Let us find out more about the darkness, and turn it also into light!'

The Emperor Charlemagne, King of the Franks, A.D. 768–814

The most important kingdom of northern Europe was that of the Franks, in part of what is now called France and Western Germany. The Franks were converted to Christianity when their king, Clovis, married the daughter of the king of a neighbouring Christian country, Burgundy. Clovis ruled the Franks from A.D. 482 to 511.

With Christianity went a desire to keep alive the old traditions of learning. The earliest known manuscript, written by hand and with beautiful decorated capital letters, comes from this period in France. As early as 591 the history of the Franks was written down by a monk named Gregory of Tours.

By this time, Muslim armies had started to cross from Arabia into Europe and Asia, conquering fresh territory for themselves 'in the name of Allah'. We shall hear more about their new religion, Islam, in Chapter 18. It was largely because of the great rivalry between the two religions, that the Christian countries of Europe flourished at all. For they had to unite in peace for their own protection, rather than conduct endless wars among themselves. In 751 the Pope in Rome was offered help by the Franks, and in return the king of the Franks, Pepin the Short, was given the title 'Father of the Romans'.

Pepin's son received even higher honours. He was called Charles the Great, or Charlemagne. He was crowned king of the Franks in 768, and from then onwards he spent his reign in improving the standard of civilization, and defending his borders against pagan tribesmen in the east, and Muslim Arabs in the south. He was so successful that by the end of his reign his empire extended over most of western Europe.

Pope Leo III was impressed by Charlemagne's strength. The eastern and western Christian churches had split apart by this time, and the Pope did not feel obliged to recognize the Roman emperor in Constantinople as his 'overlord'. (In any case, the Roman 'emperor' was now a woman!) So in 800 he invited Charlemagne to Rome, and he crowned him Holy Roman Emperor of the West on Christmas Day. Charlemagne was now recognized as the worldly ruler, while the Pope was the religious ruler, of most of western Europe.

Charlemagne himself was illiterate, but he knew the value of written works, and he had books read aloud to him. He tried to improve his people's education, and he brought learned scholars from monasteries all over Europe, including even the British Isles, to teach and advise. The language of the Franks was a kind of Latin; and since the monks who came to teach

Charlemagne

In the picture above Charlemagne, seated on the horse, watches over while a bishop baptizes some captured Saxons. The reluctant Saxons received baptism into the Christian faith under pain of death.

in France had learnt to speak Latin in their monasteries, they could already partly understand the Franks.

Christianity spread rapidly, though Charlemagne's methods of spreading it were scarcely Christian. He is said to have killed thousands of Saxons because they would not accept the new rules, one of which said:

'Any unbaptized Saxon who attempts to hide himself among his own people and refuses to accept baptism shall be put to death.'

No wonder Saxony soon became a Christian country!

But Charlemagne was quite sincere in his beliefs: his empire was built upon a religious foundation, and he probably felt that it would be dangerous to have a pagan kingdom within it.

The main towns of the empire grew up round great cathedrals, churches and abbeys. Hundreds of people served the Church, either as priests, or as monks, lay-brothers*, teachers and scribes.

The land around the Cathedral towns was tilled by farmers and labourers. In order to improve the traditional methods of agriculture, Frankish scribes studied old Roman books about farming. The farmers improved their grain crops and their dairy herds, their sheep and their vegetables, all of which they sold in the markets of the Cathedral towns.

Similar developments were taking place across the English Channel in Britain. There King Alfred made laws based on the ancient Hebrew laws of Moses. He was a learned man, and himself translated the book of songs in the Bible called the Psalms, and the prayer Jesus taught his followers which is called the Lord's Prayer, for use in his churches. But Britain was still a country divided into small kingdoms, without central government, and it did not develop as rapidly as France and Germany had done under Charlemagne.

Two hundred years after this time, the people living in one of the little kingdoms that had once been part of Charlemagne's empire, crossed the English Channel and conquered Britain. These people were called Normans (from 'Northmen'—they had originally come from Scandinavia). Their complete conquest of England is important, not only to English history, but to the history of all Europe. The Normans brought with them their own entirely different way of living, and new attitudes to law, religion and government. It is because of their arrival in Britain (and not because of the earlier Roman occupation) that so many words in the English language sound like Latin words— and in fact have Latin 'roots'.

After the Norman Conquest, England began once again to be conscious of the rest of Europe, and to imitate it. Her long period of isolation from the continent, which started when the Roman legions left at the beginning of the fifth century, was now over.

*People who lived in, or worked for, religious houses, but who had not themselves taken the religious vows.

96

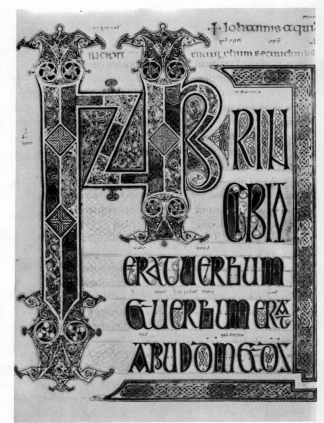

Manuscripts
An 'illuminated' [coloured and decorated] manuscript of the 8th century was a very elaborate affair. Scribes, often monks, used to sit day after day making copies for the church libraries and decorating the pages with fine brushwork in gold, red and blue. The manuscript above was written about A.D. 700 by the monks of Lindisfarne Abbey in the north of England. They wrote all the gospels in this beautiful illuminated style. The page above is the first page of the Gospel of St John.

The monks in their monasteries

We have seen how in India, Buddha preached a way of life that could really only be followed by people who went into monasteries and turned their backs on worldly things. Jesus's teaching had been different. He had shown ordinary people, men, women and children, how they could live better lives in their own homes, and while working at their old, familiar jobs.

But certain people in the early days of Christianity thought that the only way to be better men and women was to retire to a quiet place away from the towns and villages, and live alone in a cave or a hut. These people were called 'hermits'. They spent their time praying, and they only barely kept themselves alive with a little food and water. This kind of life was only suited to a very few. There were plenty of other people who wanted to follow Jesus's teachings, and who did not want to live such hard lives, entirely alone.

In the early years of the fourth century, a man named Pachomius gathered together a number of young men who wanted to pray and fast (eat very little), and he built a monastery for them on an island in the river Nile. There they worked on the land, made their own furniture, wove baskets and cloth, tanned leather, and studied the Gospels. Pachomius drew up a list of Rules for his monks, and they were used as the basis of all future monastic Orders (or communities).

The idea of monasteries spread. In 480 there was born in Italy a boy named Benedict. His parents were wealthy, but Benedict did not care for a life of ease. When he was only 15 years old he became a hermit, but later he decided to found a monastery of his own at Monte Cassino. Here the monks had to live in poverty, owning nothing. Their beds were hard, and they had only two gowns, called 'habits', a thin black one for summer and a fur-lined one for winter. Because of the colour of their gowns, they were known as the Black Monks. Each monk had a handkerchief, a pair of shoes, a needle, a knife and a pen. That was all. Their food—peas and beans, with bread and perhaps a little fish, poultry, or eggs—was shared out equally, and they ate in a communal dining-room.

The Benedictine 'Rule'

Benedict believed that to be idle was bad for a man, so almost every hour of the day was filled with work or prayer. The monks got up at 1.30 a.m. for two church services, known as Matins and Lauds. They stayed in the monastery church when Lauds was over, until the next 'Office' (service) of the day, Prime, which was at about 6 a.m. At about 8 a.m. there was an assembly, at which the head of the monastery, the Abbot, addressed the monks, and they heard the notices for the day.

Now the physical work began: some monks went off into the gardens and farms, others to the craft workshops, and those who were good at writing copied the Scriptures and decorated the pages with brightly coloured drawings. Two hours later they all returned to the church for the Sung Mass, after which came a welcome

St Jerome

In A.D. 382 a Christian scholar named Jerome collected together the existing Latin translations of the Gospels, and revised them to form a new version, approved by the Pope in Rome.

Jerome was a Hebrew scholar, and later he translated the Old Testament from Hebrew into Latin. The Latin Bible thus produced is known as the 'Vulgate'. This word comes from the Latin word meaning 'to make common'; the new Bible was so called because now the ordinary people of Rome could read it.

Benedictine monk

break for dinner—often the only meal of the day.

The rest of the day was divided between more work, two more church services, and a drink or sometimes a very light supper before bed. Even if they went to sleep immediately, the monks only had time for about 5 hours' rest before the next day began. All this was demanded by Benedict's Rule, which was based on that of Pachomius. It seems a hard Rule to us now, but Benedict did not mean his monks to be treated harshly. No man, he said, should push himself beyond endurance.

Bells were rung many times a day to tell the monks when to go to church, or to meals, or into the fields. And it was because of the need for accurate time-keeping in monasteries, that the mechanical clock developed. The first big clocks were set in church towers (see p. 116).

Many Benedictine monasteries were founded, first in Italy, and later in France and England. In all of them the Abbot was the representative of God—and as such his word was law. As the number of monks grew, the Abbots sent some of them off to lesser monasteries called Priories, ruled by a Prior. The Prior in turn was under the direction of the Abbot.

Strangers who arrived at the monastery for food and shelter were the monks' only contact with the outside world. It was their duty to feed and shelter travellers, for Jesus himself had said, 'I was a stranger, and ye took me in.' So 'to all guests fitting honour shall be shown, but most of all to servants of the faith, and to pilgrims'. The monastery became a place of refuge for the very poor people, who went every day to receive food or clothing.

Wealthier people sometimes sent their sons to be educated by the monks, and in time regular schools were established, where boys learnt to read and write in Latin. Because the monks used Latin all day themselves, they did not—and could not—teach anyone to read in the language of his own country. All the books were written in Latin, and so the old language of the Romans became a common bond between educated people all over Europe. It was not until the fifteenth and sixteenth centuries that people began to think seriously about translating their holy books into local languages. When that time came, it caused sweeping changes in Europe—as we shall see later.

By working hard on their land and in their workshops, and by selling their products in the

The Christian Kingdoms of Nubia
Nubia was converted to Christianity in the sixth century when a monk named Julian was sent to Africa by the Emperor Justinian of Constantinople. The Nubians built churches and decorated them with murals in the Byzantine style like the one of Saint Anna above, from the cathedral at Faras. They wrote inscriptions and books in their own language, and in Greek. Most of the writings have now been lost. Nubia and Ethiopia were the two great North African states that accepted the eastern form of Christianity.

Robin Hood
Robin Hood, the legendary figure who robbed the rich and gave money to the poor, was a great enemy of the rich Abbots and priests. We do not know when he lived exactly, probably between 1100 and 1300. As he was an outlaw (someone living 'outside the law') he lived, in hiding, in Sherwood Forest with his band of men.

markets, the monks often made a great deal of money; they could not keep it for themselves, so the monastery itself benefited. The Abbots received gifts from the king and from rich noblemen, and in time Benedict's hard Rule became softer. Many monastery churches began to contain beautiful paintings and gold and silver ornaments, set with jewels. The Abbots often did not follow the Rule at all—they lived in separate houses and ate rich meals. Sometimes a rich noble, or even the king, might be given hospitality (received as a guest) by the Abbot, and on these occasions the Abbot's kitchens provided an enormous feast for hundreds of people. Even the monks themselves lived less strictly, for the monasteries employed servants to do the humble cleaning and cooking and gardening jobs. In some monasteries there were more servants than there were monks.

Other Orders of monks were founded in an attempt to bring back the old strict discipline; among these were the Cistercians, or White Monks, who were not allowed to have servants. Instead they had two kinds of monks, those who attended all the services, and uneducated lay-brothers who did all the manual work. The White Monks had no ornaments in their churches, and they would not accept gifts. But in time even the White Monks grew rich—by selling wool abroad—and began to live less simply. It seems that it was almost impossible for the monasteries to remain poor and 'unworldly' for long.

The hard work of the monks and the good organization of the community were bound to increase their wealth.

Religious houses for women

Women also sometimes took vows of poverty, chastity (living unmarried and pure) and obedience. Religious houses for women (called nunneries) had been in existence since Benedict's time. As a rule the nunneries did not become as wealthy as the monasteries, because the nuns did not grow crops for sale or farm in the same way as the monks did. They spent most of their time caring for the poor, healing the sick, and embroidering tapestries and altar-cloths for the churches. Many of the nuns went into the nunnery because nobody had married them. In those days people thought that an unmarried girl was unable to look after herself, and would be better off as a nun. So many of the nuns were there not because they believed in a life of prayer and meditation, but because they had no choice.

The Bayeaux Tapestry
One of the earliest tapestries we know about is called the Bayeaux Tapestry. It may have been made by nuns at Bayeaux in France, but we are not certain. The Tapestry is 69 metres (230 feet) long, embroidered in coloured wools. It tells the story of the Norman's conquest of England. In the part shown above the Normans have just crossed the English Channel to invade England. The writing at the top is in Latin, and it says: 'and [they] came to Pevensey'. Pevensey is a bay near Hastings on the English coast, where the battle was fought.

St Francis of Assisi, 1182–1226

At the very end of the twelfth century—700 years after Benedict founded his Black Monks—there came the idea of monks actually leaving their monasteries and going out to preach to the people. The first wandering monks were called Grey Friars, and they were founded by an Italian named Francis. He is now known as St Francis of Assisi.

Francis had an intense love of nature, and great gentleness. Later many legends grew up about how he talked to birds and animals, and how they came to him without fear. He called them names like 'brother Wolf' and 'sister Lark'. His self-denial* and his goodness won Francis many followers, and in 1209 the Pope gave him permission to work among the poor, with 12 disciples, just as Jesus had done. Their headquarters was a little chapel and a group of huts near Assisi in Italy, but most of their time was spent wandering throughout the country, in grey peasants' dress, working in the fields in return for their food and lodging. In 1212 Francis started an Order of nuns, who also wore grey habits.

The number of Grey Friars grew, and in time the Pope wanted them to come under some form of discipline, in monasteries, like those of the Benedictines and Cistercians. A huge monastery and church were built at Assisi, and Francis was asked to become the first Abbot. But he refused, because he had been against the formal organization of his disciples. He had all along wanted them to live simply and do good to other people, not spend most of the day praying and working to increase the wealth of a monastery. So he resigned, and went off to pray and fast on Mt Alverno in the Apennine mountains.

The Grey Friars, or Franciscans, later became the largest of all the monastic communities, and they were famous as teachers of religion and law. Most of their recruits were poor men, and in turn they looked after the poor.

In Europe today you can see hundreds of ruins of monasteries. They are often huge buildings covering several acres of land. You can see where the large church stood, and the walled garden or 'cloister' where the monks walked in silence; the 'refectory', where the monks ate, and the 'dormitory' where they slept. On the plan you can also see the store rooms,

*Self-denial is doing without things that you would like to have.

St Francis, meditating

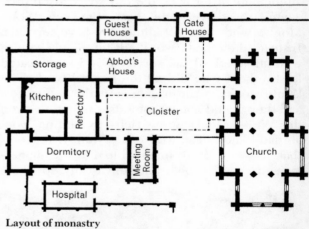

Layout of monastry

the kitchens, the guest rooms, and the infirmary or hospital where the sick and old monks were nursed with every care.

The monasteries served as centres to which people could bring their troubles, and their sick folk to be cured. The villagers were allowed to go to some of the church services, and they could appeal to the monks for food and clothing if they were destitute, that is, if they had none of the necessities of life. The monasteries were centres of learning and hard work, setting an example for the poor people of the district. As a result of the monks' hard work on the farms, agriculture all over Europe greatly improved; and because of their devotion to learning, and to creating great libraries of hand-made books, the desire for education spread.

Chapter 18 The Way of Allah

The Middle East in the Seventh Century
The three main powers of Europe and Asia in the seventh century A.D. were the Western Christians, the Eastern Christians, and the countries that made up the Persian Empire. The Eastern Christian Empire based on Constantinople we call Byzantium, after the old name of the town. For years the Byzantines had been hostile to the Persians, and often there was open war between them. This weakened both countries, and provided a great opportunity for the entry of a completely new force in the world—the followers of the Prophet Muhammad.

South of Palestine, in Arabia, there is a town called Mecca. Five hundred years after Jesus preached in Jerusalem, Mecca was a busy market town, and every day camel caravans entered and left the city carrying trade goods. The caravans travelled along well-worn roads between Egypt and the south of Arabia, or north-east to the trading towns of Asia. The merchants who met in the market place at Mecca were of all nations and all religions. Jews and Christians mingled with the pagan Arabs, and exchanged stories about their own countries and about their lives.

Sometimes, too, they talked about their religions.
In Mecca, in about 570, there was born a boy

named Muhammad. He belonged to the Quraysh tribe which controlled the city of Mecca. As he grew up, Muhammad became very interested in religion. The community in which he grew up believed in many different gods, all of whom had idols or statues for worship in the centre of Mecca. But Muhammad also liked to listen to foreigners talking about their own gods. At that time Jews and Arab Christians often visited Mecca, and he heard them speak of one God, not many. He listened to their stories of the old prophets, and he found that he agreed with their teaching. During his early life, when he was poor and later when he became a wealthy merchant, he spent his leisure hours apart from his friends, thinking about God.

One night, when Muhammad was about 40 years old, he suddenly saw a vision of the angel Gabriel, who, as he later said, 'came to me while I was asleep, with a cloth of brocade, on which was some writing.' The angel said to him, 'Read!' and Muhammad, frightened, replied, 'I cannot read it.' Three times the angel said, 'Read!' and then he said,

> 'Read in the name of the Lord your creator who has created man from a clot of blood. Read, your Lord is the most bountiful, who taught by means of the pen, taught man what he did not know.'

Muhammad was very disturbed by this dream, and told his wife Khadija what he had heard. She at once took him to see an old cousin of hers, Waraqa, who was a scholar of the Christian and Jewish holy books. He said that the angel was certainly the same messenger who had visited the ancient Jewish prophets. He persuaded Muhammad that he had been chosen to be a prophet of God.

So Muhammad began to preach about the One God, whom he called Allah. At first hardly anybody listened to him, and his only followers were Khadija, his adopted son Zaid, his cousin Ali, and his closest friends. But slowly his teachings spread, until the elders of his tribe began to be alarmed.

The Arabs had a sacred place in Mecca called the Ka'ba, which is still there today. The Ka'ba is a huge black windowless stone building, with a small black meteorite sunk into its side. Every year the tribes of Arabia came from all parts of the land to worship their gods at the Ka'ba, and to put offerings in front of the idols that surrounded it. Muhammad now said that the idols

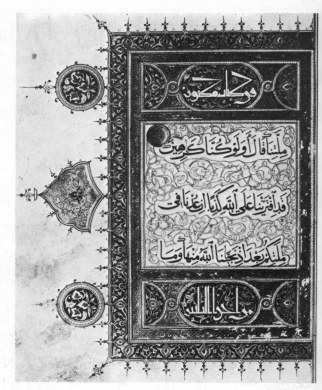

Koran
Muhammad's words were written down by scribes, and after his death the various versions were collected and 'edited' to form the Holy Koran, used by Muslims all over the world today. They believe that the words are those of Allah, spoken through his prophet Muhammad.

should be broken and Allah alone worshipped. The pilgrims who came every year to the Ka'ba were a great source of income to Mecca, and the elders and merchants of the Quraysh tribe feared that Muhammad's new religion would ruin their trade, so, in an attempt to stop him preaching, they refused to buy from or sell goods to any of Muhammad's followers. Muhammad urged his followers to emigrate to the Christian country of Ethiopia, and many of them did so. He himself remained with his family in Mecca.

In the year 622, Muhammad too decided to leave Mecca, and go 280 miles through the desert to a city called Yathrib. Muhammad had many friends there, who, whenever they came on pilgrimage to Mecca, listened to his words and believed him. Muhammad left Mecca just in time, for that very night some of the Quraysh had plotted to kill him.

Yathrib was quite different from dry and dusty Mecca. It was an oasis in the desert, surrounded by palm trees and green grass. The inhabitants grew their own food, and there was plenty of grazing for their animals. In this green city there was no jealousy from rich merchants, and Muhammad was listened to with much greater sympathy.

The new teaching

Muhammad did not claim to be founding a new religion. He said only that he was following the religion of Abraham, the prophet who had first declared the idea of One God to the Hebrews. Muhammad claimed that the Jews had spoilt their religion by adding to it teachings that Abraham never intended them to have. Moses and Jesus, he said, had been appointed by God to purify the Hebrew religion, and bring back simplicity and truth. But the Christians he had met, Muhammad said, were once again leaving God's path. He, Muhammad, had been sent to help men return to the right way of life. He called the religion 'Al-Islam' — submission. Those who followed Islam (Muslims) submitted themselves entirely to Allah.

Muhammad emphasized that it was not enough to follow a religion in name only: it was necessary to live a good life. In the Koran it is written:

'Whoever believeth in Allah and the Last Day and doeth right, surely their reward is with their Lord . . .'

Hundreds of people in Yathrib were con-verted to the new faith, and they acknowledged Muhammad as their leader. They even changed the name of their city to Medina, which means The City — *the* city of the Prophet. Up till now all the Arabs had been fiercely tribal. They fought and died for their own tribes; no man would ever kill his own kinsman, and when a man was killed by someone from another tribe, his death was quickly avenged.

But in Medina the Muslims formed a close group, regardless of tribe. They no longer recognized the old tribal loyalties, for they believed that their loyalty should first be given to Allah and their fellow Muslims. When war broke out between the Muslims and their former comrades and kinsmen from Mecca, men even killed their brothers and cousins in the name of Allah. To many of the Arabs this was displeasing, so in the Koran we read:

'Warfare is decreed for you, though it is hate-

Prayer-mat

Muslims had no altars in their mosques, no images or pictures of God and no priests. All a man had to do to achieve communion [spiritual communication] with Allah was turn towards Mecca five times each day and pray.

Muslims were supposed to kneel on clean ground to pray and so there arose the custom whereby each man or each family owned a special prayer-mat or carpet. In the picture below a family is gathered on a prayer-mat to worship in the open desert.

ful for you; but it may happen that you hate a thing which is good for you, and it may happen that you love a thing which is bad for you. Allah knows, and you do not know.'

A few years later the Muslims were strong enough to march on Mecca, but there was little opposition and Muhammad returned to his own city without a fight. When the Muslims had thrown out all the idols surrounding the Ka'ba, Muhammad told the people to come and swear loyalty to him, and obedience to Allah. From that time onwards, pilgrims came to Mecca to worship one God only—Allah.

Now that they could no longer worship other gods at the Ka'ba, many Arab tribes were quite content to worship Allah, and become Muslims. Others were more defiant, and these the new Muslim army went out to fight.

When the Arab armies conquered a tribe, or later, a foreign town, they asked the inhabitants to become Muslims, by repeating the sentence, 'There is no God but Allah; Muhammad is his Messenger.' If they were prepared to swear this, their taxation was lighter. But the early Muslims realized that it was not possible for Christians and Jews to say these words, and for the most part they were tolerant of the "People of the Book", for Muslims, Christians and Jews all believed that the Old Testament of the Bible was the word of God.

One of the strictest rules was that no Muslim should kill another Muslim. The Muslim soldiers fought against any people who stopped them from spreading Islam. More Arab tribes joined them, and soon they were fighting on the frontiers of the Persian and Byzantine Empires. A war against unbelievers outside Arabia was called a *jihad* or 'holy war'.

The Holy Wars

Muhammad died in 632, and was succeeded by Abu Bakr, one of the very first converts to Islam. Abu Bakr was known as the 'Caliph' or 'successor', and this became the title for the leader of Islam. Abu Bakr and the two Caliphs who followed him continued the holy wars with such success that within ten years the Muslims had conquered much of Persia and the Byzantine Empire. The Caliph was now the leader of a huge empire.

Once the Arab armies had moved out of Arabia, they had to camp in hostile territory. There were raids on the new Arab borders, and these troubles

Ka'ba
Thousands of Muslims go each year to Mecca to perform the *hadj* or pilgrimage. Once pilgrims either walked the whole way, or joined camel caravans to visit the Holy City. Nowadays many of them travel by 'plane.

The five 'Pillars of the Faith' of Islam
The Koran laid down these five special 'commandments':

A Muslim must have faith in Allah and Muhammad as His prophet.
He must pray five times a day.
He must give alms to the poor.
He must fast every year for a month, at the season called Ramadan.
He must go, if possible, on the pilgrimage to Mecca.

---

led the Muslim armies to invade even more territory, and so to extend the empire still further. In 639 the horsemen of Arabia turned westward towards the Nile, and began the conquest of Egypt and Libya.

The peoples that submitted to the Arab armies with their new religion, had the choice of either becoming Muslims, or else paying higher taxes for the Muslim soldiers to protect them. It is amazing that the early Caliphs managed to keep their empire together so well, for they had few soldiers actually living in the 'enemy' countries. At first the new empire was bound only by religion, and government and organization came later.

When that time did come, each new state was governed by a ruler of its own—who owed allegiance, that is loyalty and help, to the Caliph, but who occasionally behaved as though he himself were the only head of Islam, even calling himself 'Caliph' as well. These different rulers passed their titles on to their sons, and so although they were not kings in the old sense, we speak of the ruling families as 'dynasties'.

Now the Muslim empire was formed of a group of separate countries, each with a ruler who owed allegiance to the spiritual head of Islam.

Harun ar-Rashid, 786–809

In Mesopotamia, where the Sumerians, the Persians, and the Greeks had once ruled, there came to power a dynasty of Islamic rulers known as the Abbasids. Under these rulers, and particularly under the Caliph Harun ar-Rashid, Mesopotamia developed into a settled civilized country. The Arab conquerers were now rich with the revenue taken from captured cities, from the taxes that their new subjects had to pay, and from their own economic development. With their new wealth they built magnificent cities at Bokhara, Samarkand and Baghdad, where their colleges, schools, and hospitals were some of the best in the world.

Harun ar-Rashid himself lived in Baghdad, which was then the most civilized city of all. In the narrow streets shops sold beautiful jewels, pearls, gold ornaments and rich silks. There was great luxury in the houses, and women were encouraged to make themselves beautiful. To Harun's court came poets and musicians and story-tellers.

Scholars in Baghdad University collected the old Greek books and translated them into Arabic. Now they were able to build upon the learning of the Greeks, and add to it new ideas of their own. They made surveys and maps of the world from facts collected from geographers and travellers who visited the whole of the Muslim lands from India to Spain. They sent traders to the Far East, and set up small trading stations in China and Ceylon, in India, and on the coast of East Africa. Northern Europe was completely cut off from trade with these countries, and could not import gold, or spices, or silks. Charlemagne, who ruled northern France at the time when Harun ar-Rashid was Caliph at Baghdad, had to have coins made of silver, because he could not get enough gold.

Samarra minaret

The Muslims built mosques as places of worship, and one or more towers were built at the corners of the central courtyard. At each hour of prayer, the *muezzin* [a mosque official] climbed the minaret and called the Faithful to prayer. The Arabs studied the large buildings of the various countries they conquered. This minaret at Samarra in Persia, is shaped like an old Babylonian ziggurat.

Islamic design

Because Islam forbids pictures of people, Muslim artists decorated buildings with words beautifully drawn, and within a definite framework, such as a circle, or a square. They also used words to decorate plates and bowls, as this example from Turkey shows.

Chapter 19 The Muslims reach Europe

Meanwhile other Muslim armies had carried their religion northwards into Spain and France, which alarmed the Pope in Italy, and his friends the Franks. Fortunately for the Christian kingdoms, the leader of the Franks was an able commander named Charles Martel ('the Hammer').* He led his forces out to meet the advancing Muslim army, and he defeated them at the battle of Poitiers in 732. But the Muslims stayed in southern Spain, and for five hundred years the two religious groups lived side by side. Although there were minor wars between them from time to time, in fact the Christians and Muslims tolerated each other, and it was not uncommon for Christians to serve in a Muslim army.

Abd ar-Rahman III, 912–61

The city of Cordova (modern Córdoba) lies on the river Guadalquivir, in the province of Spain we now call Andalusia, but which in the tenth century was part of the much larger Muslim country of 'Al-Andalus'. By the time the great ruler of the Umayyad dynasty in Spain, Abd ar-Rahman III came to power, Muslim ideas of wealth and splendour had spread from Baghdad to Andalus, and Cordova was the great centre of world learning. (Baghdad was no longer so important.)

The Caliphs of Cordova were learned men themselves, and they wished their people to be as well-educated as possible. So they built hundreds of primary schools where both boys and girls could learn to read and write in Arabic, to do arithmetic, and to learn the Koran by heart. When they had finished at the primary school they went on to higher schools and to university, where they studied the Greek translations that had reached them from Baghdad. At home, every educated man had a library of hand-written

*He was the grandfather of Charlemagne.

The Mosque at Cordova (interior)
In Spain, Jews and Christians were often the craftsmen for their Muslim masters, and they adapted their own artistic styles to suit the new buildings, the new kinds of clothes, and the new fashions in jewellery and weapons. Cordova was retaken by Christian Spaniards in 1236, and the mosque became a cathedral.

books, often chosen for the beauty of the writing alone.

The university also gave courses in medicine. Abd ar-Rahman's own doctor was a Jew named Ibn Shaprut (even non-Muslims in Cordova had Arabic-sounding names; 'ibn' means 'son of'). He was thought to be so wise that the Christian kings of Leon and Navarre, living in the north of Spain, 'borrowed' him from Abd ar-Rahman when a member of the royal family was sick.

Cordova had half-a-million inhabitants*, and was one of the largest cities in the world at the time — far larger than any of the Christian cathedral towns of western Europe. It was clean and well-lit, and like Baghdad in days gone by, contained shops which sold beautiful luxury goods from the East. Cordova was particularly famous for leatherwork, which the Christians (who imported it) called 'Cordovan leather'. In time any leather-worker was known as a 'cordovaner', or 'cordwainer'.

Muslim rule in Spain was tolerant and useful. But during the centuries after Abd ar-Rahman's rule, the Christians of the north became stronger and tried hard to recover the land they had lost to the Muslims. Gradually they pushed the Muslims further and further south, until by 1300 only the province of Granada was left of the once large land of Andalus.

Muslim science

Ptolemy, the Greek scientist, had written a series of 13 books in which (among other things) he catalogued over 1000 stars, stated the distance between the earth and the sun, discussed eclipses, the movements of the planets, and the formation of the Milky Way. He thought that the earth was a sphere, and the centre of the Universe — with all the planets (*and* the sun) moving round it. In 827 Muslim scholars prepared the first translation of these books, which they called the Almagest (see picture on p. 111). Later, the Almagest was translated into Latin (in 1175), and the *Christian* countries began to use Ptolemy's work. As we shall see later, this led to a completely new theory of the way in which the solar system works.

In mathematics the Muslim countries were far ahead of Christian Europe, for they took over from the Indians the idea of having a *nought*. Up till now the peoples of the world had added

Numerals

The Arabic numerals used in Baghdad and later in Spain look rather like the numbers we use today. The zero was represented by a dot, which was called *sunya* by the Hindus.

A practical reason why Christian merchants preferred the Roman system was that they thought they would be cheated by the Arabic notation. Muslim merchants could change 15 to 150 by merely adding a dot, whereas in Roman numerals XV (15) looked quite different from CL (150).

numbers on counting-frames, but they had no symbol to show when a column was empty. The Indians used a dot for nought, or zero, and they called it *sunya*, meaning 'empty'.

This new symbol changed ideas about mathematics completely. Arithmetic became easier (the Romans had had great difficulty in multiplying, say, CXVIII by MDLV!), and with the nought there was the possibility of advanced mathematics — which in turn affected physics. Without the nought, much of algebra could never have developed; logarithms would be impossible, and the whole of our present-day science and engineering would never have come into being.

The Muslims were great borrowers. Besides taking over the zero from India, and astronomy from the Greeks, they learnt how to make paper from the Chinese. This meant that their books were much less heavy than the old parchment* rolls, and a library could hold more books, arranged upright on shelves. Most people in the Muslim 'empire' now spoke Arabic, just as their ancestors (who happened to be part of the Greek or Roman Empires) used to speak Greek or Latin as a *lingua franca* which bound the civilized world together.

The Christian kingdoms envied the Muslim 'caliphates' for their learning and wealth; but they could not imitate them because they said they were 'unbelievers'. For a long time they

---

*It was about the size of Nairobi, Accra or Edinburgh today.

*Parchment is the skin of a sheep or calf dried and made suitable for writing on.

did not even copy the zero in arithmetic, because they thought that it was a Muslim invention, and therefore somehow wrong. Mistrust and suspicion, added to jealousy, led to a final split between the peoples of the two religions.

A merchant goes to the East

The split into two 'rival' groups meant that it was now very difficult for Christian traders to go to the east by land, through Muslim territories. But even so, some merchants *did* manage to do so. One outstanding merchant-traveller was Marco Polo. He was the son of a merchant named Niccolo Polo, who had for many years dealt with other merchant-travellers from the east. Niccolo and his brother Maffeo made a lot of money by selling precious stones, silks and spices, in the markets of Venice.

Marco Polo was born in about 1254, and when he was 15 years old, he accompanied his uncle and his father on a great journey to the east.

Maffeo and Niccolo had travelled to Constantinople, and there they met a party of men who had been all the way overland to China, a land with a powerful king whom they called Kublai Khan. This king, they said, was wealthier than any other king in the world, and had a country larger than any of the countries of Europe. He was neither a Christian nor a Muslim, so they thought it would be a magnificent thing if they could convert him to Christianity. They returned to Venice to assemble a party of priests, but unfortunately for them, they could not persuade the Pope to send more than two men, and these soon turned back, for the journey was too hard for them.

But young Marco was more courageous. He carried on with the party, and the three Venetians stayed for many years in the country of Kublai Khan. They called this country 'Cathay', and this is the name by which China was known to Europeans for many years. The Polos became rich men, and the Khan was pleased to have them in his kingdom. Marco was sent by Kublai Khan to many other eastern countries, including India, Ceylon, Burma, Japan and Java. On his return to the court at Peking, he amused the Khan with tales of his travels.

Finally the Polos returned to Europe. It is said that they amazed the townspeople of Venice by appearing in their fine eastern clothes. After so many years in the east, they were probably the only clothes they possessed.

Christian kingdoms in the Middle Ages

The 'Middle Ages' in Europe was the time when the different countries settled down, mostly as small kingdoms under the type of government we know as the 'feudal system'. Every king (or in some countries, duke) had under him a group of knights, who owed allegiance to him; the knights were owners of large amounts of land, which was farmed for them by peasants. Besides working for his lord, each peasant had his own strip of land, which he cultivated for his own needs, and the whole village shared a common field for grazing their animals.

At this time the rule of the king was supreme. In times of war, each knight had to collect together horsemen and foot-soldiers from among his tenants, to fight for the king; when there was no war, the knights practised fighting on horseback, archery (shooting with bows and arrows), and learnt an elaborate code of 'chivalry' — that is, correct and courteous behaviour.

Having chivalrous knights in armour was very romantic, and very necessary in times of war, but in peace time the knights had nothing very much to do, and they often quarrelled among themselves. Various European rulers went to war with each other, usually over the possession of territory. If you look at a modern map of Europe, you will see that Italy, Spain and France all have good natural boundaries of seas and mountains. In the Middle Ages all three countries were divided up into small kingdoms, which could change possession overnight when a king died, or — as often happened — when a duke's lands were given away as part of the dowry* of a princess.

The Crusades

In the tenth and eleventh centuries the Muslim dynasties in Europe and Asia were in trouble, for a hitherto comparatively unknown people called Turks swept across from the east and captured some of the Muslim cities of Asia. The Turks were also Muslims. They took the holy places of Palestine and they made war on the Byzantine Empire, threatening the Christian stronghold of Constantinople. In 1095 the Byzantine emperor appealed to the Pope in Rome for help, and the Pope decided it was

---

*A dowry is the money, land or other possessions a woman brings to her husband on marriage. In some countries it is called 'bride price'.

Painting of farming in the Middle Ages
The painters of the Middle Ages liked to paint pictures of their friends and neighbours at work in the fields, as this old illustration shows. Sometimes they painted a whole series of pictures showing the farming activities for each month in turn. The picture above was painted in the 10th century, for the month of August.

indeed time to help the eastern Christians. He thought he might perhaps be able to reunite the two branches of Christian faith by recapturing Jerusalem—and he could certainly give employment to the quarrelling knights and kings of Europe.

So the Pope preached a crusade—a war of religion—against the Turks (known then as 'Saracens'), and thousands of knights and foot-soldiers answered his call. Three armies set out from France, and another from Italy, and they marched right across Europe to Constantinople where the Byzantine emperor helped them to cross over the Sea of Marmara to meet the Turks in Asia Minor. After a lot of hard fighting and long thirsty marches they reached Jerusalem and captured it in 1099, three years after they left their homes.

Most of the crusaders went back to Europe, but some stayed to live in the new Christian kingdom of Jerusalem. As there were not many of them to guard their conquests, the crusaders fortified the cities of the Holy Land and built several castles of great strength. The idea of fighting for religious reasons became widespread in Europe, and during the next 170 years Christians organized six more crusades against the Muslims. But the success of the first crusade was not repeated and most of these crusades were failures. Gradually the Muslims became stronger, and in 1187 Saladin, the sultan of Egypt, recaptured Jerusalem.

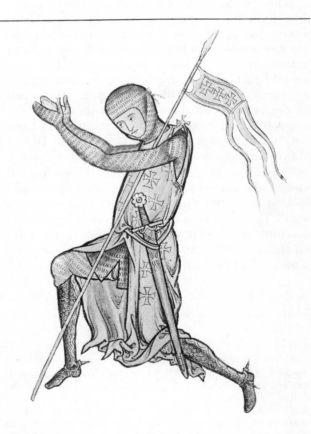

Knights
The knights wore chainmail which gave them very good protection and allowed plenty of movement. Over their armour they wore cloth tunics with their own personal markings embroidered on them. They carried shields painted with the same design. The soldiers could thus recognize their own knights in battle, and keep near them.

Baibars, Sultan of Egypt, 1260–77

One of the crusaders' most deadly enemies was another sultan of Egypt, known as Baibars. He was a huge man, very energetic and able, a great athlete, and a devout Muslim. He was determined to rid the Middle East of the Christians from the west and the new Mongol invaders from the east. He was very successful against both these enemies, and by the time he died in 1277, most of the crusaders' castles and towns had been retaken.

The Christian countries of Byzantium, Sicily, and two kingdoms of northern Spain were anxious to remain friendly with so powerful a man, and the king of France even sent messengers to greet him. But he was unwilling to stop the war before all the former Muslim lands had been regained and the crusaders had returned to their own countries.

Some of the knights and soldiers from Europe had joined the crusades for religious reasons; others because they enjoyed fighting, or because they were criminals who dared not stay in their own countries. In those days all soldiers hoped to add to their pay by looting the towns they captured; and they thought that all the lands of the east were wealthy and prosperous. They expected rich rewards from loot, and also from making important prisoners pay ransom. In fact the opportunities for 'getting rich quick' were not so great as they thought; and determined rulers like Baibars showed them that they could not expect to recapture Jerusalem without a hard fight. The Christian countries gained hardly any territory in the east, and in 1453 the whole of the Christian world suffered a great blow when the Turks at last captured Constantinople.

Saladin

Saleh al-din, or Saladin, sultan of Egypt, is famous for his wars against the crusaders during the reign of England's King Richard the Lion-Heart. His own courtesy greatly impressed the crusaders, and the fine behaviour of many of the Muslim leaders led to new ideas of chivalry in Europe. It is said that when King Richard's horse was killed in battle, Saladin sent him a horse of his own, and forbade his men to fight until Richard had mounted it.

Cairo

Cairo, in the Middle Ages, was one of the great cities of the world. It was a city built within walls, in which were magnificently carved gates, one of which could be used only by the sultan. Inside the walls the houses had overhanging windows, and balconies, overlooking narrow twisted streets. The houses were generally built round courtyards with fountains and gardens. The family lived upstairs; the women were separated from the men, and they rarely went outside the houses.

The overhanging windows did not have glass in them. Instead they had a criss-cross pattern of carved wood, which let in air but kept out the fierce rays of the sun.

The photograph on the right shows buildings dating back to the Middle Ages which are still to be seen in Cairo today.

Chapter 20 Islam in Africa

In the seventh century A.D., some Muslims had already settled in Morocco, in North Africa. They spread the teaching of the Prophet, and traded with the neighbouring tribes. From Morocco, explorers and travellers marched south through the deserts with their camels, until they came to a town called Sijilmasa, where they traded their copper and cotton, tools and swords, and their strong Arab horses for gold, ivory and slaves.

The gold trade of Sijilmasa was very old. The gold itself came from an African kingdom far to the south, situated round the forested banks of the river Niger. This kingdom, which was called Ghana*, had probably been in existence from the fifth or sixth century, but long before that time, Berbers from North Africa were trading with the south for gold to sell to the Carthaginians and Romans.

The Ghanaians did not dig the gold themselves, for the mines lay in a country called Wangara, which was inhabited by a different tribe. These more primitive Africans used to leave gold nuggets and gold dust on the border of their country, and the Ghanaians exchanged it for salt. No word was spoken in this kind of bargaining: if the people of Wangara thought there was not enough salt put out beside their gold, then they removed the gold. If they agreed to the 'price', then they took the salt and the Ghanaians were free to remove the gold. This silent trading was very old in Africa, and was the method used by the Phoenicians and Carthaginians, when they wanted to exchange goods with Africans whose language they could not speak.

Salt was a very valuable commodity† to the

Islamic Navigation
The Arabs translated Ptolomy's Greek star-maps in the ninth century A.D. The picture above is a drawing of the constellation [group of stars] *Bootes* (the herdsman) from an early Islamic manuscript of the Almagest. The Arabs used these star-maps in their navigation of the Indian Ocean and the Far East.

miners of the south. It is impossible to work—or even to live for very long—if you do not have enough salt in your body, and the Ghanaians and the workers of Wangara had no natural salt in their lands. But plenty of salt was taken every year to the markets of Sijilmasa from a place in the desert called Taghaza. So, for centuries, year after year, merchants left Ghana and travelled along recognized trade-routes northwards to Sijilmasa, where they exchanged their gold, ivory and slaves in the market-place for salt. And with the caravans, there gradually came to West Africa the faith and customs of Islam.

---

*This is not the same country as today's Ghana. It occupied about the same geographical position as present-day Mali.
†A commodity is an article of trade.

The Almoravids

In north-west Africa, at the beginning of the eleventh century, a holy man named Ibn Yasin preached to his followers a very strict kind of Islam. He said that Muslims everywhere had become too soft, and were no longer following the ways of their founder, Muhammad, who, although not poor, had always lived very simply. Ibn Yasin was a good preacher, and he soon collected a huge following of tribesmen who were prepared to join in a *jihad* against the settlements of the desert. The followers of Ibn Yasin were called 'Almoravids'.

This horde of about 30,000 warriors, most of them foot-soldiers, attacked and took Sijilmasa, and then marched north and conquered some of the civilized cities of Morocco. Ibn Yasin died in Morocco, and after his death the army split into two halves, one part going north into Spain, where they said they would help the Andalusian caliphs to defeat the Christian kings of the north. In fact they took over the caliph's power, and in the fighting, many beautiful Muslim cities, including Cordova, were destroyed, and thousands of magnificent books were burnt.

The other half of the Almoravid army went south towards Ghana. In 1054 they had reached Andoghast, a town which paid tribute to Ghana, and the soldiers killed most of the inhabitants. The Ghanaian king, in his capital at Kumbi, hurriedly collected an army, and for a time he successfully kept the Almoravids at bay. But the fierce tribesmen of the north could not be kept out for ever, and in 1076 they destroyed Kumbi and the old kingdom of Ghana was permanently weakened.

Mali

But that was not the end of local power in West Africa. Other kingdoms grew prosperous, and were ruled by Muslim kings. South-west of the old kingdom of Ghana, also on the river Niger, the kings of Mali became the new leaders in the gold trade with North Africa. In about 1300, a Muslim writer named Ibn Khaldun said of the people of Mali:

'All the nations of the Sudan* stood in awe of them, and the merchants of North Africa travelled to their country.'

*The Sudan in the Middle Ages included a much larger area of North and West Africa than it does now. Many place-names now refer to slightly different geographical areas. Mali (or Melle) was in the western part of present-day Mali.

112

Benin

Benin, on the west coast of Africa, was a kingdom noted for its beautiful bronze statues as the one in above of a hunter. The craftsmen of Benin passed on their skill from generation to generation. The king, or Oba, of Benin was a mighty ruler who had to be obeyed in all things. His young men hunted leopards, lions and elephants as training for their duties as soldiers.

Goods in Benin were exchanged for cowrie shells, and according to this account from a sixteenth century English trader, food was plentiful:

'They would bring our men earthen pots . . . full of honey and honeycombs for a hundred shells. They would also bring great store of oranges and plantains which grow upon a tree, and are very like a cucumber but very pleasant in eating.'

The greatest of the rulers of Mali was called Mansa Musa, and he ruled from his capital city, Niami, from about 1307 to 1332. It was said that his empire was so large that it took four months to walk from the western boundary to the east, and the same length of time to go from north to south. This must have been an exaggeration, but Mansa Musa undoubtedly ruled over a very large area. His great fame in Europe and Asia came about because he went on a pilgrimage to Mecca. In 1324 he set out from Niami with an enormous camel caravan, carrying gold and ivory, and followed by courtiers, warriors, servants and slaves. El-Omari, a fourteenth century writer, said:

'Twelve thousand young slaves dressed in

tunics of brocade and silk of Yemen carried his personal belongings.'

The caravan reached Cairo, a great city of learning and wealth. To impress such a city was not easy, but Mansa Musa managed to do so by his great generosity. He gave away so much gold (80 to 100 camel-loads, it is said) that for years afterwards the market-price for gold was much lower than usual. El-Omari visited Cairo 12 years after Mansa Musa's visit, to find that the Egyptians were still talking about this great king.

When he had performed the pilgrimage to Mecca, Mansa Musa returned to his own country with Arab scholars and teachers, and an architect from Andalus who built the king new mosques and palaces of brick (instead of the usual clay) at his cities of Timbuktu and Jenne. These two towns became centres of learning in much the same way as Baghdad, Cordova and Cairo had done. The university of Timbuktu still existed and was respected until the end of the sixteenth century, when invaders from Morocco destroyed the books and the buildings. But even then, Timbuktu lived on in legend, and right up to the nineteenth century, European travellers expected to find a rich and learned city there.

So the Muslim religion spread, first throughout Arabia, then to the east as far as India, to Spain and Morocco in the west, to Ghana via the ancient trade-routes, and (as we shall later see) to the coast of East Africa. Everywhere where Muslims settled, they built beautiful towns which carried on a profitable trade. They kept alive the old learning of Greece and Rome, at a time when Europe was in ignorance. But their long mastery was nearly over. Soon the European nations emerged from 'the Middle Ages', and with new-found energy provided the world's next centres of learning, of culture and expansion.

The extent of the Arab Empire – 1000 AD

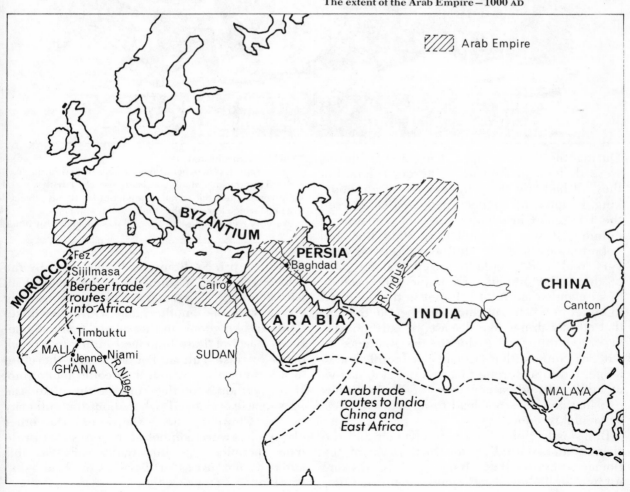

Part V Renaissance and Reformation
Chapter 21 The Old Learning Rediscovered

'Witches' being ducked
People accused of witchcraft were often ducked in the local pond. The 'ducking stool' consisted of a chair with a metal strap across the front to hold the victim in. It was attached to a hoist which lowered the stool into the water.

For very bad offences the accused was ducked many times.

During the Middle Ages, Christian countries were divided up between different rulers, but they all had one thing in common. Everybody, king, knights and common people alike, obeyed the Church. Christianity was not a matter of opinion; it was a complete way of life, and nobody questioned it. Hell and the devil were very real, and people believed that for most of them, this life was an unpleasant prelude to an even worse future. Belief in the devil led to belief in witchcraft, and many people thought that all bad things like disease, or earthquakes, or crop-failure, were due to the influence of witches. Superstition, instead of scientific knowledge, led to a Europe that was not at all active mentally. Blind acceptance of superstitious explanations does not lead to new discoveries, or mental freedom.

But slowly things began to change; and the change first started in the birth-place of the Roman Empire — Italy. Italy was now divided up into a number of city-states, each ruled by a duke or a prince. Rome itself was ruled by the Pope, who was of course also the head of all Christendom. These states were constantly at war with one another, and with other dukedoms and kingdoms in France and Spain. Sometimes parts of Italy belonged either to French or to Spanish rulers. People began therefore to ask themselves whom they could look up to. If the authority of the king, or the duke, can be so easily removed, what about the authority of the Church? The bishops and the other clergymen were supposed to be superior to other people. Was this really so? Was this authority not just as 'artificial' as the leadership of a king?

Books become cheaper

At the same time as people were beginning to question 'authority', someone invented movable type for printing. We think that the inventor was a man named Johann Gutenberg, who lived in Germany from about 1398 to 1468. This is how the new printing worked: many 'mirror-images'* of each letter of the alphabet were carved on little blocks of wood, so that the letters could be joined together to make words. In this new movable type, printers could put any letter into any position they liked. It takes a long time to put together all the letters that make up a page of type, but when it is done they can be locked together in a frame, and hundreds of pages can be printed from them. When the whole book is finished, the type can be used again and again for other books.

The earliest piece of Gutenberg's printing we know of is an astronomical calendar, printed in 1447. He also printed a Bible (the Latin 'Vulgate' or 'common' Bible of St Jerome) and several shorter books. He personally did not grow rich from his new trade, but the idea spread rapidly throughout Europe, and 50 years later there were thousands of printing presses, mainly producing religious books and histories. There was great opposition from manuscript copiers, but they could not compete with the low prices of printed books, and soon they were only employed by rich men who preferred to buy a well-illustrated hand-written book (however expensive) to a mass-produced one.

The ordinary people of Europe began to buy books, and at last education became available for the less-wealthy people. It is difficult to imagine today, when we have well-stocked bookshops and libraries in every town, how exciting it must have been to own a book, and with what care it must have been handled. A man with a whole shelf of books was no longer dependent on other people's learning, but could read for himself, and whet his appetite for more. Young lads, who had perhaps grown up thinking they would be farmers, or cordwainers, or masons, or carpenters, as their fathers and grandfathers had been, now apprenticed themselves to printers, paper-makers, book-binders and type-makers.

Some printers issued copies of the classics —

*The type letters have to be 'mirror-images' — right side to the left, left side to the right — in order to come out right way round when the frame is turned over for printing.

Here foloweth The lyf of Saynt Jherome And first of his name

Jherome is sayd of Jera that is hooly / And of nemus / that is to saye a wood / And soo Jherome is as moche to saye as an hooly wood

William Caxton, printer

At first printers copied the old hand-drawn letters, to make a printed page look as much like a manuscript as possible. Here is an example, written in English, by the printer William Caxton, in 1483. It tells of St. Jerome.

Later, printers copied the simpler Roman letters, which are still used today. Germany, however, kept the old 'Gothic' letters right up to this century. This is what a printed line in an early twentieth century German book looked like. Compare it with Caxton's page above:

Ich sage hinfort nicht, daß ihr Knechte seid; denn

that is, the writings of Romans like Cicero, Julius Caesar and Virgil and of Greeks like Plutarch and Homer. Only a very small part of the works of these authors had been preserved in Italy, but there were many more in the Greek city of Constantinople. Scholars from Constantinople found plenty of willing pupils in Italy, and when Constantinople fell to the Turks in 1453, hundreds of other Greek-speaking scholars joined those already in Italy, and brought with them some of the old manuscripts.

All these books were eagerly read by all literate people, and so began the movement known as the Renaissance or 'rebirth' of learning. There was tremendous interest in finding out about how people lived in the past. Scholars tried to see how ancient Greek ideas fitted in with the teaching of Jesus. At last people once again began to think for themselves, instead of believing what the priests and the nobles told them, and their new thinking slowly changed Europe completely. The questions they asked led to new discoveries in mathematics, science and astronomy; and their new critical way of looking at the Church led to the Reformation and the Counter-Reformation, about which we shall be talking in the next two chapters.

During the fourteenth, fifteenth and sixteenth centuries the modern world was born. Instead of regarding people with new ideas as magicians, or devils, or even just plain mad, people began to respect them as scientists and philosophers — even if they did not agree with them. And when at last men and women emerged from a frightening world of superstition, they had new dignity and self-respect: they could look forward to the future with faith and hope.

The world of Copernicus and Galileo

We have seen how the Arabs improved navigation by studying the old Greek star-maps. But the Greeks, following Ptolemy, had thought that the whole Universe moved round the Earth. The Christian Church liked this idea, because it seemed to point to the importance of man, the most intelligent creature on Earth. God had created man 'in his own image', and he had created the Universe as a sort of background to his chief creation.

But Renaissance astronomers, looking at the stars year after year, could see that Ptolemy's system was incorrect. The planets did not behave as he had shown in his diagrams. Some of the astronomers began to think that perhaps the Earth was not the centre of the Universe after all.

One of the earliest astronomers to suggest that the Earth might be revolving round the sun was the Greek Aristarchus, about 250 B.C. In the middle of the fifteenth century A.D., Nikolaus Krebs tried to convince people of the same idea. But it was another Nikolaus who finally suc-

Old playing cards
Printing began when the Chinese carved wooden blocks, pressed them on to an inked pad, and then on to a piece of paper — rather like the rubber-stamps used in offices today. The idea eventually spread to Europe, and wooden blocks were used for printing playing cards, and Bible pictures. The playing card above is French, early sixteenth century.

Fourteenth century iron clock
Early mechanical clocks were large and driven by weights. This clock was made by blacksmiths in the fourteenth century for Wells Cathedral. Clocks were a great improvement on sundials, because they went on telling the time — even on cloudy days and at night. Time began to be important after the sun had set. The word 'clock' comes from the French word *cloche*, meaning bell. Why should a bell and a clock be connected in this way?

ceeded in spreading this theory, and then only after his own death. He was a Polish priest called Koppernigk—better known to us as Copernicus. He published a book shortly before he died in 1543, describing the solar system, and showing that the Earth was a planet of the sun.

Copernicus's work was carried on by a great scientist named Galileo, who in 1610, with the help of a home-made telescope, saw that the planet Jupiter had moons or satellites of its own. He immediately realized that this could be thought of as a little model of the Copernican idea of the solar system. He also found that Venus passed through regular patterns, called phases, which clearly proved that the planet must be revolving round the sun, inside the Earth's own orbit. He wrote to the prince of Florence:

'I am filled with infinite astonishment and also infinite gratitude to God that it has pleased Him to make me alone the first observer of such wonderful things, which have been hidden in all past centuries.'

But Galileo experienced the opposition of the Church. He sent his critics telescopes, so that they might see the moons of Jupiter for themselves. But these unscientific people refused even to look through the telescopes.

Galileo was so sure of his discoveries that he resolved to publish them, whatever the consequences, and fortunately many of his writings survived. But he himself was condemned by the Church, and kept confined to his house until he died in 1642. He was bitterly scornful of this childish attitude, and he wrote:

'I believe that there is no greater hatred in the whole world, than the hatred of the ignorant for knowledge.'

Michelangelo, 1475–1564

One of the outstanding things about the Renaissance in Italy was the new interest in sculpture, in architecture, and in painting. Artists were in great demand by the rulers of the Italian cities, who wanted new buildings built and decorated—sometimes to their own honour and glory. So good painters found that they were engaged by noblemen to paint pictures on the walls of churches, and to carve huge statues to stand in the squares of the cities.

One of these painters and sculptors was Michelangelo, some of whose paintings still exist. In his choice of subjects he followed

Galileo demonstrating his telescope to the Doge of Venice in 1609

In Copernicus's system, the planets, which included the Earth, move round the sun. We now know that there are countless systems like our own in the Universe, in which each star is a sun, and many millions must have their own planets.

Later, Galileo, with the help of his telescope, proved that Venus, the brightest 'star' in the sky, shone with reflected light from the sun, and was not a ball of fire as everybody thought. All planets shine only with reflected light. The spacemen who landed on the Moon saw our own Earth shining in this way.

the more traditional artists of earlier times, whose themes were almost always religious. But he succeeded in making these themes more alive, and more 'natural'. He was a wonderful artist, and even in old age he practised pencil and chalk drawing. He was what we call a perfectionist, a man who was never satisfied with what he had done but was always seeking for the possibility of improvement.

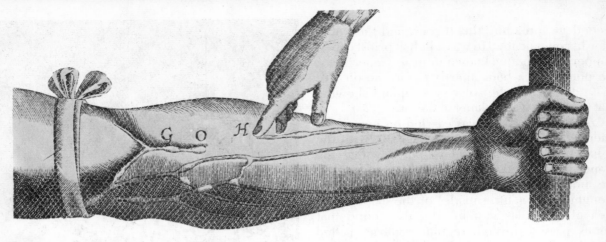

Leonardo da Vinci, 1452–1519

But great though Michelangelo was, there was one other man from Florence who was perhaps greater—one of the real geniuses of the world for all time. His name was Leonardo da Vinci. Besides being a brilliant artist, Leonardo was also keenly interested in science, and had an extraordinarily inventive brain. He wanted to know how things worked, and he complained that he could not paint properly unless he had first mastered the laws of science. He personally dissected, that is, cut up, dead bodies and discovered how the muscles worked, and where they lay. He examined the heart, found out its purpose, and he almost discovered how blood circulates round the body. Dozens of his drawings have survived, and even today, when we know so much more about anatomy (the structure of the body), we are amazed at Leonardo's knowledge.

Remember that in the fifteenth century, schoolboys did not learn science at school at all, so people had no idea of chemistry, or physics, or even biology. Leonardo, on his own, found out that air was not just one gas: he said that there were two, and that without one of them men would not be able to breathe. We now know that there are in fact more than two, but it is true that without one of them (oxygen) people would die. Another 'guess' was that sound travels in waves, which we know to be true.

These studies led Leonardo to an interest in the development of machinery, and if he had known about a fuel such as petrol, there is little doubt that mechanical devices would have been invented nearly 400 years earlier than they were.

Leonardo became the chief engineer to a prince of Italy named Cesare Borgia, and he travelled all over the country advising him on

Circulation of the Blood
William Harvey was a doctor and teacher of anatomy. He encouraged his students to dissect bodies of humans and animals, rather than rely on book-learning. In 1628 he published an article on the circulation of the blood. The picture above is an illustration from the article, showing the blood vessels of the fore-arm. His discovery helped doctors and surgeons understand more about the human body.

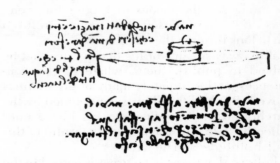

Leonardo da Vinci's submarine
Leonardo told nobody about the submarine he designed because of 'the evil nature of men who would practise assassination at the bottom of the sea by breaking ships in their lowest parts'. This is exactly what happened when submarines were invented 400 years later.

how to build fortresses and canals. Although he hated the wars that tore Italy apart, his interest in machinery led him to draw diagrams for many new types of weapons, including a kind of armoured tank on four wheels, a helicopter, and a submarine! His inventions were later regarded just as being odd, and nobody bothered to follow them up. The principles he thought out could not be put to use because the world had not yet advanced far enough in its technical skill. It is only now that we realize how forward-looking Leonardo was.

Machiavelli, 1469–1527

Machiavelli, a leading politician of Florence, was always looking for new ways in which to bring together the Italian states. In his later years, he wrote: 'Because there is only one Master in heaven, there ought to be only one master on earth.' He knew there could be no lasting peace in Italy while the cities quarrelled among themselves, and they could not keep the French and Spaniards out if they did not have a united army. He was a great admirer of the old Roman system, whereby one man was the ruler, or dictator, of the whole empire. He wanted to see one man made dictator of Italy. He did not care much how this dream came about, and for this reason he has always been thought of as a schemer, cruel and ruthless (pitiless). He thought Cesare Borgia might be his ideal ruler, and he wrote a book called *The Prince* showing how such a man could rule by being firm, but without pity and without a conscience. Although Cesare Borgia fitted this description, he was not strong enough to become Machiavelli's ideal 'dictator'.

Machiavelli was the first Christian politician to study politics as a science. (Ibn Khaldun had done something of the same sort in the Muslim world.) He looked upon the history of the world as a great road along which mankind was travelling — not always in the right direction, but with some sort of purpose. Human beings, he thought, remained much the same throughout the centuries, but circumstances forced them to behave differently. In the Middle Ages, they had not used their talents to the full, whereas in the ancient world they had built splendid civilizations through their loyalty to a great leader. Machiavelli wanted to change the circumstances under which his fellow-Italians lived, and to create conditions where a new civilization might flourish.

Portrait of Machiavelli
Machiavelli wrote: 'Although a prince can sometimes afford to be virtuous, flattery, deceit and even murder are often necessary if the prince is to stay in power.' But Machiavelli himself was not a cruel man, and he did not mean that violent means were necessarily good.

The new merchants

There were great opportunities for businessmen to grow rich during the Renaissance, and often whole families rose to power in the politics of their city because of their great wealth and standing. These families often used their money to 'buy' positions in the government, and even to influence the cardinals* in their choice of a Pope.

Only a few families controlled the banking system, the wool and weaving trades, and the shipping. It was these families who had the money and the leisure to employ artists like Michelangelo and Leonardo da Vinci. They lived on huge family estates, with great libraries and collections of statues in the grounds. They built churches and universities, hospitals and schools.

The spread of education helped the spirit of enquiry to grow. One result was a great discussion that went on all over Europe, in palaces and churches, in private houses and in taverns, about the Church and its place in the world.

*A cardinal is a Prince of the Church, a member of the Pope's Council or Sacred College which elects the Pope.

Chapter 22   A Split in the Christian Church

Right from ancient Egyptian and Sumerian days, the only people who really knew the 'secrets' of religion were the priests and the scribes. The laity, or common people, were told what they should believe, and they were often punished if they did not obey. So an important effect of the new printing presses was that ordinary men and women could learn the knowledge of the priests.

The translation of the Bible

Gutenberg's Bible was the Latin version, and could not be read by anyone who was not highly educated. In Switzerland in 1516, a great scholar named Desiderius Erasmus collected together several Greek translations of the New Testament, and produced a new Greek version. But again, this could be read by very few people. New translations were needed in the common languages of the people of Europe.

As early as 1388, a man named John Wycliffe had produced an English Bible, translated from St Jerome's Vulgate. But the clergy were not willing to allow the laity to read the Scriptures, and the English version was forbidden to be read in church until 1530. Between 1525 and 1535 William Tyndale used Greek sources to make another translation into English. He said:

'I would have women read the Gospels and the Epistles (letters) of St Paul: I would have the ploughman and the craftsman sing them at their work; I would have the traveller recite them to forget the weariness of his journey.'

This is exactly what happened all over Europe, for the Bible was now translated freely in every country. At first Bibles were scarce, and they were chained to reading desks in churches, but the printers worked night and day to produce copies which ordinary men and women could own and read in their own homes.

The Bible in English

This is the first page of the Old Testament translated from the original Hebrew into English by William Tyndale. It was printed in 1530.

Criticism begins

For hundreds of years, Christian kings and princes in Germany, in Spain, in France and in England all had to pay tribute to the Pope. Many people in these countries resented the fact that their money went out of their own country to Rome, and they suspected that it paid for the Pope's earthly glory rather than for the Church. One man, on reading a New Testament in his own language, found that there was 'little about the Pope, but much about Christ'—and that Jesus had not lived in a palace, surrounded by luxury. Even in Italy people began to criticize the Pope because he was more like a worldly prince than a religious leader, but owing to the politics of the various city-states, it was not wise to criticize too much; after all, the Pope's armies were strong enough to invade any city that disagreed with his religious policy. But outside Italy, criticism grew until it reached a great climax.

Martin Luther, 1483–1546

The person who really started the 'Reformation' of the Christian Church was a monk named Martin Luther. He was born in Saxony, part of the country governed by the Holy Roman Emperor, which included present-day Germany, Austria, Belgium and the Netherlands.

Luther was a devout man, but he was filled with great doubts about himself, and about God's purpose for the world. His father had wanted him to be a lawyer, but he decided instead to go into a monastery to try to solve the problems which troubled him. Later he wrote:

'If ever a monk got to heaven by his monkery, I would have got there. All my brothers in the monastery will testify that had I gone on with it I would have killed myself with prayers, reading and other works.'

But Luther did not believe that 'monkery' was the solution for him, and he left the monastery to go and teach in a university at Wittenberg, on the river Elbe. While he was there, he was chosen to accompany a friar to Rome.

But Luther was bitterly disappointed with what he found in the centre of Christianity. Rome was not the devout place he had imagined. The Pope was dressed in magnificent robes, and on ceremonial occasions wore a huge, glittering crown. The cardinals had enormous palaces with dozens of servants, and the common people were full of gossip about the worldly way in

John Huss

In Bohemia [now a part of Czechoslovakia], a reformer named John Huss (1369–1415) preached against sham miracles, and the wealth of the priests. His bishop forbade him to continue preaching, and his writings were taken away to be studied for 'heresy' [any teaching not approved by the Church]. But he continued to preach and write against what he thought was wrong in the church. In 1415 he was told to apologize and say publicly that he had been wrong, and when he refused he was burnt to death. The new ideas that Huss introduced into Europe led to the 'conversion' of a young monk named Martin Luther.

which churchmen lived. There had been Popes, they said, who had children of their own, although they were not supposed to marry; cardinals were sometimes chosen because they could pay more than anyone else for the privilege; even small boys were made bishops, and what was worse, they were made bishops of many different places, not just one. (All these stories were true: one man had 11 bishoprics and was the abbot of nine abbeys—and he had first become bishop at the age of three!) Naturally not all the bishops and cardinals bought their positions, and not all were interested in worldly wealth, but there were enough such cases for gossip to be widespread.

But above all these things, Luther was horrified by the way in which the Church collected money by selling indulgences. In the old days, Christians who had sinned did penance—that is, they punished themselves for it, perhaps

121

by going on a pilgrimage; or they performed some act of self-denial to make up for their sin. Now a man could buy an 'indulgence', that is, he merely had to pay money in order to keep his conscience quiet or avoid the punishment that awaited him after death. Anyone truly penitent (sorry), Luther said, would welcome punishment, and would not expect to get off lightly.

When the people of Wittenberg flocked to buy indulgences from a monk named John Tetzel, Luther's anger really exploded. John Tetzel's indulgences promised forgiveness to a man's dead relatives as well as to himself. This was really taking advantage of the feelings of poor and ignorant men, for even if they might risk purgatory for themselves, how could they bear to allow a dead father, or wife, or child, to suffer, when their release could be bought with money? 'Those who say that a soul flies to heaven when a coin tinkles in the collection-box are preaching an invention of man.' So thought Luther, and he wrote down his angry protests in a pamphlet known as the '95 theses' (or arguments) and he nailed it to the door of the parish church, where everybody going to the morning service on All Saints' Day could read it.

The year was now 1517. Luther's protests might not have got any further, but for the printing press. His theses were published, and they circulated all over Europe. He gained thousands of followers, who also believed that the Christian Church ought to be reformed. In later pamphlets, he attacked the Pope's authority, and suggested that reform should come not from the clergy themselves, but from the laity. He wanted the church services to be made simpler, and he said that the clergy were not after all superior to other people, 'for all believers are priests'.

Pope Leo X and the cardinals were furious that this young man, the son of a poor miner, should attack them in this way. The Pope ordered that his books should be condemned, and that he should be excommunicated. This meant that he was no longer a member of the Church, could not go to services, or be pardoned for his sins. People believed that to be excommunicated meant being cut off from God's mercy for ever.

In 1521 Luther was called to the town of Worms to a kind of trial, presided over by the Emperor Charles V, and there he was declared an outlaw. The emperor said: 'A single monk who disagrees with what all Christianity has said for a thousand years must be wrong!'

The St Bartholomew Massacre

In France the Protestants were called 'Huguenots'. They were persecuted by the French Catholics, and many emigrated to other parts of Europe (and later, to South Africa). Among the early refugees was John Calvin, who went to Geneva, in southern Switzerland.

The French Huguenots built churches and worshipped in their own way, but they were in great danger from a special court that was created in order to suppress them. In 1572 the French king's mother, Catherine de Medici (she was an Italian) persuaded her son to kill all the Huguenots in Paris. On St Bartholomew's night, in a surprise attack, thousands of Huguenots were massacred in the streets. It took many hundreds of years for the two branches of Christianity to live together in peace, and even now there are sometimes outbreaks of violence between them. A recent example is in Ireland.

Martin Luther at the Diet of Worms

Charles V, Holy Roman Emperor (1519–58) was a devout Catholic. He did his best to reform the Church from inside. Had he succeeded, Luther would not have had so much cause for his fiery preaching. The split in the Church led to quarrels among the princes of Germany and Charles's empire broke up. Charles retired to a monastery in Spain when he was 56. Above Martin Luther states his beliefs to Charles, at Worms.

But the priests who attended the 'Diet of Worms'* as the trial was called, did not realize how far Luther's ideas had spread. Other monks were following his example. Some started to conduct church services in German, not in Latin. Others stopped the practice of confession.† Some monks and nuns married. It was too late for reform by the Churchmen themselves. The common men were also taking up the fight, and there was now no means of stopping the break-up of the Church.

In 1555, at the 'Peace of Augsburg', a legal council declared that every city should be able to choose whether it would remain in the Catholic Church in its old form, or join the new Church (called Protestant, because its members 'protested' against the Pope's authority).

Luther had probably not intended to break the Christian Church into two halves in this way. Even some of his early supporters thought he had gone too far. Erasmus, who had been just as indignant as Luther about the sale of indulgences, at the great wealth of the priests, and about worshipping relics, could not agree with his extreme view. 'I laid a hen's egg,' he once said, 'but Luther hatched a bird of quite a different kind.'

---

*A Diet was a kind of Parliament; and in German, 'Worms' is pronounced 'Vorms'.

†The Church demanded that people should go regularly to confession, to confess their sins to a priest who had the power to forgive them in the name of God.

John Calvin, 1509–64

In Geneva, during the first half of the sixteenth century, there was a stern and strict young preacher named John Calvin who also disagreed with the old Church but strongly denied that he had been influenced by Luther. He said that God had spoken to him before he had ever heard of the fiery monk from Wittenberg. But Calvin's views on religion were as strong as Luther's, and having broken away from the Church of Rome, he himself supported a religious code which was indeed much harsher than any that Luther had advised.

Calvin not only rejected the pleasure-loving clergy of Rome—he also stopped the citizens of Geneva from singing and dancing, from gambling and drinking. He set up a Council in Geneva, in which a number of 'pastors' and 'elders' (senior laymen) looked after the moral welfare of the citizens. They had power to inspect people's houses and to order them to repair or construct drainage, and also to find out about their private lives—and if necessary, to expel from the city any who were not obeying the rules. Even school textbooks were chosen for the teachers, so that children should grow

John Calvin
John Calvin presides over a meeting of the Council of Geneva in 1549.

up thinking 'in the right way'. So, in spite of the great scholars of the Renaissance and Reformation, freedom of speech and freedom of action were still not the natural right of most of the peoples of Europe. Under the Peace of Augsburg, a *city* might decide its religious beliefs, but an individual could not. This acceptance of 'majority religion' by a state or by a city led to a great deal of cruelty in the following century.

Calvinism spreads to Scotland

Calvin's strict rule was taught to a great number of young men in his Geneva Academy, or school for priests; and they later went out to other parts of the world to spread the new form of Protestant Christianity. One of Calvin's followers was a preacher named John Knox, who introduced a stern Protestant faith into the kingdom of Scotland; it was very soon accepted by the whole country. England, south of the border, also became Protestant, but for a different reason. The person who brought this about was not a preacher, but the king himself.

The Church of England

In England, Henry VIII used the split in the Church for political ends. His wife, Catherine of Aragon, to whom he had been married for 18 years, had had many children, but only one, a girl, had lived. It was important that the king should have a male heir, for England had already had many years of wars about who should rule.

Henry asked the Pope for a divorce, but the Pope took so long to grant it that Henry became impatient. He decided to do without the Pope's consent. There were many people in the country who had read Luther's works and who sympathized with reforming the Church. Henry talked to them, and he even appointed a Protestant sympathizer named Thomas Cranmer as Archbishop of Canterbury. Cranmer showed his thanks by declaring that Henry's marriage had never been legal, and by allowing him to marry instead a girl named Anne Bullen (or Boleyn).

The Pope was furious when he heard the news; he excommunicated Cranmer, the bishops who had assisted him, and finally Henry himself. But Henry was no longer worried. He had decided to take over his country's Church and to make himself its head. Every bishop in the country had to sign a paper saying that Henry's marriage to Anne was lawful, and very few refused, although by signing it they were really agreeing that the Pope need not be obeyed.

The following year, Henry appointed an ambitious politician named Thomas Cromwell to look into the affairs of the Church. Cromwell sent officers to every monastery in the country, to find out how well or badly they were being run. Now, many of the great Benedictine and Cistercian monasteries were not being managed well at all. The old strict Rule was not being obeyed, the gardens were neglected, and the abbots were growing prosperous on all the goods they collected from their benefactors, and from the farmers who worked their farm-land.

One by one Cromwell closed the monasteries, beginning with the smaller ones. Over five years, from 1535 to 1540, all the monks and nuns of England were sent away from the homes they had lived in for years, and even the wandering friars who preached in the streets were ordered to find other employment.

The land that had belonged to the monasteries went to the king, who later sold it to wealthy merchants. They in turn sold much of it—at a profit—to sheep-farmers, for by now the wool

Thomas Cromwell

trade was very important in England. In only a few years, and with very little opposition, England changed from being a Catholic country, owing allegiance to the Pope, into a Protestant country with the king as the Church's leader. The Anglican Church that resulted from Henry's and England's legal need for a male heir was different from other Protestant Churches, because it did not stem directly from Luther's or Calvin's teachings. (Later, in England, there were people who said that the Anglican Church was still too like the Church of Rome, and there were further splits.) But in spite of the fact that Henry broke away from the Pope for political rather than religious reasons, many people in England were obviously ready for some sort of reform in the Church. Public opinion favoured the change, especially in the cities and the country near London.

Chapter 23 The Catholic Reformation

To the followers of the Pope, the new branch of Christianity was a terrible and dangerous heresy. A threat of excommunication by the Pope was effective only if the person threatened believed in the Pope's power. But if he was not a devout Catholic, and looked to his king, or to a Protestant leader for his religious guidance, then the threat was meaningless. The Catholic Church at last realized that it should think out its policy, and try to resist the new movement.

Heresy

The Christian Church had always tried to stop people having opinions that were different from the 'official' ones. People who questioned the Church's teaching were called 'heretics'. They were accused of the sin of heresy.

In the early days of Christianity a heretic could have his property taken from him, and he could be banished from his own country. An early Christian writer, St John Chrysostom, said, 'To put a heretic to death would be to introduce upon earth an inexpiable (unpardonable) crime.' But by the time of the Reformation, many heretics *had* been put to death, usually by being burnt alive. The Pope sent Dominican friars about the country to find people suspected of heresy. The friars were called 'Inquisitors' (investigators), and they came to be greatly feared. A man accused by the Inquisitors of heresy could be put into prison merely on suspicion. If he accused other 'heretics' he might escape with his life. But if he defied the Inquisition, then he could be tortured, imprisoned for life, or handed over to the 'secular arm' for execution. (The secular arm was the ordinary 'police force' of the country. Secular means concerned with worldly, not religious, matters.)

The Inquisition was worse in Spain than anywhere else. Just as Henry VIII had taken over

Joan of Arc
In the early fifteenth century, Jeanne d'Arc, or Joan of Arc, a French girl, believed that angels spoke to her, and told her to lead the French forces against the English army. She was captured by the people of Burgundy in France, and sold to the English, who tried her for heresy. She would not deny hearing 'voices', and she said that she obeyed the direct voice of God rather than the Church. For this she was found guilty and burnt in 1431.

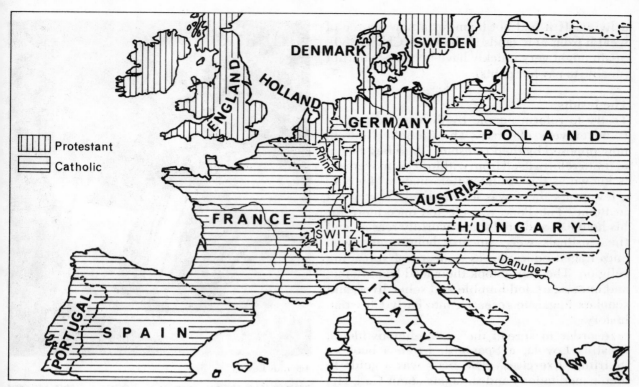

Protestant
Catholic

The division between Catholic and Protestant Countries in the seventeenth century

In some countries, such as Ireland and Germany, the decision of the rulers was not always accepted, this lead to religious wars.

the Pope's power for his own purposes, so now King Ferdinand and Queen Isabella of Spain took over the idea of Inquisitors to keep Spain a Catholic country, and to get rid of the last remaining Muslims in Granada. There had been great friendliness between the two religious groups in the past, but now people were encouraged to give information against Muslims and even Jews. Their lands were seized by the King and Queen, and as both Jews and Muslims were often good business men, the Crown became very wealthy. The chief Inquisitor, a cruel monk named Torquemada, even accused bishops of heresy and had them imprisoned.

Now, although the King and Queen acquired great estates as a result of the persecutions, business in Spain decreased, because rich men could be reduced in a single day to poverty. Everybody wanted immediate payment instead of allowing credit*, for who knew if the man who owed you money would ever be able to pay it? Tomorrow he might be in jail, and his wife and children left to live as best they might, turned out of their homes and without any way of earning

*To allow or give credit means to accept a buyer's promise to pay at a later date.

Jewish moneylender

Jews were regarded as 'different' from other people, because they kept to their own communities and they had different customs and beliefs. People who are different in these ways are often regarded with suspicion and even hated by those among whom they live. The Jews have had more than their fair share of hatred throughout their long history.

Muslims were not allowed to lend money for interest but Jews were, and many grew rich by money lending.

127

a living. If it had not been for a new source of wealth from new lands in the west (Chapter 30), Spain might very quickly have become bankrupt (unable to pay her debts).

The Jesuits

To try to reform people by threats and torture is never very effective. The Catholic Church, now opposed by the Protestant Churches, began to try to reform itself from within. This movement is known as the 'Counter-Reformation'. In only a few years there was a completely new spirit in Rome. The Pope was elected once more for his holiness, and not for any worldly reason, and the cardinals were sincere, honest men who encouraged education as a means of spreading religion. The clergy took their lead from Rome, and once again led humble and sober lives; and scholars began to research into early Christian history.

In order to spread the new religious ideals, Ignatius Loyola, a Spaniard, wrote a book of 'Spiritual Exercises'. The book was a guide to men's meditations and thoughts about God. His main theme was, 'We must serve God as if everything depended upon ourselves; but we must pray as if all depended upon God.'

Loyola was a monk, and a university teacher. In 1534 he and a small group of friends met together in a French church, and vowed that they would take up the ideals of the early Christians. They would live on the charity of others, owning no property, and having no fixed homes. Above all, they would teach other people, convert the 'heathen', and try to go on a pilgrimage to Jerusalem.

This little band of men (only about seven or eight of them at first) walked all the way to Rome, and had an audience (a formal interview) with Pope Paul III. This Pope was one of the first to return to the old spiritual ideals of the Christian Church, and he welcomed Loyola and gave him money to continue his work. Loyola formed the 'Society of Jesus', and in a short time he had gathered many followers. In later years they

Ignatius Loyola

Universities
Until the time of the Reformation, European universities were mainly run by the Church. They taught Latin, Greek, mathematics and philosophy. When the students successfully completed their course of learning they obtained a doctor's or master's degree, which meant they were qualified to teach in a university if they wished.

were known as 'Jesuits', and they penetrated almost every country in the world. They spread the new Catholic ideas, and they founded schools and colleges in order to combat Protestantism. Their schools were so well run and became so famous for their learning that wealthy parents had no hesitation in sending their sons to the Jesuits. In particular they tried to build good schools in Protestant countries such as Germany, so that they could educate priests to replace those who had become Lutherans.

The Council of Trent
Charles V, the Holy Roman Emperor, was one of the first people in authority to be concerned about the wrong practices in the Church. He urged the Pope to call together a council to discuss ways and means of setting things right. The result of his concern was the Council of Trent, which met many times over a period of several years to set down the beliefs of Catholics, and to end the differences of opinion of Catholics in different countries. The council was not a complete success, because there were always more Italians in the sessions than there were representatives of any other country, and so they could out-vote the rest. But the Jesuits sent their best scholars of all nationalities, and the council did strengthen the power of the Catholic Church in Europe.

Neither the Catholics nor the Protestants were very sure of themselves, and for this reason both sides were often intolerant. Bitter quarrels broke out between scholars and between churchmen, and hundreds of good people on both sides were executed for no other reason than that they believed in the 'wrong' kind of Christianity. The religious quarrels of the sixteenth and seventeenth centuries led to the various European countries competing in other things as well. Catholic and Protestant countries were rivals in the search for new lands, and in opening new markets with the East, and with the newly-discovered America—as we shall see in the following chapters.

The Arts
During the fifteenth, sixteenth and seventeenth centuries, Europeans became more conscious of a need for using their brains as well as their hands. People wrote books, painted pictures, learnt about medicine, astronomy, history and geography. And just as *everybody* in ancient

William Shakespeare
The greatest English poet and playwright of the age was William Shakespeare. His works include historical plays about the kings of former times; tragedies about the downfall of great men; and comedies which are sometimes like fairy stories. Shakespeare's players acted in the Globe Theatre, London this had a circular stage which allowed the audience to sit all around the actors.

Greece went to plays, talked politics, took part in athletic exercises, and played a musical instrument; so now, after the Renaissance, all educated people could sing, write verse, ride horses, and appreciate beautiful buildings, parks and gardens. They learnt foreign languages, read Latin, danced and practised fencing. They were aware of the current events of their time, and they took a great interest in the achievements of their fellow-countrymen.

These last few chapters have been about the things people *thought* about, and how they broadened their knowledge by using their brains; in the next section we shall see how these same centuries also produced explorers, adventurers and people willing to endure pain and great discomfort for the sake of an ideal.

Part VI Exploration and Conquest
Chapter 24 Looking beyond the Sea

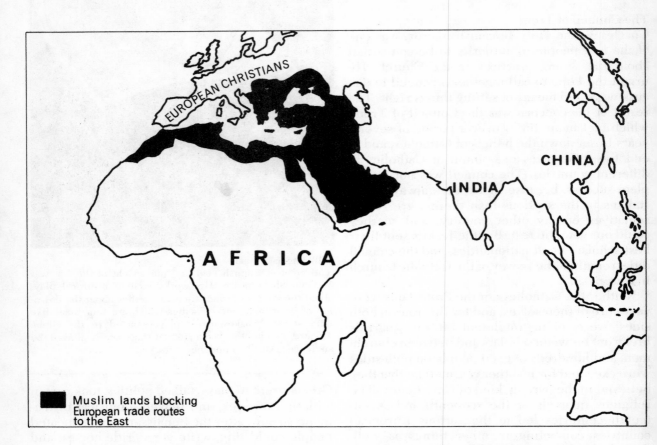

Muslim lands blocking
European trade routes
to the East

By the time of the Reformation, the great Muslim conquests were over. After that, battles between Christians and Muslims were less important to the history of the world. Lands sometimes changed hands, but in general, Muslim and Christian countries left each other alone.

There was a block of Muslim countries around the Mediterranean Sea (see map), which cut off Christian Europe from the countries of the East. The two main Christian ports of Venice and Genoa grew rich by buying goods from Muslim traders, and selling them to their northern neighbours.

For the most part, Muslims and Christians did not meet at all. But in various ways Christian countries were reminded of what they were missing by being separated by the Muslim block from Africa and the lands of the East.

The first real contact with another way of life came with the Crusades, one important result of which was that those Europeans who returned from the East brought with them new ideas of comfort and luxury. They had seen the palaces of Constantinople and Damascus, and enjoyed the hospitality of Eastern nobles. They also brought back new foods, and new ideas of how to flavour food with pepper and other spices. The demand for these Eastern goods increased, and money poured into Muslim lands to pay for them. The European knights and soldiers all learned new and less harsh ways of life. A prosperous and ambitious middle class of traders and merchants began to realize its own strength and importance. They were no longer content to be servants (almost slaves) of the wealthy. They wanted more rights and privileges. They became more independent than they had ever been before and more likely to seek adventure. The 'spirit of enquiry' of the Renaissance encouraged people to read for themselves the old Greek books about astronomy and geography. Old maps were brought out and studied. An increase in trade with other countries led to better boat-building. As seamen sailed farther and farther from home, so the shipbuilders tried to build ships to meet the greater risks of long voyages.

The second way in which the two cultures met was when Christians went on pilgrimages to the East. This was one way in which the well-to-do citizens took a holiday. They made their way down to southern Italy or Venice, and sailed across the Mediterranean to Palestine, the land in which Jesus had lived. When they returned to Europe they entertained their friends with tales of the strange things they had seen in Palestine and Syria, Egypt and Arabia. Just like modern tourists they brought back presents — silks imported from India and China, Persian carpets, spices, and carved ivory. Damascus, in Syria, was now the most important trading centre in the Middle East, and if they could afford it, travellers to Syria could buy all the luxuries they wanted.

The third sort of people who visited Muslim lands were perhaps the most adventurous of all. These were the merchants who travelled long distances on foot and on horseback, to find the *sources* of the wealth of cities like Damascus. One outstanding example of a merchant-traveller was Marco Polo, but there were many others. When Marco Polo finally returned to Europe, he wrote down all he could remember of the lands of the East, and so excited the interest — and the greed — of those who read his book that soon the governments of Europe were eager for their merchants to visit and trade with these lands.

So interest in the East developed in all the countries of Europe. But along with this interest,

Kublai Khan

Kublai Khan, the emperor of China in Marco Polo's time, was not Chinese. He came from Mongolia in the north, and he led an invasion of Mongols into China and overran it. The Mongols were expert horsemen, and no ordinary foot-soldiers could withstand them. In the far-off west, they had already invaded and conquered much of what is now Russia and Poland.

Kublai Khan made himself the emperor of the whole of China, and built his capital at Peking. In spite of the warlike manner in which he had gained the throne, he ruled wisely, and soon China was again famous for its art, poetry and peaceful ways. The Khan built beautiful palaces and gardens, and encouraged his people to unite and live together in harmony. He brought religious leaders and teachers to his capital, because he thought they would have a civilizing influence on the country.

there was a spirit of rivalry. Kings by now were becoming powerful, and there was competition between the new nation-states. In time the new split between Catholics and Protestants made the rivalry stronger. Each country wished to profit as much as possible from the trade with the East and to exclude others from it. It was important therefore to get through the Muslim barrier and reach the 'treasure-countries'.

But it was almost impossible for any expedition to go through Muslim territory. A few merchants were allowed to do so, but they had to pay so much in customs duties and taxes that their goods were very expensive to buy in Europe. The Christian countries saw this as good money getting into the hands of 'unbelievers'. If there was no way through by land, then the countries of Europe had to find a way round by sea. And the first European country to have any clear ideas on the solution to this problem was Portugal.

Henry the Navigator, 1394–1460

Henry the Navigator was a prince of Portugal. He had a great interest in exploration, and in anything to do with ships, though, in spite of his nickname, he was not himself a sailor. When he was a young man, Henry went to fight the Muslims at a place called Ceuta in North Africa. While he was there he saw the arrival of caravans from the centre of Africa, caravans which had come all the way from the towns of Songhai and Timbuktu, south of the Sahara. He realized that a country as small as Portugal could not possibly capture this trade from the Muslims; but was there any reason why they could not sail round the coast of Africa, and find another route to the gold-mines? With this idea in mind, Henry spent all his time consulting old maps, talking to sailors and adventurers, and encouraging his inventors to improve the existing compasses and other aids to navigation. Henry's first objects were to find Africa's gold and to convert Muslims and heathens to Christianity.

Soon, as a result of this one man's interest and imagination, the ship-builders and sail-makers, the traders and craftsmen of Portugal, were talking about the possibilities of voyages and trade-routes to new, and as yet undiscovered countries.

The reasons for exploration were all in existence: the desire to convert or to overcome the Muslims; the knowledge that there were rich cities in the East; and the lure of gold in Africa. Before long the exploration began.

The Way South

One of the questions that faced the Portuguese was, 'How safe is it to sail southwards round Africa?' Ptolemy, the map-maker of the Greeks, had said that it was impossible to live in the tropics, and many legends had grown up about how men turned black, or were shrivelled up like a leaf in a fire, when they crossed the Equator. In a world full of superstition, fear of the unknown was very great. But if Henry the

Henry the Navigator

Prester John
The legend was that Prester John (probably 'Priest John') was a powerful Christian king whose kingdom was somewhere in Africa, or Asia, or India—nobody quite knew where. He was said to be successfully keeping the Muslims out of his kingdom, so the Portuguese felt that he would be a powerful ally. Everywhere they went, they asked for news of Prester John. None of the inhabitants of Africa or India knew whom they were talking about, but they tried to be helpful. Many Portuguese, and many converted Africans, were sent inland on hopeless searches for the legendary king.

Navigator's dreams were to be fulfilled, these old theories had to be put to the test.

Year by year small, fast sailing-ships called caravels made their way down the west coast of Africa, first calling in for supplies at their newly-colonized Cape Verde Islands. Each expedition tried to push a little further southward, always asking for news of Prester John, and looking for new kingdoms with which they could trade.

In 1482 a sea-captain called Diogo Cão anchored in the waters of the river Congo, having successfully crossed the Equator without bursting into flames, or even noticeably changing colour! He left four Franciscan monks at an African village, with orders to look for the ruler of the Congo kingdom, and to discover whether this large river led to Prester John's country. He then returned home to Lisbon, with several Africans whom he had taken as hostages* for the safety of his Franciscans. These Africans were trained by the Portuguese in Lisbon so that they could act as interpreters and guides when Diogo Cão returned to the river Congo. Five years later the Africans were home again. Together with Cão and his sailors, they paddled up the river to the king's town, which was the capital of a large state. The Franciscans were well and happy. The king waited for his guests, seated on his wood-and-ivory stool, and surrounded by his councillors and advisors. Altogether it looked as though the Portuguese and Congolese would be able to bring each other considerable benefits. Trade in ivory, gold and slaves started almost straight away—a trade which was eventually to lead to the downfall of the kingdom of Congo. Later we shall see why this was so.

Overland to Calicut

Meanwhile, another Portuguese explorer was travelling overland to try to find out all he could about the west coast of India and the spice trade. His name was Pero de Covilhã†, and he went through Arabia disguised as a merchant. He joined a party of Arab merchants, without arousing suspicion (a remarkable feat), and so passed through all the dangers of the route in company with people who had been there before. He reached India, and set to work to discover all he could about the Muslim trade between India

*A hostage was a prisoner held as a guarantee of good behaviour by the people from whom he was taken.

†Also spelt Covilhão and Covilhan.

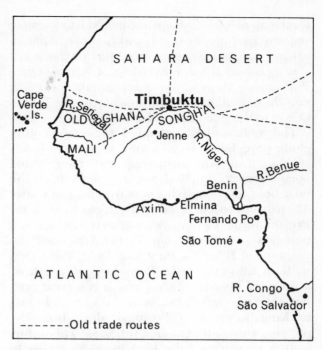

The West Coast of Africa

There had already been in Africa more splendid towns and palaces than those of the Congo Kingdom. Between the rivers Senegal and Niger, the kingdoms of Ghana, Mali and Songhai had grown rich by trading with the people of North Africa. Their trade routes through the desert were centuries old, and the fame of their kings had spread to Europe.

When the Muslim king of Mali went on a pilgrimage to Mecca in 1324, he took an enormous amount of gold with him. Dealers had to drop the price of gold because it was now so plentiful. A fourteenth century writer said: 'Twelve thousand young slaves dressed in tunics of brocade and silk of Yemen carried his personal belongings.' This king, whose name was Mansa Musa, returned to his own country with Arab scholars and teachers and schools in Timbuktu and Jenne became famous for their learning. The scholars taught history, religion and law.

These facts were forgotten in later centuries, and the European explorers of the nineteenth century talked of 'darkest Africa', and expected to find only savages there.

and East Africa. He saw horses from Arabia being taken ashore at Goa, and at Calicut the gold and ivory from East Africa being unloaded. The boats used by the traders were small and frail, sewn together with strips of coconut palm, and with no nails at all. They had triangular sails, and looked much less seaworthy (fit to go to sea) than the vessels of Covilhã's home country.

Covilhã had an opportunity to find out for himself how well these little dhows could sail across the Indian Ocean; he paid for a passage in one of them, and went to Sofala, in south-eastern Africa.

(See map on p. 135) He was the first European to see any part of this coast, and he heard enough of the local gossip to convince him that there was a way round the southern tip of Africa. Once Portuguese ships could reach Sofala, he knew that they could easily continue across the Indian Ocean to the rich lands of India and China.

The trading dhow unloaded its cargo of cotton cloth, porcelain (china) plates, wheat and beads at the East African ports, and then sailed northwards to the Red Sea. Covilhã got off the boat here, and made his way overland to Cairo. Then he decided to go to Ethiopia to look for Prester John. Twenty years afterwards, when a delegation arrived from Portugal to visit the emperor of Ethiopia, they found him still there, with an Ethiopian wife. Pero da Covilhã left no account of his adventures, which is a great pity, but before he left Cairo, he had sent back letters to King John II of Portugal, describing the pepper, clove and cinnamon trades. This information encouraged the king to go on trying to find a way round Africa to the Indian Ocean, and in 1487 he sent the navigator Bartholomew Diaz with instructions to continue down the coast until he found the southern end of Africa.

The voyage of Bartholomew Diaz

It is difficult for us now to know exactly how Bartholomew Diaz's crew fared on this journey, for all the reports and maps were kept strictly secret by the Portuguese of the time, and they have since been lost. The Portuguese did not want other nations to find out what they were doing. By Portuguese law passing on maps or information about trade-routes was an offence punishable by death.

Bartholomew Diaz's little 'lateen rigged' (triangular-sailed) ship was blown away from the course his pilot had set, and the sailors knew that they were much farther west than they wanted to be—but they didn't know *how* much farther. When the wind dropped, they sailed eastward again, and were astonished at not reaching land. In great fear, they turned the boat towards the north, discovered land, and to their amazement realized that they had found the route round Africa. They were in the area we now call Mossel Bay.

Diaz was delighted to find that they had achieved their purpose, and was eager to go on towards the north and up the new coastline. But his men panicked and refused to go any farther. They were now in an unknown sea, and who knew what dangers they might have to face? They had very little fresh water, and food was scarce. They did not know whether they would meet friends or enemies, and they were not armed for battle. Bartholomew Diaz was finally persuaded that he had gone far enough. So they returned, and saw for the first time the harbour we now know as Table Bay. Diaz called the southern tip of Africa 'The Cape of Storms', because he was unlucky enough to arrive there in bad weather. His king renamed it 'The Cape of Good Hope', because now it seemed that there was a promise of new and exciting voyages.

Map showing voyage of Bartholomew Diaz, in 1487–8, during which he reached the Cape of Good Hope

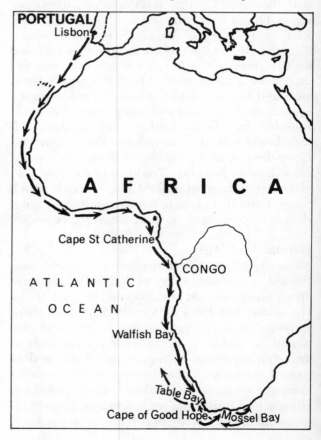

Chapter 25 The Land of Zenj

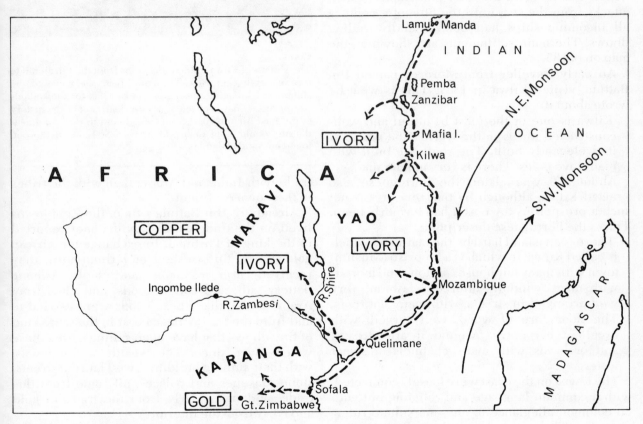

In the days of the early Portuguese voyages of discovery, East Africa was already well-known to the Muslims from south Arabia (and others who had settled on the west coast of India) as the 'land of Zenj'. (It is also sometimes spelt 'Zinj' or 'Zanj'.)

From about the ninth or tenth centuries, traders from Arabia had made small settlements along the east coast of Africa. Then, probably about the thirteenth century, a number of Muslims from towns in Somalia, north of present-day Kenya, emigrated to these settlements, and built new towns of their own. They cultivated

The Land of Zenj

The people of the coast traded with the interior along several different trade routes. In the north, the Maravi (Malawi) traded ivory with Arabs who travelled up the Shire River. Ingombe Ilede was once a flourishing trading town where Arab merchants bought ivory. The ivory was carried to the coast by African men, some of whom were probably sold as slaves at the end of the journey.

Further south, Arabs exchanged their cloth, beads and knives for gold from the country of Monomatapa.

crops, kept livestock (domestic animals), and fished in the cool waters inside the coral reefs which protect the harbours and inlets of the coast.

There was frequent intermarriage between the Arabs and the Africans of the coast, and they started to create a new kind of culture, which was a mixture of the Arab and African ways of life, yet different from both. These people became the rulers of the towns, and the wealthy merchants. The rest of the population were Africans, most of whom were probably not converted to Islam. They kept to their own customs, and did not copy the richer people very much.

Most of the settlements were built on islands, as protection against raids from inland tribes. There was no need to fortify the islands against attacks from the sea; until the fifteenth century all incoming ships had been friendly trading dhows. The main settlements are shown on the map on p. 135.

An early traveller from Morocco named Ibn Battuta, visited Kilwa in 1331. This is what he wrote about it:

'Kilwa is one of the most beautiful and well-constructed towns in the world. The whole of it is elegantly built. The roofs are built with mangrove poles. There is very much rain.'

About 250 years later, the Portuguese also praised Kilwa, although by that time it was not such a prosperous town as it had formerly been. This is the Portuguese description:

'There is an island hard by the mainland which is called Kilwa, in which is a Moorish (Muslim) town with many fair houses of stone and mortar, with many windows after our fashion, very well arranged in streets, with many flat roofs. The doors are of wood, well carved, with excellent carpentry. Around it are streams and orchards with many channels of sweet water.'

The towns on the coast were loosely connected, with a common language and religion, but with no common allegiance to any one sultan (ruler) or nation. The people had little to disturb them. Craftsmen wove cloth, carved wood, built stone or wooden houses and mosques, and made jewellery and ornaments. The weather was good, there was enough rain for the crops, the sea was full of fish, and the coconut palms gave food, drink, matting and roofing. There was no need to work very hard in order to be fed and clothed on a tropical coast. Perhaps because of this, and because a hot moist climate does not make people very energetic, the Muslims of the coast made no attempt to build towns inland. They were a sea-board* people, more interested in their

Coins
The sultans of Kilwa minted tiny coins from the thirteenth to the sixteenth centuries. The coins bear the name of the sultan, and sometimes also a prayer to Allah for the sultan's prosperity. Today archaeologists can learn about the history of the East African coast from coins found in ruins and near the sites of old 'Zenj' towns. There were 569 coins in this pot, found on Nanda Island in 1964.

trade with India and Arabia than with the tribes in their own continent.

Already in Ibn Battuta's time, the Zenj towns lived on the trade which Covilhã later reported to the king of Portugal. In exchange for African gold, ivory, tortoiseshell and rhino-horn, they received iron weapons and tools, Islamic pottery, silk and cotton goods, and glass from Arabia and India. These goods were carried to and from the East African coast in the same kind of tiny dhows that have been sailing across these waters ever since. The wealth of the towns, with their shining buildings, well laid out streets, stone mosques and palaces, all came from this trade, and particularly from the trade in gold and ivory from the interior.

The main route by which the gold came was along the great river Zambezi, and southwards to the port of Sofala. The sultans of Kilwa were powerful enough to rule over Sofala, and take most of the profits of the gold trade for themselves. The country from which the gold came was ruled by a king called by the Portuguese, Monomotapa, and his people were the Karanga. Their descendants still live in present-day Rhodesia. ('Monomotapa' was the Portuguese way of pronouncing 'Mwinemutapa', which

*The sea-board is the strip of land nearest the coast.

means 'the plunderer'. It was a praise-name given to him by his own people because of his great conquests.)

The ordinary coast-people's contact with the outside world was limited to the news they got from the crews of sailing dhows, which arrived on their shores between December and April; the dhows stayed on the coast until the north-east monsoon blew, and the sailors returned to India during April and May. The crews brought news from the Spice Islands (the East Indies), from India, and even from China. They brought no news from Christian Europe, so the coming of the Europeans was an unexpected shock.

Strangers in the Indian Ocean

Ten years after Bartholomew Diaz's voyage, three little sailing ships made their way round the Cape of Good Hope and sailed northwards, looking for new countries, Prester John, and opportunities for trade. The Portuguese—though they did not know it, or in any way intend it—were about to put an end to the prosperity of the East Coast of Africa.

The leader of the expedition was Vasco da Gama, a soldier and mariner, now about 37 years old. His navigator was the real hero of this voyage. He had sailed on a course that took them far away from the west coast of Africa, and by doing so he had avoided the worst of the contrary winds. During the ten years that had passed since Bartholomew Diaz rounded the Cape, ships' designs had been slightly altered, and ships' instruments had been improved. But they were still very inadequate for such danger-

Trade with the Far East
The dhows came to the coast towns of the Zenj between the months of December and April. With them they brought news from the East and the goods and wares for which they had traded ivory.

The square-rigged carrack
The square-rigged carrack was adopted by Vasco de Gama as an improvement on the caravel as used by Bartholomew Diaz. The caravel carried two lateen (triangular) sails and one small square sail. It sailed well in shallow water and could anchor very close to the shore. The carrack, fitted with up to five square-rigged sails was more fitted to the open seas.

ous journeys, and the crew relied completely on the skill and knowledge of their navigators.

This little group of ships arrived at Mozambique in March 1498, and saw in the bay a line of canoes and four large trading dhows. The dhows were a surprise to them, and so indeed was the sultan himself, who later came to greet them with full ceremony. Vasco da Gama's men were amazed at the prosperity of Mozambique. This created a difficult situation for the

Portuguese, because the only presents they had in their ships were things like beads, bells, and cheap cloth. And here were the inhabitants of Mozambique, unloading beautiful silks, cottons and porcelain from the dhows of India and Arabia! However, the citizens of Mozambique treated their visitors with courtesy and kindness, and the Portuguese ate their fill of oranges and limes, and also coconuts, which were something new to them. The sick men began to recover, and everyone's spirits rose at the sight of the riches of Mozambique.

For explorers searching for the Christian kingdom of Prester John, it was a disappointment to find that the inhabitants spoke Arabic, and were Muslims. They kept their own religion secret, and for a while the islanders thought they were Muslim Turks. Trouble started when they discovered their mistake, and the Portuguese left in a hurry, taking with them two pilots who knew the coast well.

Northwards along the coast they went, missing Kilwa because the winds blew them past the harbour. But even so, the dhows from Mozambique sailed faster than the Portuguese fleet, and their crews warned the inhabitants of the more northerly coastal towns that they were about to have Christian visitors. This is what an Arab historian, writing in about 1520, had to say about the Portuguese arrival:

'After a few days there came word that the ships had passed Kilwa and had gone on to Mafia. The lord of Mafia rejoiced, for he thought they (the Portuguese) were good and honest men. But those who knew the truth confirmed that they were corrupt and dishonest persons who had only come to spy out the land in order to seize it. And they determined to cut the anchors of their ships so that they should drift ashore and be wrecked by the Muslims.'

Each side was quick to suspect the other of treachery because of their different religious beliefs, and in view of what happened later, the Muslims were quite right to do so. The Mombasa islanders were cautious about accepting the Portuguese as friends, though they allowed them to have fruit, meat and water. But the news from Mozambique had its effect, and the islanders did try to set the ships adrift. A Portuguese account says:

'Those who swam to the *Berrio* began to cut the cable. The men on watch thought at first

Vasco da Gama

that they were tunny fish, but when they perceived their mistake they shouted to the other vessels. The other swimmers had already got hold of the rigging (the ropes of the sails) of the mizzen-mast*. Seeing themselves discovered, they silently slipped down and fled. These and other wicked tricks were practised upon us by these dogs, but Our Lord did not allow them to succeed because they were unbelievers.'

The same author did not seem to think it at all 'wicked' that the Portuguese had that same day poured boiling oil on the skin of two Arabs, to make them confess any treachery against them.

Malindi had also had news of the visitors. But here the Portuguese received a better welcome, for the sultan of Malindi was an old enemy of the sultan of Mombasa, and he must have said to himself, 'The enemy of my enemy is my friend.'

Only a few Portuguese sailors were allowed

*The mizzen-mast is the mast nearest to the back of a three-masted ship.

138

on shore, and Vasco da Gama himself refused to meet the sultan anywhere except out at sea. But in spite of this lack of trust, the people of Malindi were completely friendly to the Portuguese. They gave them a pilot to assist the navigator on the journey to India, and a quantity of square water containers, such as they used on their own dhows. Then with many friendly farewells, they watched the strange European ships sail away with the monsoon winds.

The Portuguese reach India

The merchants of Arabia and the Malabar coast of India were the people who every year received the ivory and gold, tortoiseshell and rhino-horn, from the ports of East Africa. In Calicut, the chief trading port, Arab merchants made contact with others all the way round the coast of India, as far as the Spice Islands and even China. Trading ships from these Far Eastern ports reached India, and there the goods were either sold inland, or sent across the Indian Ocean to pay for more African gold. The Indian traders were busy men, for they had a great continent to deal with. The rulers of the many Indian states liked to have rich silks from China, and jewellery made from the gold of Sofala.

The 'zamorin' or king of Calicut was a Hindu, but the traders were Muslims. There was great tolerance in India for different religious beliefs; but the Muslims there became just as unfriendly towards Christian traders as their kinsfolk everywhere else.

Vasco da Gama's men arrived in Calicut on 21 May 1498. The traders were accustomed to foreign trading ships, and sold the Portuguese some pepper and cinnamon. But there was something about this expedition that the Arabs did not like. It looked as though the newcomers wanted to take their trade from them, rather than use them as trading partners. The zamorin was in a fix; the prosperity of his city depended upon trade, yet he knew that if he granted the Portuguese trading-rights, his Arab traders would be angry. On the other hand, the Portuguese ships were all well armed with guns, which they might easily decide to use on his city.

In the end he asked the Portuguese for customs' duty, and when they refused to pay it he imprisoned some of the ships' crew. Vasco da Gama immediately captured some Indian citizens, and kept them as hostages till his crew members were returned.

The Padrão at Malindi

Everywhere they went the Portuguese put up stone pillars or *padrãos*. The padrão at Malindi has been cased with coral rock, but part of the original pillar may still be inside. The cross is made of stone from Lisbon, so it is probably the original one.

The sailors who went ashore spoke of Malindi enthusiastically. The well-laid out streets were lined with large houses, each having a wooden verandah. The rulers wore Arab dress, and there were also some Gujerati traders living there. The town remained loyal to Portugal for 100 years.

Today Malindi is just a small fishing village, with a row of 'tourist' hotels along the beach. Nearby is the old Arab town of Gedi, which, although in ruins, gives a good idea of the sort of stone buildings in which the coastal peoples used to live.

The Portuguese were obviously not welcome, but this did not discourage them. Vasco da Gama returned to Portugal to report to King John, and within a year a second expedition was on its way. The zamorin was going to have many worries in the future.

Chapter 26 The New World in the West

During the time that they had been pushing south along the west coast of Africa, the Portuguese were so concerned with their new 'factories' (trading stations) there, that Christopher Columbus, the greatest explorer of his time, could not get them to listen to him. He had an entirely different plan: he wanted to sail westward, and get to the Spice Islands and China (he called it Cathay) by sailing straight across the Atlantic Ocean.

We now know that this was impossible, because the continent of America lies between Europe and China; but Columbus and a few others had come to the conclusion that China was only about 3,500 miles away. They imagined the world to be smaller than it really is — the true distance from Portugal to China is more than three times as great as Columbus supposed. Only a few highly educated men believed the old Greek geographers, whose ideas of distance had been more exact.

Disappointed that Portugal would not give him ships, Columbus went to Spain to try his luck with King Ferdinand and Queen Isabella. They received him kindly, but at first they were too busy to take much notice. Their wars against the Muslims of Granada (southern Spain) were to them more important, and paying their troops had used up a great deal of public money. But finally the Spaniards took Granada and, in 1492, five years before Vasco da Gama rounded Africa, Columbus set sail. The Spanish king and queen had provided him with three ships, because they at last realized that Portugal was already ahead of them, and that they had better hurry up and discover new trade outlets of their own. Portugal would resist any Spanish attempt to sail round 'their' land; the Spaniards could therefore only hope that there was indeed another route to the Spice Islands and Cathay, as this mariner Christopher Columbus said.

For two months the three Spanish ships sailed west, seeing no land at all. Columbus sailed in the largest ship, the *Santa Maria*. They ran into an area now called the Sargasso Sea, where for days the sea was completely calm, and the sails hung idly without picking up a breath of wind. Nowadays ships set a course which avoids the Sargasso Sea, because besides being windless, it is full of floating weeds. Columbus thought the sea-weed meant that they were near land. But almost anything encouraged him to think they had nearly reached Cathay. He saw birds, a whale and flying-fish, and each time he assured the sailors that land must be only a short distance away. He even tasted the water and told them that it seemed to him to be 'less salty'!

Land, when they found it, was not part of a great continent; it was the island of San Salvador. The explorers gave thanks to God for their safe arrival, and began to look for fresh water and fruit. There were no palaces or even large buildings on the island — only small palm-thatched huts — and Columbus reluctantly had to admit that this was not Marco Polo's Cathay. But perhaps, he thought, it was a part of India? The natives had long, straight hair, so this was certainly a possibility. Columbus regarded it as a fact. He called the natives 'Indians' and they have been called 'Indians' or 'West Indians' ever since.

When they had explored the island, they set off again to find Cathay and the Khan. But at island after island they found only poor villagers, and although some of them wore gold ornaments, earrings and bracelets, there did not seem to be any evidence of a great civilization. This is how Columbus described the islanders:

'They are very well built, with very handsome

bodies and thin faces. Their hair is coarse, almost like the hair of a horse's tail, and short. They wear their hair down over their eyebrows, except for a few strands behind, which they wear long and never cut. Some of them are painted black ... and some of them are painted white, and some red, and some in any colour that they find. Some of them paint their faces, some their whole bodies, some only the eyes, and some only the nose.... They are all generally fairly tall, good-looking and well proportioned.'

Columbus kept on trying to make the Indians understand that he wanted to find the Khan and gold, and they always pointed out to sea to some other place far over the horizon. At each new island a little ceremony was held, whereby it was formally taken over by Columbus on behalf of the king and queen of Spain.

The men were always glad to get ashore, and to eat their fill of the strange new plants they came across; the sweet potatoes and pineapples they found particularly delicious, and they took samples of them back to Spain. There was wild cotton, with which the natives wove cloth, and with which each made for himself a hanging bed which they called a 'hamac'. (We have now changed the spelling to 'hammock'.) Before this time, sailors had always slept on the bare decks of their ships. Now they copied the Indians' hammocks to make a dry (and rat-free) bed above the level of the dirty and often wet deck.

But the king and queen of Spain could hardly be expected to regard a few fruits and vegetables or a bed made of some kind of netting as great treasure—they wanted news of gold and silver and precious stones, and to make the journey seem worthwhile, Columbus's men collected all the gold they could find.

Then came disaster: on a reef off their new 'possession', Española, the *Santa Maria* was wrecked. Fortunately nobody was drowned, and the now homeless men built a fort on the island, using the ship's timbers. Columbus decided to keep the fort as a permanent colony, so that later voyagers would have a place to buy food. He asked for volunteers to start the colony, and 39 men decided to stay. The rest, including Columbus, returned to Seville in the other two ships, taking with them some of the Indians, samples of gold, and spices, weapons, cotton and parrots. After a terrible voyage, with raging storms almost tearing the little boats to pieces,

Christopher Columbus, bearing the Spanish flag, sets foot on the New World.

An Indian *hamac*

141

Los Cayos
San Salvador
CARIBS CARIBS
Juana
ARAWAKS
Santiago
CARIBS
ARAWAKS
Santiago
España
Santo Domingo
ARAWAKS
San Juan Bautista
CARIBS
CARIBS
ARAWAKS
ARAWAKS & CARIBS
Antigua
Guadalupe
Dominica
Martinino

CARIBBEAN   SEA

ARAWAKS
S p a n i s h   M a i n
CARIBS

The West Indies in the sixteenth century
The peoples of these islands were Arawaks and Caribs. The Caribs have given their name to the Caribbean Sea. Some of the islands now have different names from the ones the Spaniards gave them. Can you say which are different, and what the present names are?

they arrived home. Columbus was given a grand welcome, and immediately became famous. Spain was in the 'exploration-race' at last, and at any time might discover the land of Cathay. To keep peace between Portugal and Spain, the Pope drew a line across the map of the world (see map on page 143), giving Portugal the non-Christian lands in one half and those in the other to Spain. But later, when other countries wanted to sail ships to explore lands across the oceans, they were angry that the Pope had reserved the new discoveries for the Portuguese and Spaniards, especially as the Pope who made the ruling was himself a Spaniard.

Columbus made three more voyages to the West Indies, but he had more disappointments than encouragements. The greatest disappointment of all was that he never reached Cathay. The colonists on Española were all dead when he returned, but he persevered and started other settlements. He proposed to send home each year as much gold as the settlers could find, and spices and slaves. The Spanish king and queen were not much in favour of having 'Indian' slaves, but the gold was a different matter.

By now, the ships' crews were getting tired of exploring islands that all seemed alike to them. They became greedy for gold, and they got into fights with the Indians. There were no game animals and not enough wild fruit to provide them all with fresh food, and the Indians did

not see why they should continually give away food from their own stocks. So the sailors started to steal. From now onwards the Indians were suspicious of the white men, and not at all willing to let them have everything they asked for.

Columbus was often sick on his later voyages, and had a lot of trouble with his eyes. His old enthusiasm died. He even landed on the coast of mainland South America, and took it for granted that this was just another island. Even when he reached a mighty river (the Orinoco) he did not realize the truth—although such a great river could never have been found on an island. Columbus was getting old and tired. Spain was disappointed by his inability to produce large quantities of gold, and he no longer received a royal welcome when he returned from a voyage. He died poor and unrewarded in 1506.

History has been kinder to him. We now realize that his discoveries, even though he never reached China or India, were to lead to a future expansion far greater than that pioneered by the Portuguese explorers. His navigation was as perfect as it could be with the instruments in his ship. Time after time he set off for a particular place, and accurately arrived there. His achievement

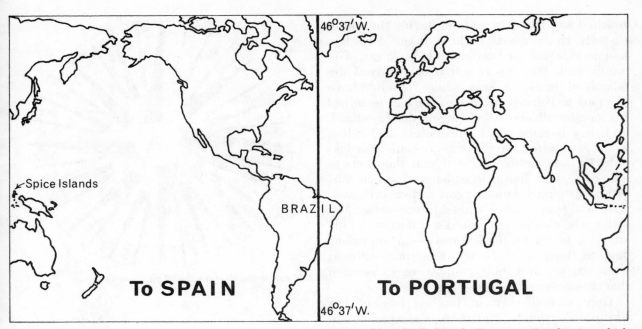

To SPAIN

To PORTUGAL

46°37'W.

46°37'W.

Spice Islands

BRAZIL

The world as divided by the Pope in 1494, showing which areas belonged to the Spanish and which to the Portuguese.

was far more remarkable than the later one of da Gama. He had no local pilots to help him, and there were no known trade-routes.

Columbus's strength of character was such that he could persuade his men to continue even when they were dying of scurvy, and nearly mad with starvation, and terrified by hurricanes and of imaginary sea-monsters. As a sailor and navigator Columbus had no equal: as an administrator he was not so clever, and his settlements were not a success.

Vasco Nunez de Balboa

Even though Columbus was no longer honoured by Spain, the Spaniards did not hesitate to follow up his discoveries. They had a bigger country and more men than Portugal, and they sent fleet after fleet out to the west, using Columbus's charts and profiting from his experience.

Seven years after Columbus's death, a soldier named Vasco Nunez de Balboa was led by Indians across the narrow strip of land that separates the Atlantic and Pacific Oceans. The mystery was solved: Balboa saw that this new country could not be in Asia at all. Asia must lie even further away, across another great sea. He himself was standing on a narrow neck of land that might perhaps join two huge unexplored land masses. In full armour, holding the flag of Spain aloft, Balboa performed the now-familiar ceremony of claiming the land for Spain.

Into the new sea

It was now clear that there was no way of getting a ship from one ocean to another without a passage through or round the new continent. Ferdinand Magellan was the first to discover the passage round the south of South America, and by using this route, one of his ships even managed to sail all the way round the world.

Magellan was a Portuguese sea-captain, who had earlier followed Vasco da Gama's route to Calicut; and then went farther, round Ceylon, and even to the 'Spice Islands'. He had been dismissed from the Portuguese service for trading with the Muslims. So, like Columbus, he went to the Spanish king, and asked if the king would help him to find a westward way to the Spice Islands. The king was pleased to have a commander who already knew so much about the Portuguese possessions, and he gladly agreed. You can follow Magellan's voyage by reading the notes on the map on page 145.

Sailing through the Straits was a frightening experience, and one which not many later explorers dared to repeat. But at last they were through, and Magellan's fleet sailed out into a blue, calm ocean. It was Magellan who named the sea 'Pacific', though later voyagers discovered that it was not always as peaceful as the name suggested. Once in the new ocean, Magellan's little fleet sailed for 98 days before they reached any land—in spite of having the south-easterly trade winds to help them. Magellan had no idea that the Pacific would be so vast. The winds took him on a course that missed the islands of the South Seas, where he might have stopped to refresh the crew. He had to forbid his men to talk about the dangers that lay ahead, and they became even more silent and sullen as the food rotted and the water became undrinkable. By the time they sighted land, they were in a terrible state, living on stinking water, crumbs of biscuit mixed with maggots and rat-dirt, sawdust, and even leather soaked in sea-water. Any sailor who caught a rat could sell it to one of his starving mates for half-a-crown—an enormous sum to those men. Nearly everyone suffered from scurvy, and their gums were so swollen that they covered their teeth.

They disembarked at last on one of the Philippine Islands, and there a quarrel broke out with the islanders. That was the end of the journey for Magellan: he and 40 of his crew were killed, and many others wounded. The survivors had more trials to face before they reached Spain again by way of India and South Africa. The whole journey lasted three years, and only about 20 men out of the original 270 arrived home. The rest had died of disease and starvation, in fights, or as prisoners of the Portuguese in the Spice Islands. These 20 men were the first people ever to sail right round the world.

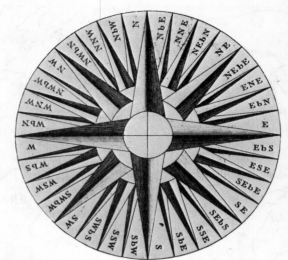

Old engraving showing the 32 points of a compass

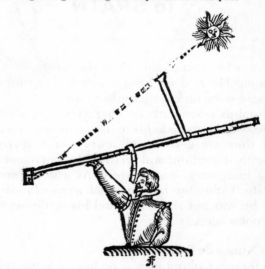

Above: cross-staff   *Below:* astrolabe

Aids to Navigation

The compass contains a magnetized steel needle which always points to the *magnetic north*. There are 32 points (positions) marked on a compass and from it the sailors could tell which way they were going but not how far they had gone.

The cross-staff: the shorter piece of wood of the cross-staff could be moved up and down the main bar, which was marked like a ruler. The user pushed the cross-piece along the bar until it covered the distance between the horizon and the sun. He could then work out the *latitude* (the distance north or south of the equator) from the measurement recorded on the bar. He would know from this how *far* he had gone, provided he was travelling in a north-south direction.

The astrolabe also calculated the latitude. The calculations were taken from the positions of the stars, or heavenly bodies. It was more accurate than the cross-staff. At this time there was no way of finding the *longitude* (distance in degrees east or west of a fixed point of the earth's surface). This was because mechanical clocks for use on ships had not been invented.

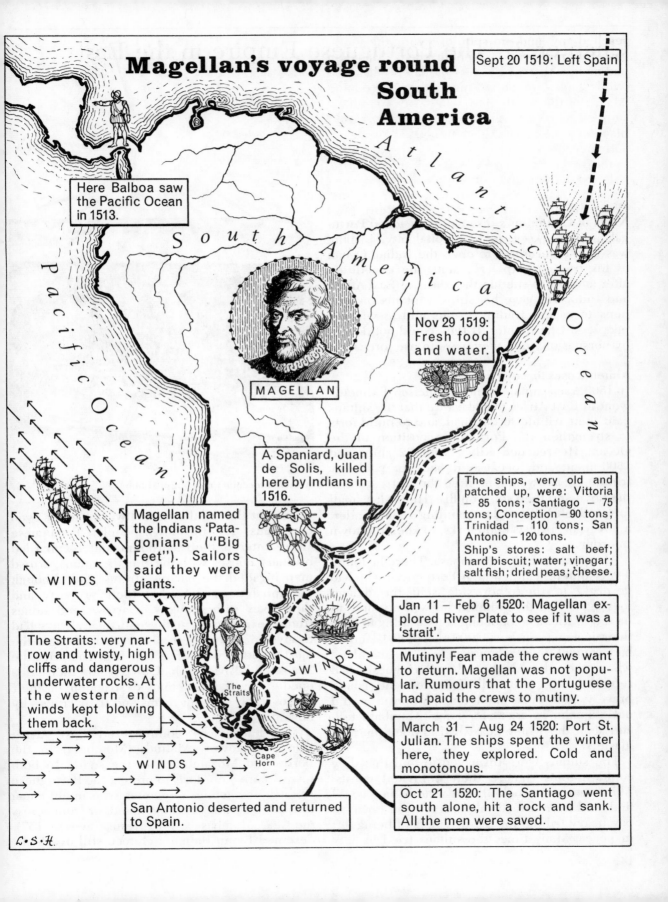

Magellan's voyage round South America

Sept 20 1519: Left Spain

Here Balboa saw the Pacific Ocean in 1513.

Atlantic Ocean

South America

Pacific Ocean

MAGELLAN

Nov 29 1519: Fresh food and water.

A Spaniard, Juan de Solis, killed here by Indians in 1516.

Magellan named the Indians 'Patagonians' ("Big Feet"). Sailors said they were giants.

WINDS

The Straits: very narrow and twisty, high cliffs and dangerous underwater rocks. At the western end winds kept blowing them back.

WINDS

The Straits

Cape Horn

WINDS

San Antonio deserted and returned to Spain.

The ships, very old and patched up, were: Vittoria – 85 tons; Santiago – 75 tons; Conception – 90 tons; Trinidad – 110 tons; San Antonio – 120 tons.
Ship's stores: salt beef; hard biscuit; water; vinegar; salt fish; dried peas; cheese.

Jan 11 – Feb 6 1520: Magellan explored River Plate to see if it was a 'strait'.

Mutiny! Fear made the crews want to return. Magellan was not popular. Rumours that the Portuguese had paid the crews to mutiny.

March 31 – Aug 24 1520: Port St. Julian. The ships spent the winter here, they explored. Cold and monotonous.

Oct 21 1520: The Santiago went south alone, hit a rock and sank. All the men were saved.

L·S·H.

Chapter 27 The Portuguese Empire in the East

News of Columbus's discoveries reached Portugal, and the king, in his capital city, Lisbon, was now determined to open the Indian Ocean to his trading ships. He sent one expedition after another to subdue the coasts of East Africa and India. He gave his ships' captains instructions to secure trading profits and to win the people to Christianity. If they could not do this by persuasion, then they were to use force.

Almeida uses force

In 1505, a sea-captain named Francisco d'Almeida went to East Africa to make sure that the sultans paid their tribute to Portugal, and to build forts to strengthen the Portuguese position in the Ocean. He reached Kilwa with 22 ships and 1500 men, and, because it had not paid any tribute for two years, he fired the ships' guns at the town and then set it on fire. He built a small fort, and left 150 people, including a commander, a governor, priests and clerks, to keep the town in order.

Almeida went on to Mombasa. There he found a very different situation. A Portuguese who had deserted to the other side sent the defiant message: 'Tell the Admiral he will not find, as he did in Kilwa, a lot of chickens waiting to have their necks wrung, but 20,000 men.' The islanders had brought in extra bowmen from the mainland when they heard that the Portuguese had returned, and they all defended the island bravely. But even such tough opposition did not stop the invaders for long – Mombasa fell, and soon the whole coast had to obey the new masters.

The sultans were dismayed to find that they could not just ignore their uninvited guests. The Portuguese took all the wealth they could find, and even forced the East African towns to pay heavy tribute for the privilege of being left in peace. Many times the sultans tried to defy

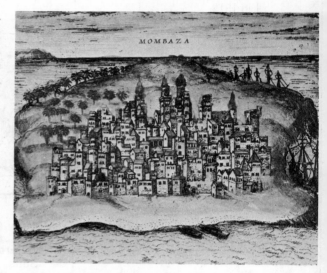

A sixteenth-century drawing of Mombasa

them, but the results were always bad, or even disastrous, for the townspeople. Portuguese ships entered their harbours and bombarded ordinary houses with the ships' cannons; armed men invaded the narrow streets, and although the inhabitants defended their property and their lives with showers of arrows and stones from the rooftops, in the end they always had to give in. Then there always would come the most dreadful weapon of all – fire. The price the Arabs and Africans had to pay for their 'disobedience' was the total destruction of their homes, their coconut palms and their crops – by burning.

The Portuguese administered East Africa from two towns – Malindi (Mombasa) in the north, and Mozambique in the south. In both towns there were forts to protect the Portuguese from their enemies – enemies who might come at them from the local mainland, or from across the sea. Mombasa's Fort Jesus (See p. 157), designed by an Italian architect, still overlooks the narrow stretch of water between the island and the mainland. It was not completely safe however; Arabs from the Persian Gulf captured it twice in later years and flew their red flag over the battlements. Once the Arab victory followed a long siege, during which the Portuguese defenders starved and died by the hundreds from disease.

The fort at Mozambique also saw some bitter fighting, not between Arabs and Portuguese, but between the Portuguese and newcomers to the coast—the Dutch. The Mozambique fort always suffered from lack of proper care and repair; its Captains were too busy enriching themselves by sending trading expeditions up the Zambezi to the lands of the Monomotapa.

The worst restriction for the Arabs in East Africa was that they were not allowed to trade without Portuguese licences. The Portuguese now knew exactly how much profit was made on the trading journeys, and they seized as much of it as they could. In time their greed and lack of foresight led to their own downfall. They had been told by their king to 'secure trading profits', and for a time they had done so. Had they allowed the East African towns to continue to earn a good living by trade, the Portuguese themselves would have been able to stay in the area longer. But the local people were naturally not interested in trading if they could not profit from it themselves.

In 1600, only 100 years after the Portuguese first landed on the East African coast, a Franciscan friar wrote about Mombasa:

'The inhabitants are Moors, who, although formerly rich, now live in utter poverty— their most usual occupation is that of making mats, baskets, and straw hats so perfectly finished that the Portuguese bring them out to wear on feast days.'

Although individual Portuguese traders or soldiers must have learnt a little Swahili, Portuguese documents about East Africa do not mention the language at all; the majority were only interested in trade and they did not realize that to trade with people you have to try to understand them; and to understand someone, you must first try to learn his language.

Great Zimbabwe

The ruins of Great Zimbabwe are very interesting. They date back to the early Middle Ages and were probably built by a Bantu tribe. A Portuguese writer, Joao be Barros said about the gold-bearing country of the Monomotapa:

'The mines are the most ancient known in the country, and they are all in the plain, in the midst of which is a square fortress of masonry (stonework) within and without, built of stones of marvellous size, and there appears to be no mortar joining them. . . . The natives of the country call all these buildings "zimbabwe".'

India

After Francisco d'Almeida had sacked Kilwa and Mombasa, and left some soldiers to hold these towns for the Portuguese, he sailed on to India. He built a fort and a house for himself at Cochin, and became the first 'Viceroy* of India', though in fact he only ruled over a few Indian coastal towns.

In these towns the traders were very alarmed when they saw that the Portuguese meant to stay permanently. There was so much to lose that they looked for allies to help them drive the Portuguese away. At the other end of their trade routes, the Egyptians, Turks and Arabs were also anxious not to lose their profits—and farther north, the Venetians became worried.

Venice had for centuries been the great market-place for Muslim and eastern goods, which were sold to the more northerly European countries. The Venetians had to try to stop the Portuguese taking Chinese and Indian luxury goods back to Portugal, and creating a new 'market-place' there. In haste the Venetians helped the Egyptians to build a fleet of 12 ships in the Red Sea. This fleet sailed out into the Indian Ocean to do battle with the Portuguese, and at Diu they joined the tiny fleet of the Zamorin† of Calicut. They learnt that the Portuguese were not to be driven away so easily. The Portuguese carracks sank the Turkish ships, which would take much time and money to replace. Almeida's sailors had won the first round for Portugal; they now had mastery of the Indian Ocean. Almeida wrote to King Manuel, 'As long as you are powerful at sea, you will hold India.'

Albuquerque becomes Viceroy

Almeida's successor was a man named Afonso d'Albuquerque. He wanted Portugal to be much more than just 'powerful at sea'. His aim was to build more new trading-posts on the Indian coast, and to strengthen the Portuguese position on land all round the Indian Ocean. Goa—which Albuquerque seized—became the centre of trade in the eastern ocean, and the capital of the Portuguese empire in the East. Albuquerque

Portuguese ships in the sixteenth century
Portuguese ships stood higher in the water than Venetian ones. This meant that the Portuguese could fire down on their enemies, and so had advantage over them.

There was no timber in Arabia for ship-building, so the people of Ormuz (on the Persian Gulf) could not even put one or two pirate ships into the Indian Ocean without much preparation and spending a lot of money. Later the Turks built long, low, narrow, oar and sail driven ships, called galleys, in the Red Sea with materials that had to be carried across the isthmus of Suez on camels and donkeys. But still the Portuguese ships were better, and had more guns.

In the sixteenth-century illustration above you can see the sailors navigating the ship, using an astrolabe and a cross-staff.

himself lived there, and from Goa ruled over his scattered empire. His Captains* at Malindi and Mozambique took orders from him, and not from Lisbon, and he built and kept in touch with forts in Ceylon, Malacca, the east coast of India, and even China.

Albuquerque was both a great sailor and a great administrator; he laid the foundations of the empire well. Had there been others like him, the Portuguese might have lasted longer in the East. But the men sent to Goa as viceroys after Albuquerque were often harsh and ruthless. It took a long time for news to reach Goa from the distant forts: East Africa, for instance, was completely cut off for half the year, when the

---

*A viceroy is a man appointed by a king to rule an overseas territory for him. Columbus was called 'Admiral of the Ocean, Viceroy and Governor of the Indies'.

†Zamorin was the title used for the sovereign of Calicut.

---

*The Captains of Malindi and Mozambique were governors —they were not necessarily 'sea-captains'.

GOA *fortissima Indiæ vrbs in Christianorum potestatem anno Salutis 1509 deuenit*

monsoon winds were blowing in the wrong direction. But in any case the Portuguese had no firm policy for their empire. They were interested in trading, but they did not see that it was necessary to be on friendly terms with the local people. Their trading-posts were like little islands, ignorant of the life around them. The native rulers were allowed to have power over their people, so long as they did as they were told, and produced the yearly tribute. If they refused, punishment was harsh and swift.

The trading-post in Ceylon
South of India is the beautiful island of Ceylon. The island was divided into seven tiny Buddhist kingdoms when Francisco d'Albuquerque, Afonso's son, first went there to build a fort. One of the kings granted him land at Colombo, on the west coast, but the whole time the Portuguese were in Ceylon, one kingdom after another tried to drive them away.

Ceylon was famous for its semi-precious stones, moonstones, sapphires and rubies, and for its cinnamon. The centre of the island is mountainous, and up in the hills lies the town of Kandy. Here the Buddhists kept a holy relic of Buddha—a tooth. The king of Kandy fought the Portuguese, who said they had carried off the sacred tooth, and burnt it at Goa. (The Sinhalese—they are the Buddhist inhabitants of Ceylon— denied this, and they still claim that the tooth is in the Buddhist temple at Kandy.)

In spite of this the Portuguese made a favourable impression in Ceylon on the whole. They successfully converted hundreds of humble fishermen and land-workers to Christianity. They intermarried with the local people, and— as in Goa—today there are many people living in Ceylon who have Portuguese names.

Goa
Goa traded with Persia and Ormuz, and each trading-ship brought cargoes of horses, dates, almonds and raisins. Albuquerque spent time and thought in building his capital. Goa even had equal privileges with Lisbon itself. The Catholic priests built churches, and a cathedral which is still used for worship today. In 1542 a famous Jesuit, St Francis Xavier, arrived in Goa to preach and baptize. Many people from other parts of the Portuguese empire in East Africa and the East were sent to Goa to be educated.

Although Goa is now part of India, it contains many traces of the centuries of Portuguese rule. Most Goans are Catholics and most have Portuguese surnames such as Ferrao, Gomes, Pereira, Fernandes and Almeida.

Malacca*
Albuquerque wanted Portugal to control all the trade-routes of the Indian Ocean, but most ships from South-East Asia and China came through the Strait of Malacca where they paid tribute to the sultan. Malacca was a rich port which had for a long time been the capital of a powerful Malay empire. The sultan had a large army, but in 1511 Albuquerque arrived before the city with a fleet and, after hard fighting, captured it. Then he built a great fortress called 'A Famosa' (The Famous) to hold Malacca for Portugal.

The fort at Malacca provided a convenient base for further exploration. Albuquerque sent explorers south-westward and they built settlements in the Moluccas (the Spice Islands) and on the coast of China. As a trading centre, Malacca was more important than Goa, because it controlled the route to these new forts, and

*Look up the Moluccas and Malacca on the map on p. 150, so that you know the difference between the two.

149

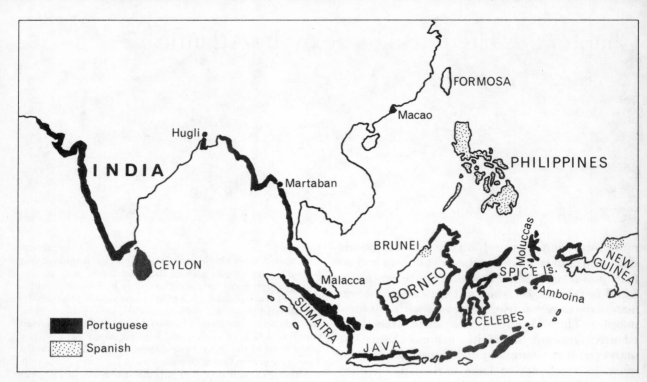

Portuguese possessions in the Far East, 1498–1580

under the rule of the Portuguese it continued to grow and prosper. But as a place to live in, it was uncomfortable. The west coast has many mangrove swamps and it is very hot and wet. From October to February the soldiers and civilians in the fort were cut off from their sea-routes by high seas and contrary winds. They could not go far inland because of thick tropical jungle, inhabited by wild animals, and by tribesmen armed with blow-pipes and poisonous darts. For the most part the soldiers stayed in their forts, which they had to defend from time to time against the attacks of the Malay sultan.

The Spice Islands and China
The islands of the Moluccas and several ports on the China coast were already carrying on a flourishing trade with the Persian Gulf when the Portuguese arrived. The Muslims had established themselves as the chief traders and rulers, and so once again there was a religious clash. The Portuguese built a fort at Amboina, but after Magellan's voyage, the Spaniards declared that *they* really owned these rich islands. Finally they allowed the Portuguese to buy them!*

---

*Look at the map on p. 143 and see where the Pope's division comes. On which side of the line are the Spice Islands – the 'Spanish', or the 'Portuguese' side?

There was so much nutmeg, cloves and pepper in the Spice Islands, and so much cinnamon in Ceylon, that in spite of the long journeys and the expense of fitting ships and maintaining forts, the trade was very profitable. The Portuguese succeeded in taking over the Muslim trade in several Chinese ports, and in 1557 the Chinese officially allowed them to build a fort at Macao. This is the only port they still hold on the mainland; the rest of their Far Eastern possessions, apart from part of the island of Timor, have gradually been lost.

By 1550, the charts show that on their return journey, ships used to sail far north before turning westward, in order to take advantage of the north-eastern monsoon. Then the well-laden fleet sailed home to Lisbon. The Indian Ocean was now controlled by the Portuguese, for Albuquerque followed up the success of the battle of Diu by raiding the Muslim town of Ormuz on the Persian Gulf. He built a fort there, and left a garrison of men to guard the town. Now it was Lisbon, not Venice, that became the market-place for spices from the East.

Chapter 28 The Portuguese in the Atlantic

In the countries we now call Ghana and Nigeria, the Portuguese made contact with the local chiefs and kings. Most of the chiefs did not mind the Portuguese caravels trading with their people, but they were very unwilling to let the Portuguese build forts. One chief, named Caramansa, reluctantly agreed when the Portuguese leader, Diogo de Azambuja, persuaded him that the fort would make it easier to carry on trade. But misunderstandings arose because of language difficulties and lack of local knowledge; the Portuguese, not realizing what they were doing, took rocks to build their fort from a hill which Caramansa's people regarded as sacred. Caramansa was furious, and his warriors attacked the Portuguese. Then the fort had to be finished quickly for their protection, and it is not surprising that the Africans were suspicious of these foreigners, shut up inside their stone enclosure.

This Gold Coast fort, built in 1482, was named Elmina, meaning 'The Mine', because of its nearness to the gold mines. Smaller forts were maintained all along the coast, and the Portuguese imported and planted oranges and lemons from their own country, and rice from the East. Later they also brought new plants from America: guavas, pineapples, maize, tobacco and cassava. The news of their forts spread to the inland tribes, and the African chiefs sent messengers to see the strange white men. The Portuguese then sent messengers of their own to the interior, to find out where the gold came from. Though in most cases they did not succeed, they tried to persuade the Africans with gifts of cloth, beads, small bells, and glass to show them the mines. These were also the 'trade-goods' which they exchanged for gold, ivory and pepper.

One of the Portuguese forts was near the African state of Benin. This vigorous kingdom was friendly to the new arrivals, and trade flourished.

Elmina Fort

This is a sixteenth-century account of the preparations for building Elmina Fort:

> Once the building of the fort was decided upon, he [the king of Portugal] ordered the equipping of a fleet of 10 caravels and 2 barques ... to carry hewed stone, tiles and wood, as well as munitions and provisions for 600 men, one hundred of whom were craftsmen, and 500 soldiers.

Nobody in West Africa had much use for ivory or gold except as decoration, so there was plenty to spare for trade. The people of Benin were quite willing to exchange such things for the Portuguese trade-goods, which were a novelty to them. But after only about 50 years the trade changed on both sides. The Europeans wanted to buy men and women to re-sell as slaves; and the Africans wanted weapons, metal and alcohol. Then the peaceful and innocent trading days were over.

The Congo Kingdom

Forty years after Diogo Cão landed at the mouth of the river Congo, the Mani-Congo (king of the Congo country), whom the Portuguese called King Afonso I, was eager to Europeanize his kingdom, and he was pleased when his new European friends sent him missionaries, soldiers and traders. At first all went well. The king and his court dressed in European clothes, and were given Portuguese titles. The Portuguese aim was to set up a Christian kingdom in Africa. They were quite sincere in their desire for peace and good relations between the two countries. For one thing they would have a base from which to start looking for Prester John; and the Africans would receive European goods in exchange for the gold which they did not value very highly.

King Afonso did everything in his power to be a friend to the Portuguese, and to make the new alliance work. He wrote letter after letter to his 'royal brother' in Lisbon, asking for medical supplies, teachers, and a ship of his own. On his side, the Portuguese king wanted peaceful trade, but his servants in Africa were often concerned only to help themselves rather than to help either their own country or the Congo kingdom. Afonso refused to give up hope. He sent many of his young men off to be educated in Lisbon. Some of them, however, never got farther than São Tomé, an island off present-day Gabon. The Portuguese had made this island their chief port of call in the south, and all their ships went there rather than to the mouth of the Congo. So passengers and letters for Lisbon all had to be taken by boat to São Tomé first. The Portuguese had started to plant sugar-cane on São Tomé, and they did not have enough cheap labour to work the plantations: so when Afonso sent young men there, the Portuguese kept many of them as slaves.

One of the young men who *did* get farther than São Tomé, and who was eventually educated in Lisbon, was Afonso's son Henrique. He was trained to be a priest, and he even became the first African bishop, and was ordained* by the Pope himself in Rome. Henrique returned to the Congo kingdom, full of admiration for the European way of life, only to find that the Portuguese in his own country did not share his high ideals.

*To ordain means formally and ceremonially to give somebody the title and responsibilities of a priest or, in this case, of a bishop.

Portuguese soldier
This is how the bronze-workers of Benin saw the Portuguese soldiers. With guns ready to fire they were seen as a threatening force and not the peaceful traders that they were first thought to be.

By the end of his reign, in the 1540s, Afonso was cut off from Lisbon, because no ships came direct to his kingdom, and his letters remained unanswered. (Probably many of them never even left São Tomé.) The slavetrade, which removed hundreds of young men and women from Congo and nearby Angola to São Tomé and the Americas, caused terrible hardship and havoc in West Africa. In 1526 Afonso wrote a very polite and friendly letter to King John III of Portugal, imploring him to stop the slavetrade, which was ruining his country. But his letter was ignored. The slave trade got worse, and went on and on for the next 250 years, leaving a once prosperous land empty and poverty-stricken.

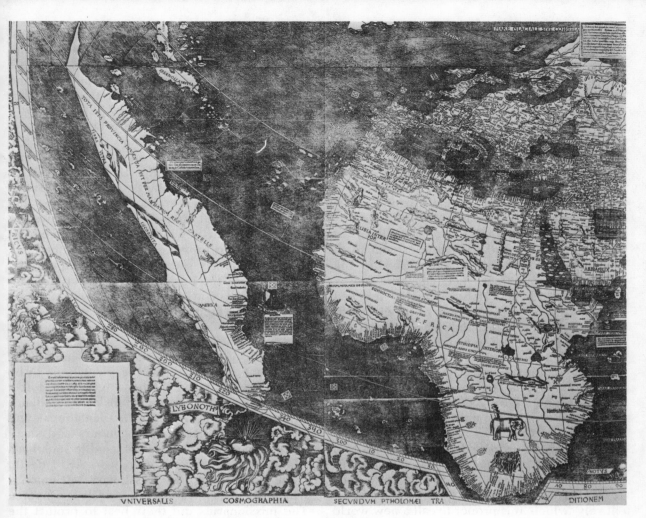

UNIVERSALIS COSMOGRAPHIA SECUNDUM PTHOLOMÆI TRA DITIONEM

Three reasons why the West Africans did not benefit from their contact with the Portuguese

1. Portuguese sailors were discovering and occupying *too many* overseas ports. Portugal is a small country, and there were just not enough good people to administer so great an empire. Portuguese administrators were often more interested in making money for themselves than in honest trading for their country.

2. The produce of the Spice Islands, and later the produce of Brazil in South America, was more profitable than the gold or ivory of Africa. Consequently, if the Captain of the Spice Islands and the Mani-Congo *both* asked for doctors, or preachers, or a new ship, then the Spice Islands were supplied first. The Mani-Congo was often not supplied at all.

3. Africa became more important as an exporter of human beings than of any other commodity. The slavetrade finally ruined the West African states.

America

In 1507 a German mapmaker named Martin Waldseemüller published a map of the New World, the southern part of which he called America, after Amerigo Vespucci. The name has stayed and it was soon to be used for the northern United States as well. Waldseemüller might more justly have called the new land 'Columbia' after the first mariner to set foot on its shores; without the inspiration and example of Columbus, Vespucci might never have sailed westward at all.

The Portuguese discover Brazil

In 1500 a Portuguese sea-captain named Pedro Alvares Cabral set sail from Lisbon, and followed Vasco da Gama's route to the south. He was supposed to be on his way to India, but he sailed so far westward that he reached the mainland of South America. Some historians say that this was an accident, and he was blown farther west than he meant to go; others say that the Portuguese had

153

found out some of the Spanish secret information about the western Atlantic, and Cabral was *told* to look for a coastline in the west. Whichever story is true, Cabral certainly found himself in the country we now call Brazil. He landed, and laid claim to Brazil for Portugal. He sent one of his supply ships back to Portugal with news of this new land; then he sailed away again.

Cabral went back across the Atlantic and continued his journey to India, and Brazil's next visitor from Europe was an Italian named Amerigo Vespucci. Vespucci had become a Spanish citizen, and he had helped to prepare ships for Columbus's voyages. He picked up a great deal of information about navigation, and in 1499 he went to the West Indies as navigator in a Spanish ship. Like Columbus, he was convinced that the coast of America was a part of Asia: on his return to Spain he asked if he might take an expedition to look for Ceylon and India. The Spaniards were unwilling to give him permission, so he went to Portugal, where he was more fortunate. (Many mariners of this time went from country to country looking for someone who would finance them on their exploring journeys. Columbus and Magellan were not the only ones.)

On Vespucci's next voyage (paid for by the Portuguese), he explored a great deal of the coast of South America, and he saw the true nature of the newly-discovered land. This, he said, is not Asia. It is a different continent entirely, which 'it is proper to call a new world'.

Portugal at this time was more concerned with building up connections in the East, where the trade in silks, precious stones, pepper and spices was so profitable, than with exploring this new territory. Spain had almost finished *her* conquests in America before Portugal decided to find out more about Brazil. The unexplored area was enormous, and it had many great rivers, between which there were dense forests and high mountains. The Portuguese divided the vast land into 15 parts, each of which was to be governed by a Captain. As in East Africa and India, the Captains were favoured courtiers, and not pioneers or administrators. Only two of the 15 Captains were really successful in making their captaincies thrive. The first of these settlements was São Vicente, near present-day Santos, established by Martin Afonso de Souza. He built a port and from there went southwards, exploring and mapping the coast. The Captain of the second successful settlement was Duarte

Coelho, a farmer who set up sugar-plantations, and started to export sugar to Europe. His captaincy was in present-day Pernambuco. Sugar and tobacco became the main Brazilian crops, and where they were well-managed, the plantations flourished.

The division of Brazil into captaincies was a mistake, because without any central control they all suffered from attacks by Indians*, and raids by French pirate ships. So in 1549 Tomé de Souza, a man who had had experience in India, arrived in Brazil to unite the captaincies into one country. He built a capital town at Salvador, and brought in new immigrants—people who were prepared to work hard and farm the land. Soon the country started to be self-supporting. Here, at last, the Portuguese had a settlers' colony, instead of a little 'factory' in an already-developed foreign land.

The search for labour

The country was too vast, and the number of immigrants too small, for the plantations to be worked without some other big labour force. The Portuguese started by enslaving Indians, and making them work on the plantations—and later in the mines—for long hours and small wages. The Indians were not used to such hard labour and they were often worked to death. Some fled to the new missionary settlements, which were always glad to receive converts. The missionaries did their best to protect the Indians from plantation owners, who began to look elsewhere for slaves.

Over on the other side of the Atlantic Ocean, their Portuguese fellow-countrymen in the Congo kingdom and in Angola were already shipping a few African slaves every year to Europe and the Middle East. On hearing that Brazil was short of manpower, they decided to transport African men and women to Brazil and sell them there. By 1600 Tomé de Souza's capital had a population of 2000 whites and about twice as many African and Indian slaves. The Spaniards, the British, the French and the Dutch all fitted out ships to carry the new human cargo, and did a tremendous trade in all the newly-colonized parts of America. The terrible sale of human beings became more profitable

---

* The natives of South America were also called 'Indians'—in fact the word meant almost the same as 'native' to the Portuguese. They have kept the name ever since. The 'Indians' in this chapter are all South American Indians.

and important to the European nations than the trade in gold and ivory.

Because there were people to convert in the interior of the country and perhaps because they could be more independent there, the Jesuit missionaries were not content to remain on the coast near the rich settlements. They penetrated far inland, and thousands of Indians came to work on the new mission plantations. Almost the first building in any Portuguese or Spanish town was a church. The converted Indians were treated with care and understanding by the missionaries, and taught to grow crops and raise cattle.

Many of the white immigrants to Brazil did not have the money to buy or run plantations in the rich sugar-growing districts, and they too went inland and started to farm there instead. But there were not enough Indians to work for them locally, and the African slaves who were now arriving were too expensive for them. So the white men organized themselves into armed gangs, known as *bandeirantes,* and raided villages and mission settlements for slaves. They were particularly eager to carry off converted Indians, for these had already been taught how to farm by the missionaries. As time passed the *bandeirantes* went even farther for slaves, and started to raid the neighbouring Spanish territories.

Over the next 200 years the Portuguese had to fight off attacks by other Europeans, the Dutch, the English and the French. The Dutch took possession of the north of Brazil for some time but were eventually expelled. To the south the Portuguese and Spaniards fought for possession of the territory that is now called Uruguay, which the Portuguese finally lost.

During this time many Portuguese settlers intermarried with Indians and with Africans and in time people did not say they were 'Portuguese' or 'Indian' or 'African' but were proud to proclaim that they were all Brazilians.

South American Indians
The consequences of the arrival of Europeans in America were terrible for the South American Indians. Before the 'civilizing' white men came, the Indians wore very little clothing (sometimes none at all). The missionaries taught them that it was 'not decent' to be naked. They made them wear cotton clothes. These clothes got wet in the torrential rains of South America; but they did not dry nearly so quickly as the Indians' naked bodies had done. Before long the Indians were dying in hundreds from chest diseases and other illness brought on by being chilled. They were sent down mines and used as slaves and many suffered and died from exhaustion because of this unfamiliar work. The white men, without knowing it, also brought diseases such as small-pox and measles which had a fatal effect on the Indians. These diseases had never been known in South America before.

Chapter 29 The Dutch rival the Portuguese

By the end of the sixteenth century, most of the European nations were sending ships to West Africa, and French and English ships were even reaching the Indian Ocean and the East. But the nation which at that time competed most successfully with the Portuguese was Holland.

The Dutch had made their country into a strong sea-going nation in a very short time. Until 1579 Holland had been part of the Netherlands states, which were under Spanish rule. But she had at last won her long war for independence from Spain. Now the Dutch entered the world scene—not as adventurers and discoverers, but as businessmen and traders.

Portugal brought spices and silks from the East, then by arrangement, Holland took them and distributed them to other European countries. Had Portugal been bigger and richer, she might have been able to buy the spices in the East *and* distribute them. As it was, the Portuguese sailors took all the risks, and the merchants of Antwerp made most of the profits. Holland soon became a very wealthy country.

But in 1580, when Spain and Portugal became united, Philip II, King of Spain, refused to let the Dutch enter Portuguese harbours. He hoped to destroy their trade and their prosperity. The Dutch however were not so easily defeated— they decided to make their own way to the Spice Islands. The Pope had divided the world between Spain and Portugal, but this did not worry the Protestant Dutch. The Portuguese had managed to keep the route secret for a full century by hiding their maps, and by spreading tales about the dangers on land and at sea. But the Dutch had no trouble in rounding the Cape, and in 1595 they quite easily found their way across the Indian Ocean.

From the beginning the Dutch had great success in the East. Their trade-goods were better than those of the Portuguese, and at first they were careful to make no enemies. By 1602, only seven years after their first voyage, they had taken a large part of the trade in the Spice Islands, in China, in Malaya and in Ceylon. They soon realized that the Portuguese empire was much weaker than anybody had thought. The Portuguese Captains were urgently warned to be on their guard, but it was too late. One by one their forts fell to the Dutch—often with the help of the local people. In 1641, after a long siege, the Dutch captured Malacca. It had been the richest port between India and China, but its great days were now over; the Dutch neglected it and soon Malacca became small and unimportant.

The only trading-posts left to the Portuguese were Goa, Diu and Daman in India; Macao in China, and part of Timor. The East had never brought them as much wealth as they had hoped; and King John IV of Portugal once cried: 'I wish to God that I could rid myself honourably of the East Indies.'

The Dutch East India Company

In 1602 the Dutch government formed the East India Company. This company owned all the ships trading with the East Indies; no merchant was now allowed to trade on his own account, or to form a rival company. In this way both profits and risks were shared by the whole country.

The East India Company was also partly the navy of Holland. The ships were all armed, and manned by soldiers as well as sailors, and they were quite ready to do battle with Spanish or Portuguese or English ships, and to fight or besiege enemy forts from the sea. The Company also administered the new possessions overseas. All the governors, traders, soldiers and lawyers were under the rule of the Company, and each new Dutch territory was self-governing.

Fort Jesus, Mombasa
This was the main fort of the Portuguese on the East Coast of Africa, built in 1593. The Dutch never attacked it—probably because it was the strongest Portuguese fort on the coast—and the Portuguese stayed in Mombasa for another 100 years.

The officials were paid high salaries, and forbidden to become businessmen themselves. This was a much stronger and far more efficient system than that of the Portuguese, whose whole Eastern empire was governed from Goa, and whose officials were allowed to make money from private trade.

The Dutch and the King of Kandy

Although the Portuguese had had great success in converting the coastal fishermen and farmers in Ceylon, they had one great enemy there. Up in the hills lived the fierce King Rajasinga of Kandy. King Rajasinga hated the Portuguese, and he sent an army to help the Dutch to remove them from the island. The Portuguese governor of the time was an arrogant and cruel man. It is said that he 'would hang up the people by their heels, and split them down the middle.... Lesser malefactors (wrongdoers) he was merciful to, cutting off only their right hands.' This man swore to treat the Dutch in the same way, but the Dutch were too clever for him. Behind their army they placed a row of cannons: when the Portuguese thought they had pressed the soldiers back, they found themselves right on top of the cannons—which the Dutch then fired.

The Dutch besieged all the east coast ports of Ceylon in 1607, and the west coast ports soon after, but it took over 50 years for them to take the whole country from the Portuguese.

Jan Pieters Coen and the Moluccas

Coen was the able governor who first started to create a Dutch empire in the East. He was a hard man, who believed in using force to get what he wanted.

The Dutch needed a place where the produce from the Spice Islands, from Ceylon, India, China and Japan could be collected and stored. Ships went back to Holland only twice a year, in December and February, but the local trading-ships visited the various ports of the empire more often. Coen found an ideal place for a central 'store-house'. It was a port on the island of Java, which belonged to the sultan of a kingdom called Mataran. Coen seized the town, and renamed it Batavia.

Soon settlers went out to live there, in newly-built stone houses with fine furnishings. They built forts, churches, offices and roads. The law in all the new towns was Roman-Dutch law, the same as in Holland. With their excellent business sense, the Dutch soon created a very prosperous empire.

157

Trade monopoly

Coen was supposed to follow instructions from Holland; but of course it took about 18 months for replies to his requests to arrive in Batavia. This meant that he was really in control in the East. Any unwelcome instructions from home could always be quietly forgotten!

The people of the Spice Islands thought they would be better off under the Dutch, but they were mistaken. They were forced to sign a treaty which gave the Dutch the monopoly (sale control) of the spice trade. This meant that the Dutch could buy the spices very cheaply, because nobody else was allowed to buy them. So the people of the Moluccas found that they were now poorer than they had been under the Portuguese. Their own imports — rice, sago and cotton — had been brought to them in Japanese ships, but now the Dutch themselves were the only people officially allowed to bring goods to the Spice Islands. They bought cotton and silk from the west coast of India, and rice from China and Japan, and exchanged these goods for spices. Similarly the pepper from the east coast of India was used for trade with the Persians (who had retaken Ormuz from the Portuguese). In this way the Dutch avoided having to bring all their trade goods from Europe (see map opposite).

On the whole the Dutch monopoly was very profitable but they were continually having to fight off ships of other nations, and keep a watch for pirates and smugglers. On the coasts of India, moreover, there was often much resistance from the local zamorins and sultans.

The Dutch land at the Cape

Before crossing the Indian Ocean on their way to the East, the Dutch ships needed somewhere to obtain fresh water and food, and a place where their sick men could recover. (The number of deaths at sea, from scurvy, dysentery and fever was always very high indeed.) The Portuguese used Mozambique and the East African towns for this purpose, and for a long time the Dutch also tried to gain a foothold there. But the Portuguese managed to keep them out of Mozambique. This had a far-reaching effect on the history of Africa, for the Dutch decided instead to build a landing-place at the Cape of Good Hope.

In 1652 Jan van Riebeeck and a small party of tough Dutchmen landed at the Cape, and built a small settlement there. They had no intention of looking for gold, or of trading in ivory and

Dutch ship
The Dutch were determined that they should be the only European traders in Africa and Asia. They built sturdy ships and engaged tough sea-captains.

slaves — they merely wanted to plant vegetables and raise cattle, so that their trading-ships could take fresh supplies on board.

The settlement was not very successful at first, for the Cape is not an ideal place for a port of call. There are terrible storms at sea in this area at some seasons of the year, and a lot of rich Dutch cargoes went to the bottom because of shipwrecks. But in calm weather the sailors enjoyed a brief rest in their seven-month long journey to Batavia. Later, the port became well established, and ships of all nationalities called there, so the Dutch merchants did a good trade by selling vegetables and meat to their rivals.

Soon pioneers started to 'trek'* far inland to find more good farming country. Slaves were imported from Madagascar, Mozambique and Malaya, and their descendants still live in South Africa today. Later, the more northerly African tribes were also made to work for the Dutch. The system of 'white supremacy' (European rule over Africans) in southern Africa was already beginning. Van Riebeeck's original small settlement became a Dutch colony, and from it grew what was eventually called the Union (now the Republic) of South Africa. The Dutch language, in the course of time, changed in both pronunciation and grammar, and today we know it as Afrikaans. The Dutch word for farmer — Boer — became the word for all South African Dutchmen.

*Trek — this word came from Dutch South Africa and meant to make a journey by ox wagon.

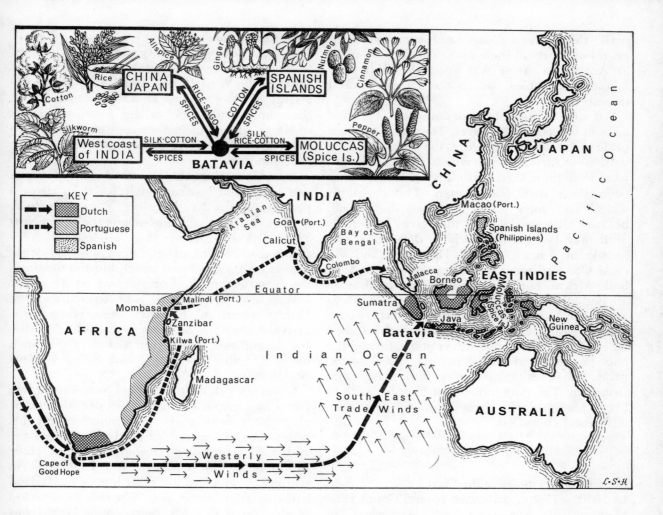

Religion in the Dutch empire

The Portuguese had sent thousands of priests to the East and to West Africa; the Dutch sent hardly any. Dutch priests were called *predikants*, and they were helped by lay-preachers—often people of quite poor education, who simply read parts of the Bible aloud to others, and sometimes taught in schools. They did not have a great deal of success in converting the native peoples. Those who had already been converted by the Portuguese were specially stubborn. The Catholic faith, with its ceremonies, was much nearer certain Eastern faiths, and some of the people of the East took to it easily. The *predikants'* religion seemed colourless by comparison. The Dutch were tolerant of all the Eastern religions, and they allowed worship in the temples and mosques to continue. But they would not allow Catholic churches to hold services because Holland had suffered many years of oppressive rule by Catholic Spain.

West Africa

'Gold is your god!' the West Africans said to the Dutch traders. They could see that these new arrivals were not even going to try to improve the African states. They just wanted money. In 1595 a regular trade in gold and ivory started, and soon forts were being built all along the coast. The Portuguese had to accept the existence of two Dutch forts, Fort Mouri and Fort Butri, one on each side of their own fort at Elmina. Worse still, the Dutch sold weapons to the African tribes, so that they could fight the Portuguese. But the Portuguese did not give in without a struggle. They managed to keep Elmina until 1637, when, after several attacks, the Dutch seized the fort for themselves.

The Dutch forts were all better defended than the Portuguese ones had been, and ships of other nationalities were unable to drive their occupants away. The English, Danes, Swedes, Germans and French were all now sending ships to trade

159

with 'the Guinea Coast' and some of them even built forts of their own. The Dutch fort of St Antony at Axim was specially built near inland gold mines, which the Dutch worked themselves.

But most of the forts were doing an increasing amount of business in slaves. There was so much profit in the slavetrade that all the nations trading with West Africa were trying to find chiefs who would sell them their prisoners — and sometimes even their own countrymen. Those nations which had forts were obviously better off, because they could keep the slaves locked up until they had enough to fill a slave-ship. The people of Angola, Congo, Dahomey, and the Gold Coast all went in fear of the slavetraders, both African and European, who would seize anybody they could find, and sell them overseas at a profit. In return the chiefs received firearms and alcohol. This terrible trade, which reached its height in the eighteenth century, turned the once-peaceful African villages into half-deserted ruins, whose inhabitants were full of hate and suspicion. The governments of Europe were to blame for letting the trade go on — for years they all 'turned a blind eye'.

Dreams of an empire in the West

In 1630, a Dutch nobleman named Count John Maurice of Nassau-Siegen*, embarked at Amsterdam for the long voyage across the Atlantic Ocean to Pernambuco. Six years had passed since the Dutch first tried to take a part of Brazil from the Portuguese. Now they had seized Pernambuco, and Count Maurice was on his way to take up the post of governor.

The Count had a very clear idea of how he wanted to govern Pernambuco. In the first place he proposed to make peace with the Portuguese, and work side by side with them. He argued that there was room for everybody in South America, and that the best way to benefit both Holland and Brazil was by tolerance.

Unfortunately for Count Maurice, the governors of the Dutch East India Company were more interested in making quick profits. They refused to support the far-seeing Count, and in 1644 he resigned and left the colony. Soon afterwards, the Dutch left Brazil altogether.

New Amsterdam

But Brazil was not the only territory in the West to be claimed by the Dutch. They had several ports in the West Indies, and during the seventeenth century, many Dutch Protestants left their homes to settle in the promising lands of North America. Another company, the Dutch West India Company, was formed to look after their interests.

In 1607, an Englishman named Henry Hudson was employed by the Dutch 'for to discover a passage by the North Pole to China'. Instead, he discovered what later became the site of New York. Other explorers had missed this very favourable landing-place, because of the dense forests on Long Island, which hid the mouth of the river. Henry Hudson stepped ashore in red ceremonial dress with gold trimmings; the North American Indians* remembered his arrival for scores of years, and could describe his magnificent clothes in detail. The Dutch made a settlement here, and called it New Amsterdam.

Governor Peter Stuyvesant of New Amsterdam ruled his people strictly and under his leadership the colony grew. But unfortunately his religion was a very narrow kind of Protestantism, and he disapproved strongly even of other Protestants. The Quakers and Lutherans in particular, who had left their homes in Holland because they were not allowed to worship freely, found that life in the New World was even harder. There was a good deal of discontent, and the local town councillors fought Stuyvesant's decisions.

During his governorship, the Indians began to realize that the Europeans would soon take away all their land. It was not only the Dutch: settlers from England, France and Spain were also pouring into North America. Three times Stuyvesant had to take out his hastily recruited troops to fight against Indian warriors. Often lonely farms were raided, and the farmers and their families brutally killed by the Indians. There was cruelty on both sides, and sometimes the Dutch burnt whole villages. Stuyvesant tried to stop the Dutch from selling guns and alcohol to the Indians, because he argued — quite rightly — that this was just asking for trouble. Because of these upsets, New Amsterdam never became a properly settled community. In 1664

*The island of Mauritius had been named after him in 1598.

*North American Indians are often called 'Red Indians'.

t' Fort nieuw Amsterdam op de Manhatans.

New Amsterdam
A view of New Amsterdam at the beginning of the Dutch settlement.

an English fleet landed troops in the mouth of the river, and the captain claimed the island in the name of King Charles II of England. Stuyvesant had had no warning of the English approach, and he had to hand over the town. It now became known as New York.

Holland

In Holland, the people had never been so prosperous. The housewives baked meats and puddings with the new spices, the dressmakers and tailors were busy turning the silks and cottons of the East into rich clothes. With new foods, and with beer and wine to accompany them, the wealthy merchants and landowners lived easy lives. After meals, the men brought out their clay pipes and smoked the new weed called tobacco, brought to Europe from America. The making of pipes became a very large industry.

The Dutch had money to spare for luxuries, especially for works of art, with which they decorated their houses. Many houses, whether in Holland or in far-off Batavia, had beautiful pictures of indoor and outdoor scenes on the walls, and huge portraits of the master and mistress of the house.

Peter Stuyvesant, Governor of New Amsterdam

Chapter 30 The Thirst for Gold

The Portuguese had discovered that the South American Indians of Brazil were not very advanced culturally, or politically. The Spaniards, exploring to the north and west of Brazil, found a very different state of affairs.

They landed on the coast of Yucatán, and there found that instead of naked savages, the inhabitants were civilized people living in stone houses and wearing woven clothing. If that had been all the Spaniards noticed, they might have gone away again. But everywhere they looked they saw gold; gold ornaments, gold bracelets and necklaces, and gold coins for money. Yet the people of Yucatán were not in fact as rich as they had been once, and even more wealthy people, called Aztecs, were living in their own small kingdom in Mexico. When the Spanish general Hernando Cortez heard about these people, he set off at once to find the Aztecs.

'We Spaniards suffer from a disease that only gold can cure,' Cortez is supposed to have said. And he sent a message to King Montezuma of the Aztecs, asking for a meeting. In return, Montezuma sent so many rich and costly presents to Cortez, that the Spaniards' 'disease' grew worse. They had to have the riches of Montezuma's golden city, Tenochtitlán, for themselves.

Cortez and his small army started off from Vera Cruz (which Cortez had founded) in 1519. The journey was long and mountainous, and often the army had to fight its way through groups of hostile Indians shooting arrows from the dense jungle trees. But they also had to cross lands belonging to a tribe called the Tlaxcatec, and this turned out to be fortunate for the Spaniards: the Tlaxcatec were unwilling subjects of Montezuma, and they were quite prepared to see him overthrown, so their warriors joined the Spanish army.

South and Central America

This mixed force struggled through jungles and over high steep mountain passes, and then suddenly, while they were still many miles away, they saw the glittering city of Tenochtitlán. 'We didn't know what to say, or whether it was real, with all the cities on the land and in the lake, the causeway with bridges one after the other, and before us the great city of Mexico.'

So wrote Bernal Diaz, the official diary-keeper of Hernando Cortez. They crossed the causeway and the bridges, and as they entered the city, a strange thing happened. The Aztecs welcomed them with great joy, and even seemed prepared to worship them. Montezuma and his priests had decided that the Spaniards were their gods, returned to earth in human form. By tradition, the feathered serpent-god Quetzalcoatl was supposed to return in this way together with a race of white 'supermen'. The return of Quetzalcoatl was to be the end of the Aztec kingdom, and the beginning of the Aztec 'heaven'. Tragically, Cortez' arrival certainly meant the end of the Aztec kingdom, but no heaven was put in its place. Montezuma was persuaded to recognize the king of Spain as his overlord and to hand over vast quantities of gold as tribute. Efforts to persuade him to become a Christian were not successful.

Meanwhile, Cortez had to leave the capital and return to Vera Cruz, where fighting had broken out. When he reached Tenochtitlán again, he found that his soldiers had been misbehaving, and were being besieged in a palace which Montezuma had set aside for their use and in which the Spaniards held Montezuma as a hostage. The Aztecs were in an angry mood. Cortez furiously ordered Montezuma to stop his people from attacking the Spaniards, and Montezuma, who only wanted peace, appeared on the palace wall and began to speak to the Aztecs who were attacking it. Then someone threw a stone at the king, inflicting a wound from which he later died. There was no longer any hope of a peaceful occupation of the city. The Spaniards had to fight every inch of the way back over the causeway to escape the fury of the Aztecs.

Two years later Cortez, with a new army, defeated 200,000 Aztecs and captured the city. As before, the Aztecs were terrified of his horses, and of the cannons and metal weapons of the invaders. Iron was unknown to them and their light weapons were quite inadequate; after a bloody fight the power and glory of the Aztec kingdom disappeared for ever. The priceless gold and silver treasures of Tenochtitlán were simply melted down and the metal shipped to Spain in blocks instead of in the form of beautiful ornaments.

Aztecs

Montezuma was ruler over a great many of the tribes of Mexico. His priests were very knowledgeable people, and gifted in astronomy and mathematics. Their religion demanded human sacrifice, and every year thousands of people were killed by having their hearts cut out from their bodies.

The Incas

Far to the south, on the west coast of South America, another American Indian tribe had become famous and great. The Incas of Peru had conquered much of the mountainous country to the east of them, and had built a magnificent capital city at Cuzco, 3466 metres (11,370 feet) above sea-level. The Inca kingdom was a difficult one to administer, because it was so vast, and because the highland peoples were completely different from the lowland peoples — yet all were one kingdom. Their clothes and their houses and even their food had to be different, because of the great differences in climate. On the coast, sun-dried mud houses with thatched roofs were adequate: in the cold hills, the people developed a way of building stone houses and palaces and temples, that even survived earthquakes. The stones were fitted together so exactly that no mortar was needed to keep them in place.

The Incas worshipped a sun-god, whose representative on earth was their ruler, the Sapa Inca. The Sapa Inca (or Sole Inca) and his queen ruled a people who worked together like bees in a hive: each man knew his job, and contributed to the good of the community. All farm produce was collected and stored in communal granaries and storehouses, to be given out in equal shares. Even the children, and the old people, had their jobs and their rewards.

163

Every male member of the tribe, and of the tribes that paid tribute to the Sapa Inca, had to do a period of military service. He put on the padded tunic, and wooden helmet covered with bronze, and was taught to use spears, pikes, axes and clubs. Iron was unknown to the Incas as it was to the Aztecs, and the weapons were tipped with bronze. The army was fed from special store-houses, which were used by the rest of the population only in an emergency.

Everyday food for all the Incas consisted of maize, millet, potatoes, sweet peppers, bananas and mangoes. Sometimes runners from the coast brought fish to Cuzco, wrapped in seaweed to keep it fresh. Occasionally the people ate the meat of a llama, or killed one of the little guinea-pigs that they raised for food.

Between the towns and the villages there was a well-developed system of roads. Parts of the mountain roads were paved and stepped where necessary; the coast roads were made of clay and protected by walls to keep them from being covered by sand. The llama-drivers, and the king's messengers, used these roads frequently. There is a great deal of difference in the amount of oxygen for breathing, and in temperature, between the coast of Peru and Cuzco. In the mountains, the water is so cold that it has to be warmed before it can be drunk comfortably. A coast-dweller who travelled the whole way might feel ill and faint at Cuzco; and a city-dweller from the mountains would feel most uncomfortable in the heat of the coast. So the country's messengers used to work in relays. One messenger ran from the coast perhaps ten miles to a village where another messenger took over from him. *He* travelled to the next staging-post, and a third messenger carried on. So each man remained at the altitude best suited to him.

The men in iron arrive

Just before the Spaniards arrived in Peru, an event had occurred which completely disorganized the Incas. For the first time, on the death of a Sapa Inca, there were two people who claimed the throne. They were half-brothers, both sons of the Sapa Inca. The son with the greater claim was killed by his brother Atahualpa. This was the ruler who now had to fight the new threat to Inca power—the Spaniards.

Francisco Pizarro, Spanish governor of New Castile, first heard about the wealth and glory of the Incas when he was in the lands bordering the Gulf of Mexico. Eager to see this land for himself, he took a small force of men and horses, and sailed down the west coast to an Inca port called Tumbez. Like the Aztecs, the Incas far from resisting the strangers, gave them food served on gold plates, wine in gold cups, and gifts of gold ornaments. This, Pizarro thought, was the city of gold he had heard about. So he was astonished to hear the inhabitants of Tumbez talk of a much richer city called Cuzco, high up in the mountains. There, they said, the temple of the sun-god was covered with sheets of gold, and all the people wore gold and silver as a matter of course.

Pizarro did not have the equipment to take an expedition into the Andes, so he returned to Spain to collect men, horses and supplies. Two years later, in 1532, he made the exhausting and dangerous journey through steaming jungles and over freezing mountains. Pizarro at this time was nearly 60 years old, and he was attempting a journey which killed many of his young followers. The dangers from Indian arrows, from disease, hunger and cold were so great that most of his men were only persuaded to go on by the promise of gold.

At last they reached Caxamalca (Cajamarca) where Atahualpa had camped; he and his courtiers came to meet Pizarro in the large central square of the city. Pizarro's party came into the square with their daggers well concealed. Armed soldiers were hidden all round the square. The Incas were unarmed. This, they thought, was to be a friendly ceremonial meeting. But when Pizarro told Atahualpa he must accept the Spanish king as his lord, and give up the sun-god for the Catholic religion, the Sapa Inca angrily refused. Pizarro shouted to his men and they seized Atahualpa and massacred his followers. Pizarro agreed to let Atahualpa free on payment of a roomful of gold. But even when this colossal amount of gold had been paid, Pizarro still did not keep his part of the bargain. He found an excuse for trying the Sapa Inca and had him executed.

The death of Atahualpa marked the end of the Inca kingdom, although the Spaniards tried to keep some of the former organization going for another century. They introduced horses and cattle, pigs and sheep, and grew vines, wheat and olives on the slopes of the mountains.

But they demanded too much tribute from the people, and the ordinary peasants became little more than slaves. The upper classes mixed freely with the Spaniards, and there was a good deal of intermarriage. Here, as in Brazil, a mixed breed of 'mestizos' came into being.

The Mayas

The people whom Cortez had first met in Yucatán had once been even more highly civilized than the Aztecs. Their weaving, pottery-making, stone-carving (without iron tools) and building were as great as anything produced by the ancient Egyptians. They were completely cut off from the rest of the world, yet quite independently, and without copying any other peoples, they managed to build observatories, and to study the stars so well that their astronomy was even more accurate than that of the Greeks.

They built pyramids and temples, many of which still stand today. They had a highly organized religion, which included human sacrifice. In their ancient cities, priests wearing jaguar*-skin tunics, elaborate feathered headdresses and many colourful ornaments, interpreted the Maya calendar to the people. They predicted eclipses, and (like the Egyptian priests) controlled the all-important crop-planting. But unlike Egypt, the land of the Mayas had no river, and their towns grew up near deep natural wells.

By the time the Spaniard, Francisco de Montejo, arrived with an army in 1540, the Maya civilization was declining. Catholic churches were built in new Spanish towns, and the Mayas were needed as an endless supply of cheap labour. They worked in the fields, and in the mines. But their gold was taken, and added to the gold from Mexico and Peru. Spain became richer as the 'conquistadores' (conquerers) took possession by force of the wealth of civilizations that were older and in some ways finer than their own.

Naturally, having found three such rich kingdoms in Central and South America, the Spaniards thought that there must be others. They sent many expeditions to the Gulf of Mexico, and explored both the east and the west coast of North America. Inland, they sent parties of men right across the continent, from Florida to California. From Cuzco, men went north, south and east, in search of more wealth. They now had a legend to drive them on — a story told by the Indians that somewhere there was a man dressed all in gold. They called him 'El Dorado',

Quipus

As well as carrying verbal messages, Inca messengers carried a rod on which were tied a number of coloured knotted strings. This was called a *quipu*. Each string and each knot could be changed to alter the meaning. They could be used to record history, keep accounts, or work out measurements for buildings. People who knew the language of the *quipus* could 'talk' to each other even if they belonged to a different tribe and otherwise spoke another language.

the golden one. He was as imaginary as Prester John, and the search for him cost the Spaniards hundreds of lives. Many of them died of hunger and cold; many more become prisoners of the Indians.

Pizarro's brother was lucky to return from a terrible march through thick jungle and mosquito-filled swamps. On their arrival in Quito in 1542, his men were 'clothed in skins, on foot, without shoes, worn out and so thin that they scarcely knew each other'. It is amazing that so much exploration was achieved in conditions like these. It was the greedy desire for gold that forced the Spaniards on, but they never again found a rich civilization to spoil* and plunder.

Meanwhile, colonists were building new towns on the ruins of Cuzco and Tenochtitlán. Catholic churches replaced the pyramid temples, and palaces decorated in the Spanish style took the place of the plain buildings in which the Sapa Inca and Montezuma had lived. Explorers like Cortez and Columbus died poor; the administrators who followed them often became very wealthy in their new homes.

---

*The jaguar is the South American leopard.

*Spoil in this sense means to take property from a defeated enemy.

Chapter 31   England joins the Exploration Race

The English first heard about Columbus's voyages from a Venetian sailor named John Cabot, who arrived in England about 1484. The king of England, Henry VII, decided to send Cabot westward on an expedition of his own. Cabot set sail from Bristol in 1497 in a ship called the *Matthew*, reached what is now called Cape Breton Island, and discovered the rich fishing grounds of Newfoundland. But he did not bring home any gold or spices, and he did not find Cathay, so the king's interest died.

After Cabot's voyages, the English made no really important voyages of discovery westwards for 50 years. While Spain and Portugal were conquering their 'new worlds', the English remained at home. Henry VII's son, Henry VIII, was too busy with English affairs to bother with explorers; and his daughter Mary, who succeeded him, was a Catholic, who married King Philip II of Spain. So during *her* reign the English were allies of Spain. But after Queen Mary's death, her half-sister Elizabeth (a Protestant) came to the throne. Queen Elizabeth I is one of the most famous English monarchs, and under her rule, many important English voyages of exploration took place. It is impossible to tell the story of all these adventures, and we can do no more than mention a few of the outstanding Elizabethans.

By this time, of course, it was common knowledge that America was a new world between Europe and Asia, and many explorers now looked for a northern route to the East. Sir Hugh Willoughby tried to find a passage to India by sailing northwards round Russia. He failed, and was frozen to death in the bitterly cold northern seas. On the same voyage, his friend Richard Chancellor, separated from Willoughby by bad weather also sailed north round Norway, and discovered the White Sea. He then travelled overland to Moscow, and had dinner with the tsar of

Queen Elizabeth I

Russia. On his return he described his experiences in Russia, and the customs of the Russians. He was particularly interested in the ladies, who painted and powdered their faces in such a fashion that he said they resembled millers' wives, 'for they look as though they were beaten about the face with a bag of meal, but their eyebrows they colour as black as jet'.

The result of Chancellor's journey was that England and Russia began to trade with each other, and the Muscovy Company was formed. For a time the English concentrated on trading with Russia, and also in defying the Portuguese by trading with the Muslims of North Africa (which they called 'Barbary'), and the Levant (countries on the east coast of the Mediterranean). Richard Hakluyt, who wrote down the stories of many Elizabethan sailors and explorers, says:

'The Portugals were much offended with this our new trade into Barbary . . . and gave out that if they took us in these parts, they would treat us as their mortal enemies.'

The English in Africa

Attempts by the English to sail down the West Coast of Africa were timid at first, partly because the Portuguese were their 'mortal enemies'. (They would much rather have found a north-west or north-east passage to the East for themselves.) But gradually the English sea-captains learnt to avoid Portuguese patrol ships, and sometimes they even managed to find Portuguese navigators who were willing to lead them past the forts, and into deserted harbours. They traded with Africans for ivory and gold, and one of these early traders, John Lok, observed:

'Whoever would deal with them must behave civilly, for they will not traffic (trade) if they be ill-used.'

The trade in 'pepper and elephants' teeth, oil of palm, cloth made of cotton wool very curiously woven, and cloth made of the bark of palm trees' was sufficiently profitable for the English to start yet another trading company. This company, founded in 1618, was called The Company of Adventurers of London trading into Africa. The Company built forts of its own on the West Coast, and agreed to supply 30,000 slaves every year to the West Indies.

But before the formation of this Company, 'gentlemen adventurers' working on their own had already begun to trade in slaves. The first Englishman to do so was John Hawkins, a member of a famous ship-building family in Plymouth. There was no demand for slaves in England, so he took them across the Atlantic and sold them to the Spaniards. The Spanish settlements in the West Indies had been forbidden to trade with the English, but the slave-traders in the Caribbean were so eager to have slaves that they secretly bought John Hawkins's cargo.

The English in the Indian Ocean

The first voyages round the Cape to the East brought many disasters and deaths. The English did not have the Dutch captain's excellent maps to help them, and they had to make their own charts from their own experience.

Early explorers sailed up the East African coast as far as the Comoro Islands and Zanzibar, where they were received cautiously. The East Africans did not know what to make of a second European power in their harbours, and the Portuguese forbade foreign ships to enter East African ports after an incident off Pemba. This is what happened: a member of the crew of a

East Indiamen
The ships of the East India Company, known as 'East Indiamen', were a little larger than the early exploring ships. Men still suffered from scurvy and ships had to call in at islands constantly in order to take fresh water, vegetables and fruit on board. Otherwise they lived on mouldy biscuits and maggot-ridden salt meat. Rats and cockroaches swarmed all over the ships and were even eaten by the sailors in emergencies.

The seamen wore their ordinary clothes on board, usually without shoes or stockings. There was no waterproof clothing and during the monsoon rains, or in Atlantic storms, the sailors were hardly ever dry. Besides this, they suffered great discomfort from fleas and lice. It is not surprising that, on long voyages, the captain considered himself lucky if *only* one-fifth of his men died.

Because of the rich cargoes they carried, sailors had to be alert for pirate ships and ready to man the guns in a fight. There was also the danger of collisions with other ships; in foggy weather the seamen banged drums, rang bells and fired their muskets to warn other ships of their presence.

ship called *Ascension* went ashore to fill a water-barrel. For some reason he was seized and killed. The English captain immediately thought that this was the beginning of a Portuguese attack, so he quickly put to sea. Next day the *Ascension* captured three dhows, and took the crews on board. From an account of the disaster that followed, it seems that the African sailors drew their knives, probably in an attempt to escape. Whereupon all 30 of them were killed by the *Ascension*'s crew. After that, English ships usually went straight across the Ocean to India, after stopping for water at the Cape of Good Hope.

In 1601 the English founded an East India Company of their own. This Company was first granted a monopoly of all trade for 15 years, then later King James I optimistically renewed it 'for ever'. By James's reign the Company was doing good business, and gentlemen in England were keen for their sons to join the 'East India-men' as apprentices. For the young apprentices* it was an adventurous life, and on their return they had many exciting stories to tell, of pirates, fights with the Portuguese, storms at sea and shipwrecks. Trading ships reached Java, the Moluccas, and Surat in India. On all these expeditions, the English ships had to try to avoid both the Portuguese and the Dutch.

In 1623 the Dutch and English came to blows at Amboina, and many English merchants were killed. After that the English stayed away from the Spice Islands, and turned their attention more and more to India. Their new settlements in Bengal, Bombay and Madras became the foundation of their Indian Empire.

Gradually the Dutch and English recognized certain trading areas as Dutch and others as English, and local quarrels became less frequent. Their colonial ventures in the East now had firm roots.

Pirates in the Caribbean

The riches of Peru were taken by the Spaniards up the west coast of South America to Panama, then put on to mules and carried in long 'trains' across the narrow strip of land to the Atlantic coast. From there the treasure went to a Spanish island called San Juan de Ulua, opposite the settlement of Vera Cruz which Cortez had

founded. Mexican gold was also sent to San Juan, and once a year a huge Spanish treasure-fleet took this enormously rich cargo across the Atlantic Ocean to Spain.

One day the English captain John Hawkins arrived at San Juan, after his ships had been nearly battered to pieces by a storm just outside the Gulf of Mexico. He sailed boldly into the harbour, and asked permission to land and make all necessary repairs. The Spaniards agreed, and the sailors gratefully went ashore to find water and fresh food. Suddenly, without warning, the Spaniards attacked them. Many of the English sailors were killed and many more were captured. Hawkins escaped from San Juan de Ulua, and so did Francis Drake, then a young captain on board one of his ships. Drake was shocked by the treachery of the Spaniards and for the rest of his life he carried on a personal battle against them.

'The Dragon'

Drake's exploits around the 'Spanish Main' sound like a boys' adventure story. In 1572, after many voyages, he attacked the town of Nombre de Dios on the Isthmus of Panama, captured a treasure ship and returned safely to England. Queen Elizabeth had to pretend not to notice that one of her sea-captains was behaving like a pirate. She assured the Spanish ambassador in England that any sea-captain caught raiding Spanish ships or settlements would be punished. But at the same time she gave Drake money for his voyages, and received the best pieces of Spanish jewellery for herself!

Drake was a very skilful seaman, and an excellent organizer. He insisted that his officers and men shared the work equally, saying: 'I must have the gentleman to haul and draw (work) with the mariner, and the mariner with the gentleman.' He was strict with his men, but they all loved him and respected him. He made sure that all his sailors knew how to fight on land as well as sail their ships, and consequently did not crowd his ships with soldiers as the Spaniards did.

Drake's navigation was as good as that of any of the earlier explorers of the Atlantic and Pacific Oceans. In 1578 he followed Magellan's route through the Straits and out into the Pacific, with a small fleet of ships. Hakluyt wrote, 'The Strait of Magellan is the gate of entry into the treasure of both the East and the East Indies.'

Once through the Strait, a gale blew Drake's

---

*An apprentice is a beginner, a boy or young man learning a trade or craft from an employer to whom he is legally bound for an agreed number of years.

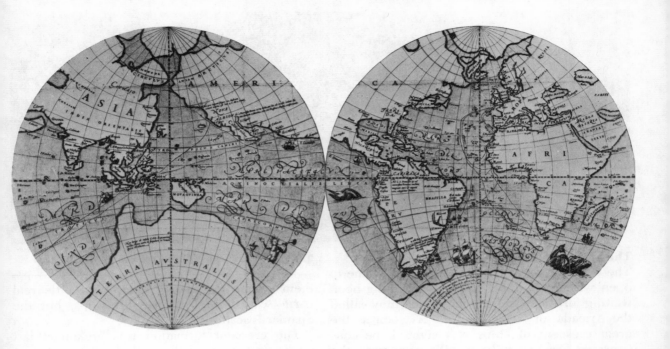

Sir Francis Drake's voyage round the world
This is a map of Drake's voyage around the world. It was printed, about ten years after his return to England, in 1590.

ships southwards, away from the coast of South America, and for weeks he and his companions saw no land at all. Everyone believed that Tierra del Fuego was the *northern* tip of a huge new, unexplored continent called 'Terra Australis' on the maps of the time. But Drake's own ship, the *Golden Hind*, was blown so far south that Drake was able to say that the geographers were wrong. One ship in Drake's little fleet disappeared for ever, and another managed to struggle back to England through the Strait. But Drake battled against the wind and eventually returned to the western shores of South America.

Now came his chance for a really profitable piece of piracy. The Spaniards had built a fleet of ships at Panama, which they sailed up and down the Peruvian coast, and northwards to their new settlements in North America. Naturally they did not bother to keep a lookout for enemy ships, because there had never been any on this coast. So as they sailed northwards, the English sailors stopped in the Spanish harbours and raided the unsuspecting settlers. One man was sleeping out in the open, with several bars of silver beside him. The raiders managed to take away the silver without even waking him! There was panic among the Spaniards when they realized that the dreaded Drake, whom they

called the 'Terrible Dragon', was in the Pacific. All the ports were alerted, but they were not able to prevent the Dragon from his most successful piece of piracy. He captured a Spanish ship which was so full of treasure that the little English ships were unable to take it all on board. Then they sailed northwards, to see if they could find a northern passage home, but finding that the coastline turned westward, Drake decided to follow Magellan's example and sail west, right round the world.

In the Moluccas the English fleet added six tons of cloves to their already overloaded ships, and then continued their voyage round Africa and home to Plymouth. Unfortunately for Drake, this was the year (1580) in which Spain and Portugal united. Spain was thus the most powerful nation in Europe, and Queen Elizabeth dared not offend King Philip. She had therefore to pretend to be displeased when Drake sailed into harbour with many thousands of pounds worth of Spanish treasure. He was officially ignored by the Court, but in fact he became a hero to everyone. The queen herself relented, and in spite of Spanish disapproval, Francis Drake was knighted the following year, and he became Mayor of Plymouth.

169

The Spanish Armada

The Spaniards and the English finally came to open warfare in 1588. England had long been waiting for the Spanish fleet (which they called the Armada, or 'armed force'). As soon as the great crescent of ships was sighted, beacons (warning fires) were lit on hilltops to carry the news throughout the country. (The English were still using this kind of signal, a thousand years after the Romans first used it.)

The Spanish ships carried so many soldiers that they might themselves have been able to attempt an invasion. This is what the English expected and their ships, quicker and easier to handle than those of the Spaniards and Portuguese, kept between the Armada and the coast all the way up the English Channel. But in fact the king of Spain had ordered the Armada to sail to a position where it could help and protect an invasion of England by the army of the Duke of Parma from the Netherlands, then under Spanish rule. Neither the king nor the admiral knew how unprepared he was for such action.

The Spanish admiral, the Duke of Medina Sidonia, led his fleet up the English Channel, strictly obeying the orders he had received in Spain. The English captains had to prevent invasion but did not know where it might be attempted. When the Armada sailed in a close, crescent formation the English found it very difficult to attack and little damage had been done to it by the time it anchored off Calais. The Spanish admiral knew that was a bad place to stop but by now he needed water, food, cannon-balls and, above all, information about the Duke of Parma's plans. This was the English captains' opportunity. That night they deliberately set some supply-ships on fire, and let the wind blow

The English ships attacking the crescent-formed Armada

them among the enemy fleet. Very little real harm was done by these fire-ships, but the Spaniards scattered.

The crescent formation was broken at last when, next morning, they sailed up the east coast of England, trying to shake off the English ships, which for the first time were able to inflict serious hurt on some of the enemy vessels. Then came a wind that blew the Armada steadily north. The English followed as far as the coast of Scotland by which time it was clear that there would be no invasion. Storms, disease, starvation and lack of water afflicted the Spanish fleet as it went round the north of Scotland and south past Ireland where more ships were wrecked. Of the 130 ships that left Lisbon only 67 got back to Spain.

While the Spanish fleet was being blown towards Scotland, Queen Elizabeth went to Tilbury, near London, to review her troops. In the speech she made to them, she said:

'I know I have the body of a weak and feeble woman, but I have the heart of a king, and a king of England too, and think foul scorn that Parma or Spain, or any prince of Europe, should dare to invade the borders of my realm.'

The defeat of the Spaniards at sea was a turning-point in the history of Europe, and perhaps also of the world. Had Spain won, Spanish influence would have spread over far more of Europe, Asia and America. The enormous English-speaking areas of the world today might have spoken another language, and adopted another culture. As it was, the English, free from the danger of invasion, set out to increase their queen's realms, while Spain declined in importance.

Chapter 32 Settlers in North America

The Spaniards had established themselves firmly in Central America by 1533 and had conquered the Inca nation in South America. In northern North America, at about the same time, a French explorer named Jacques Cartier landed at the mouth of the river St Lawrence. The French were still trying to find a northwest passage to the Pacific, and they thought the St Lawrence mouth was the beginning of a Strait. Cartier sailed up the river as far as an island near Quebec, and there he encountered a tribe of friendly Indians. By signs he asked them the name of this place, and they replied 'Canada'. Cartier thought that this was their name for the whole country; it was in fact their word for a village.

The Indians also told Cartier about a rich country called Saguenay, where there was gold and precious stones. When he returned home and told King Francis I of France about Saguenay, the king thought that he was going to be the lord of another great empire like those of Peru or Mexico. He was very happy to supply Cartier with more ships and men, so that he could explore the river St Lawrence properly. Cartier went on two more expeditions, but he never found Saguenay. In fact, it did not exist. But he decided that the land near the river would be wonderful for settlement, and he turned his mind to trading with the Indians, and colonizing the new land. His main settlement was on the site of present-day Montreal.

Almost 50 years after Cartier's death, in 1603, the French sent their first governor to Canada. His name was Samuel de Champlain. He had already been on expeditions to the West Indies and South America, and he was the first person to suggest that a canal should be cut across the Isthmus of Panama. But that was all Spanish territory, and there was very little that a French-

man could do to make such a dream come true. He continued Cartier's work of exploring the St Lawrence, and tried to find a way past the many rapids and waterfalls on the river. He founded the city of Quebec, and started many other small settlements where fur-traders could buy and sell their goods. They bought all kinds of animal skins from the Indians, cured (preserved) them, and sold them to merchants who sailed up the river to their trading-stations. These settlements remained small; besides fur traders there were only fishermen and peasant-farmers living in them. At this stage, Champlain did not want settlers who would not contribute to the development of the settlements.

Champlain was a great believer in keeping friendly with the Indians, and they liked and trusted him. He found out a great deal about their way of life, and once he even joined a war-party of Indian braves (warriors) of the Algonquin tribe. Their enemies the Iroquois turned to the English for help, and so Europeans became involved in Indian quarrels.

Champlain's exploring trips took him far to the west, and he was the first white man to see Lakes Huron and Ontario. He must have heard about the other Great Lakes, but he seems to have been misled into thinking they were not lakes, but the sea. Still thinking of the possibility of a way by water to the Pacific, he sent an expedition to find this 'Sea of the West'. No way through was discovered, but this and other expeditions (many of them led by Jesuit missionaries) found out a tremendous amount about the geography of North America. They made contact with the Spaniards in Mexico, and with the English on the shores of Hudson Bay; while westwards they reached the Rocky Mountains. The first person to cross the North American continent was a Scottish fur trader named Alexander Mackenzie, very much later, in 1793. Long before this happened, the thoughts of Europeans were turning away from the idea of making easy money in America. The land was so fertile that newcomers now arrived to build themselves homes and to farm rather than to explore.

The 'Lost Colony'

One of the first Englishmen to become interested in colonizing North America was the famous Sir Walter Raleigh. He and the English geographer Richard Hakluyt together wrote a book that gave instructions on how to start a colony. The book also suggested that new settlements should be founded by the state, and not by private individuals. Unfortunately Raleigh's attempts to build colonies were complete failures, partly because the men chosen to make their homes in America were unsuitable for such a tough and thankless task. Raleigh himself did not lead any of the expeditions.

The only attempt which might have been successful was made when Raleigh sent out a party of men with their families under the leadership of a man named John White. White was to be 'Governor of the City of Ralegh* in Virginia'. His party landed at a place called Roanoke, where Raleigh had already sent 15 settlers with stores to last for two years. The new party could find no trace of these men, which was disheartening, because they had expected to find warm houses and food awaiting them at their journey's end. Whatever the fate of these fifteen men was, it was probably the same as that of White's little colony. When supplies ran short, White took their ship back to England, promising to return almost at once. He left behind 89 men, 17 women and 11 children, including his own daughter and her newborn baby, Virginia Dare. For various reasons White was unable to return for two years. When he got back he found that the 'City of Ralegh' was an empty, overgrown, deserted clearing in the forest.

The English at home were shocked to hear that all these settlers had vanished, and many later expeditions were asked to search for the inhabitants of the 'Lost Colony'. But no definite explanation of their disappearance was ever found, though years later there was an Indian

*Walter Raleigh spelt his name in many different ways. Nowadays we usually keep to the spelling 'Raleigh'.

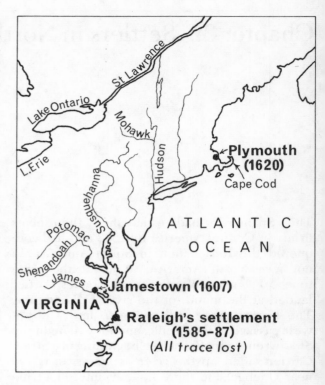

Early English settlements in North America, 1585–1620

story that all except seven of the settlers had been killed. The Indians of Roanoke were gentle people, whose main occupation was hunting and fishing: perhaps they grew tired of the Englishmen's demands for food. Or perhaps another more warlike tribe captured them. One of the seven said to have been saved was a 'young maid', who may possibly have been Virginia Dare. If so, she very likely lived for the rest of her life as an Indian 'squaw' (the North American Indian word for a woman or wife).

John Smith and Pocohontas

In spite of repeated failures to colonize the land named Virginia, the London merchants were still eager to try. So they formed the 'London Company in Virginia', and in 1606 they sent out a party of 105 colonists under the leadership of a young man named John Smith. Their settlement was called Jamestown, in honour of the new English king, James I.

But the Company was no better at choosing suitable colonists than Sir Walter Raleigh had been, and Smith had a hard time trying to keep them all alive. Sometimes Indians made surprise attacks, but Jamestown was on a peninsula, and easy to defend, so they did not do any lasting

John White's drawing of colonists landing in Virginia
John White was very interested in all he saw in the New World, and he made a collection of drawings of the people, plants and animals. He hoped that his pictures would attract more English settlers.

damage. More serious was the shortage of food. John Smith was the only member of the party who was successful in trading with the Indians for maize: other colonists tried, but they did not return. In winter they all had to live on whatever birds and animals they managed to kill.

When Jamestown became more settled, John Smith left to explore the river Chickahominy, and he then had an adventure for which he has always been remembered. He was captured by Indians, and to save himself he gave their leader a round ivory compass. The Indians had never seen such a thing before, and they watched with surprise as the delicate needle swung round under its protective glass. In his own account of the event, John Smith (who wrote about himself as 'he') said:

> 'Within an hour after, they tied him to a tree, and as many as could, stood about him prepared to shoot him, but the King* holding up the compass in his hand, they all laid down their bows and arrows, and in a triumphant manner led him to Orapaks, where he was after their manner kindly feasted, and well used.'

But that was not the end of the matter. The Indian braves performed a war-dance round him, and then fed him with great quantities of venison (deer-meat) 'which made him think they would fat him to eat him'. Then for about three days they performed a ceremony which was designed to show them whether he wished them well or not. They tried to make him their leader for a raid on Jamestown, but he told them that they would never be able to resist the guns used by the settlers.

So at last he was taken to the chief of the tribe, Powhatan. And Powhatan's decision was that he should die. Two large stones were laid on the floor, and John Smith was stretched on the stones. Just as the braves were about to beat out his brains with their clubs, Powhatan's young daughter, Pocohontas, rushed forward and laid her own head on top of his. 'Whereat,' said John Smith, 'the Emperor was contented he should live.' After this lucky escape, John Smith was given land in exchange for 'two great guns and a grindstone', and he was allowed to return to Jamestown.

Meanwhile the colonists struggled along, battling all the while against hunger and disease. It was a losing battle, and in one short year after their arrival in America, there were only 38 people left. This was a dreadful death-rate, and Jamestown would have failed completely had

*Early explorers often quite wrongly called minor chiefs and headmen 'King'; the 'Emperor' mentioned later was chief Powhatan.

173

not a ship arrived bringing fresh stores, and 120 more settlers. They were under the leadership of Captain Newport. The London Company was not so interested in making the colony self-supporting as it was in making money: Captain Newport's instructions were to look for gold, to discover a passage to the Pacific, and to find 'the Lost Colony'. Smith tried to do all these things, as well as ensuring that sufficient corn was planted, and that the Indians were treated well. It was a superhuman task, and naturally he could not do all these things properly. The London Company was constantly telling him that they wanted more valuable cargoes sent back to England.

John Smith was an excellent choice for the job of starting a colony in Virginia. If only the Company had left him to do as he thought right, he would probably have succeeded. But the policy was directed in London, by men who had never been to America, and had no idea of the difficulties the colonists had to face. It was not until colonies became independent of European Companies that the colonization of America became really successful.

The Pilgrim Fathers

King James I of England was a strange man, and not very likeable. But he was king, and he had to be obeyed. He had been brought up as a strict Protestant, but was very intolerant of those who belonged to different branches of the Protestant faith. 'You will reform,' he shouted on one occasion, 'or I will harry* you out of the land!'

One religious group who preferred to leave before they were harried out were called Separatists. They were a very extreme kind of Protestant, who thought that the Reformation did not return closely enough to a simple Christianity. The Separatists dressed very plainly, often in grey and white, and their lives were rather dull because they did not believe in dancing, or holiday fairs, or even merrymaking in private. They drank no wine, and wore no jewellery.

At first this group went to Holland, but later they decided to leave Europe altogether and become pioneers in a new country. The London merchants gave them a ship called the *Mayflower* so that they could go to Virginia. In 1620 they

*To harry is to make repeated attacks on. This sentence means 'I will keep on attacking until you leave the country.'

Pocohontas, the chief's daughter, arises to save John Smith's life by laying her head on his

The Pilgrim Fathers arriving at Virginia

The *Mayflower* was shockingly overcrowded. Each passenger had to provide his own food and the cabins were very small. A whole family slept in bunks, one above the other, with scarcely room to turn around. Even though the Separatists lived simple lives at home, they were horrified by the conditions during their two months on board the *Mayflower*. William Bradford said of their arrival:

'Being thus past the vast ocean and a sea of troubles ... they now had no friends to welcome them nor inns to entertain or refresh their weather-beaten bodies ...'

174

sailed from Plymouth in England but they missed Virginia, and instead landed at Cape Cod. They called their first settlement Plymouth, and the new colony, New England. Many years later the people of the United States of America called them the 'Pilgrim Fathers'.

These devoted people did their best to start work on building houses and collecting food. They had very few stores left from the voyage, and winter was approaching. Their sufferings during that first winter were terrible, and by the time spring came, half of them were dead. But the rest of the little band persevered, and with a man called William Bradford as governor for the next 30 years, they gradually managed to create a colony. They caught herrings, cod and mackerel, and sold them to traders. They became excellent ship-builders, and used their ships to carry goods to England from other American colonies. Their cargoes consisted of fish, wood, tobacco, hemp, sugar and wheat.

William Penn

Farther south, another Christian religious group made its home in this country. They were the Quakers, and their leader was an Englishman called William Penn. Penn's father had lent a large sum of money to King Charles I, James I's son. The king readily agreed to repay Penn on his father's death, not with money, but with a grant of land in America. Penn wanted to call his land 'Sylvania', which means 'woodlands', and it was the king who persuaded him to add his own name; the new colony became Pennsylvania.

Penn sat down and wrote a 'Last Farewell to England' (in fact he returned many times), and then sailed from Deal on the south-east coast. The journey was a nightmare, because someone came on board already infected with smallpox. In such crowded surroundings, with little room to move, nobody could escape the disease, and by the time the ship reached the shores of America, one-third of the passengers had died.

But again, from a disastrous start grew a thriving colony. Within two years there were 300 houses in Pennsylvania, built in the new town called Philadelphia, which means 'brotherly love'. Pennsylvania turned out to be a very fertile land, particularly for grain-crops like wheat and barley. Each man worked his own land, and they did not rely entirely on slave-labour, as the Spanish and English planters of the southern part of America did. So whereas in the south

William Penn trading with the Indians

there were a few very rich landowners and thousands of slaves, farther north there was a less wealthy middle class with fewer very poor people.

Penn always paid the Indians well for any land he bought (unlike Peter Minuit, a Dutchman, who bought New Amsterdam for a few yards of cloth). In return he asked that they should sell their furs and skins only to Pennsylvanians, and not to 'the enemies of England'. All English settlers at this time considered that their colonies belonged to Britain and it was, of course, the British fleet that was expected to defend them from attack.

But in spite of Penn's justice and sense of fair dealing, he was not popular in England, and was once put on trial for suspected treason. He was found not guilty, but this and later accusations affected his health. But by the time he died in 1718, British colonization of America was firmly established.

By 1732 there were 13 British colonies, spread along the east coast of North America. These colonies had many quarrels among themselves, and there were terrible wars with the Indians, who were pushed farther and farther west. Although the colonists had not yet gone very far inland, it was now certain that the time would come when all the vast, beautiful and rich territory of North America would belong to the European settlers.

Chapter 33 Terra Australis

To finish the story of the Voyages of Exploration, the discovery of one more great territory must be mentioned—that of the continent of Australia. Although, as long ago as 1578, Francis Drake had proved that the southern tip of South America, Tierra del Fuego, was an island and not part of a new continent, explorers and geographers believed in the existence of a great southern continent, which they called 'Terra Australis', for another two whole centuries. They argued that since there was so much land north of the equator, there must be an equal area of land to the south of the equator as well. So far, they had only discovered a relatively small amount of land to the south, so they thought that Terra Australis must be a vast continent, balancing the whole of Europe and Asia.

Before 1700 explorers of various countries put in at ports in the South Seas, and thought that they had reached part of Terra Australis. The Spanish explorer Torres had passed through the Strait that bears his name in 1605. Dutch seamen followed: Arnhem to Arnhem Land in 1623, Carpenter to the Gulf of Carpentaria in 1628, Tasman (who also discovered New Zealand) to Tasmania in 1642. The first Englishman to arrive was Dampier, at Dampier Land, in 1688. But none of them thought Australia was worth colonizing and its exact size and shape remained uncertain. The first person to discover that New Zealand was two islands, and to chart the east coast of Australia, was another Englishman, Captain James Cook.

Captain Cook had sailed many times to North America, and he was a great seaman. He was very interested in scientific exploration, and on his voyages he took with him experts to study the plants and animals on the lands he discovered. He was the first sea-captain to provide fruit juice for his sailors, and so to end the dread-

A Remarkable Animal found on one of the Hope Islands in Captⁿ Cook's first Voyage.

Kangaroo

Captain Cook described a kangaroo in his journal in 1770:

'I saw this morning one of these animals. It was the full size of a greyhound and shaped like one, with a long tail which it carried like a greyhound. I should have taken it for a wild dog, but for its walking or running in which it jumped like a hare or a deer. Excepting the head and ears, which was something like a hare's, it bears no sort of resemblance to any European animal I ever saw.'

ed scurvy, and to insist that his ship was kept clean and that the sailors washed themselves and their clothes. Before his time many sailors died on any long voyage, but during three years at sea in hot and cold climates, out of the 112 men of the crew of his ship *Resolution* only one man died of disease.

Cook made three great voyages into the Pacific Ocean, twice sailing round the world. In the years 1769–70 he explored the coasts of New Zealand. On his second voyage he went farther south than any ship had been before, sailing among the icebergs of the Antarctic Ocean, and proved that there could be no great southern continent. He did not, of course, come in sight of the frozen continent of Antarctica. On his third voyage he tried to find a way round the north of North America but had to turn back because of the ice in the Arctic Ocean. Then he sailed south to the Pacific islands in which he was intensely interested, but in 1779 he was killed by a group of Hawaiians on the beach of their island.

Cook had claimed Australia for Britain, and the colonization of Australia began in 1788 when the British started to use a part of the east coast, called Botany Bay, as a prison settlement. Free settlers soon followed, and after 1797, when sheep were introduced from Europe, the new colony began to prosper.

The results of the Voyages

What did all these voyages mean to the people of Africa and America? And of the countries of Asia?

The consequences of the voyages of exploration for Africans were sad. In East Africa and on the west coast of India, the Portuguese wrecked the traditional trade, and the once flourishing towns declined. In West Africa, metal knives, guns and gunpowder were handed over in exchange for gold and silver and ivory — goods of much more lasting value; and the time came when African chiefs were willing to sell their fellow-Africans into slavery. We have already seen the damage that the slave-trade did to West Africa.

In North America, trade between Indians and

Captain Cook and his men receiving an offering in the Sandwich Islands

Europeans gradually gave way to trade between white Americans and Europeans, as the Indians were pushed farther and farther westwards by settlers. In time the Indians lost their hunting grounds and their numbers steadily decreased. Today most of them live in reservations with little to do. In return, they learnt European ways, but this must have seemed a poor exchange for their old free way of life.

In Asia, very little was changed. The Europeans were established in India, Ceylon, the Spice Islands and the Philippines, but in the country districts, life went on much as it had always done.

The ships calling at the South Sea Islands left behind metal pots and pans, nails and knives; and Captain Cook brought cattle, pigs, goats and hens, because there were no native domestic animals there. He also advised the British government to allow ships to call at the islands frequently, because he realized that once the islanders got used to European utensils and weapons, they would come to rely on them. Cook was very fond of the islanders, and was perhaps the first great explorer to care what happened to people of a different race and culture.

The Christian religion of the sixteenth and seventeenth centuries did not help men to understand cultures other than their own; for the priests taught that those who had never heard of Christianity were 'heathen', and therefore inferior. They must be brought to the true faith (by force if necessary). Because of this, nobody thought it immoral to rob the heathen of their land, or to exchange a handful of beads for a lump of gold. So the explorers put up flags and erected monuments, claiming their new discoveries for this or that European country. The claims of 'inferior' people already living there were ignored.

What did all these new discoveries mean to the people of Europe? How did the voyages affect their lives?

Firstly, they enabled people to learn more about the geography of the world. Maps now included the newly-charted shores of America and Asia, and travellers' tales about foreign lands became more realistic. Gradually the fears about sea-monsters and queer half-human creatures grew less. Red Indians and Africans were taken to Europe, where men saw that these strangers were after all much the same as themselves.

Now that printing was making books cheaper, accounts of the adventures of sailors, explorers and colonists could be read by all literate people. Their world had suddenly grown larger and more interesting. King James I of England heard about America's talking parrots, and he asked to be given one. Other people with sons on the ships also had new pets from overseas.

Secondly, the discoveries made an enormous difference to the trading-pattern of Europe. Up till now, the main trading countries ringed the Mediterranean Sea. Now the main trading nations were those with coastlines facing the Atlantic Ocean: Portugal, Spain, Britain and Holland. (We have seen how Portuguese trade in the Indian Ocean took away Venice's monopoly of luxury goods from the East.) During the centuries that followed, hundreds of small trading ships sailed between Europe and America, or between Europe and the Far East.

Thirdly, gold and silver and precious stones arrived in such quantities (particularly from South America), that soon their value decreased. This meant that each gold or silver coin in a man's pocket would buy less. The rise in prices did not matter much to the merchants, because they had more money anyway. They became very important people, and the kings of Europe had to listen to their demands. They were the people who now financed the European countries, and even controlled other economies in foreign lands.

Some of these merchants began to deal in money itself, instead of in wool, or tea, or corn. They built Banks and Exchanges, lent money which had to be repaid with interest, and started the system whereby goods could be bought by cheques, promissory notes and bills of exchange, rather than by coins. Bank notes were also manufactured, in order to save people from having to carry large amounts of heavy coins about. The international financiers were so important that even kings were glad to allow their sons and daughters to marry into their families.

Fourthly, everybody got used to new customs. The merchant or courtier with his pipe and tobacco, the seamstress drinking her coffee, the child chewing a stick of sugar, the housewife preserving food with cinnamon, cloves and pepper—everybody's life was changed to some extent by the voyages.

Revision

Questions and Exercises

Chapter 1
1. Where was 'man's first home'?
2. What does *Zinjanthropus* mean? How long ago did this hominid live?
3. What is a nomad? Are there any nomads in the world today?
4. What is the scientific name of the only hominid that now exists?
5. What did early hominids eat?
6. Name three animals that existed two million years ago.

Chapter 2
1. Name three important early inventions.
2. What were the earliest grain crops ever planted?
3. Where did early men draw their pictures? What did they draw?
4. Name three kinds of early weapons.
5. Which wild animals were first domesticated?
6. What jobs did people first 'specialize' in?

Chapter 3
1. What did the Sumerians write on, and what with?
2. What is the name of the river on which Ur was built?
3. Why did the Sumerians bury the king's servants in his grave?
4. Who came first—Ur–Nammu or Sargon?
5. Which classes of people learnt to read and write in Sumeria?
6. What is King Hammurabi famous for?

Chapter 4
1. How long did Egypt's great civilization last? About 500, 1000, 3000 or 5000 years?
2. What is Egyptian writing called? Is it still used today?
3. Egypt is divided by us into three 'kingdoms'. What are they called?
4. Which Egyptian god represented the sun?
5. What was Egyptian 'paper' made of?
6. Name two metals used in Ancient Egypt.

Chapter 5
1. Draw a pyramid and a ziggurat, to show the difference in shape. What was the difference in the way they were used?
2. Where did the Egyptians import trees from? What did they use the wood for?
3. How did the priests of Egypt grow rich?
4. What new metal did the Hyksos introduce into Egypt?
5. Who tried to introduce a single god into Egypt?
6. Why did the pharaohs build such enormous tombs, and have their bodies embalmed?

Chapter 6
1. Which nation first used battering rams?
2. What was the religion of the Persians?
3. Moses led the Hebrews out of captivity—from which country?
4. What is another name for the Israelites?
5. Who made a collection of cuneiform tablets?
6. What was the capital city of the Israelites?

Chapter 7
1. Who built the earliest-known spoked wheels?
2. Draw the 'Yang-yin' sign. What did it signify?
3. Confucius, Moses, Buddha, Zoroaster. Which was born first? Which was a Hindu?
4. What were silkworms used for?
5. Which religion has been called 'the encyclopaedia of all religions'? Why?

Chapter 8
1. Who won the battle of Marathon?
2. Where did the small Greek fleet finally defeat the Persian ships?
3. Name three Greek city states.
4. Name three great Greeks, and say why they are famous.
5. What is the 'Hellespont'?
6. Put into date order: Xerxes, Cyrus, Darius. Which country did they rule?

Chapter 9
1. What is a 'democracy'?
2. Name one famous leader of the Greeks who was sent to Salamis to escape from the Persians when he was a young boy.
3. What was the name of the hill on which the Athenians' main temple was built? What was the temple called?
4. What did a Greek theatre look like?
5. Why were Spartans not allowed to trade with other Greek city-states?
6. Name four Greek gods and/or goddesses.

Chapter 10
1. What two states fought each other in the Peloponnesian wars?
2. What famous Athenian is known for his discussions and arguments?
3. Name three different kinds of cargo carried by Phoenician ships.
4. Where does our word 'alphabet' come from?
5. Who was the leader who commanded the new

Spartan fleet in 404 B.C.?

6. What is a delta? How did it get its name?

Chapter 11

1. Who was the son of Philip of Macedon? Which country did he become ruler of?
2. Which army introduced chariots with long knives fixed to their wheels?
3. Persepolis was the capital of — ?
4. Why did Alexander want his soldiers to marry Persian wives?
5. How far east did the Greek army march?
6. What was the name of the new capital of Egypt?

Chapter 12

1. What was the name of the city Aeneas is supposed to have founded?
2. Who were the Etruscans?
3. What was a Roman *corvus*?
4. In 218 B.C. a Carthaginian tried to conquer Rome. What was his name?
5. Why was Scipio nicknamed 'Africanus'?
6. Why did Hannibal want to take Rome?

Chapter 13

1. What was the *lingua franca* of the Mediterranean world in Roman times?
2. In 58 B.C. a Roman leader invaded Gaul. Who was he?
3. Caesar conquered Egypt for Rome. Name two other nations which had also conquered Egypt.
4. What is meant by 'the Ides of March'? Which dates were they?
5. What were *lares* and *penates*?
6. What was 'a century' to a Roman, and what does it mean to us? What is the connection between the two?

Chapter 14

1. What was the name of the first Roman emperor?
2. What was an 'auxiliary' in the Roman army?
3. What was the northern limit of the Roman empire?
4. Name three articles of trade brought into Rome from the provinces.
5. Write a paragraph about Alexandria in Roman times.
6. What was the name of the city buried by lava when Mount Vesuvius erupted?

Chapter 15

1. What was the Saturnalia?
2. Who was the last emperor to rule from Rome? Where did he move the capital to?
3. Who were the 'barbarians' who destroyed the Roman empire?
4. How did Roman criminal trials differ from ours?
5. Name four different kinds of buildings used by the Romans.
6. What implement did Romans write with? What did they write on?

Chapter 16

1. In which religion did Jesus of Nazareth grow up?
2. Who were the four writers of the Gospels? What does 'gospel' mean?
3. What is a parable?
4. Who were the first 'Gentiles' to whom the disciples preached?
5. What countries first became Christian, and why?

Chapter 17

1. Who founded the Grey Friars?
2. Which European king was crowned by the Pope in 800 A.D.?
3. Which people conquered Britain in 1066?
4. What was the 'Vulgate' Bible?
5. Name an African state converted to Christianity by a monk named Julian.
6. What was the Bayeaux Tapestry? Where were the boats going, and why?

Chapter 18

1. How did Islam change the way of life of the Arabs?
2. What does 'Islam' mean?
3. Where and what is the ka'aba?
4. Name three great Muslim centres in the Middle Ages.
5. Why do Muslims use a prayer mat? Which way do they face when praying?
6. Name two important inventions 'borrowed' and developed by the Muslims.

Chapter 19

1. Which country did Kublai Khan rule over? Name a European who met him.
2. Why are there no statues in mosques?
3. Name two people who took part in the Crusades. Which countries did they fight for?
4. In 1453 a great city was captured from the Christians. What was its name, and who had founded it?
5. How was a medieval knight dressed?
6. Who fought in the battle of Poitiers in 732?

Chapter 20

1. Why was the name of Mansa Musa known to Europeans? What was the name of his country?
2. Name two towns in Mansa Musa's kingdom.
3. What was used instead of money for buying goods in Benin?
4. What was silent trade? How did it work, and why was it used?
5. Are there still Muslims in West Africa?

Chapter 21

1. Who invented the printing press?
2. Name three new jobs created by the printing industry.
3. Name the scientist who, in 1610, looked through a telescope and saw — which planet?
4. Besides being an artist, Leonardo da Vinci was also an engineer. How did this affect his drawing?
5. How did the Roman and Greek civilizations affect the lives of people living in Italy in the fourteenth and fifteenth centuries?
6. Who discovered the circulation of the blood in 1628?

Chapter 22

1. What do St Jerome, Wycliffe and Tyndale have in common?
2. What were 'indulgences'?
3. Who wrote the '95 themes'? Where did he put them, so that people might read them?
4. Why was the break-away church called 'Protestant'?
5. Name two Protestant reformers in Switzerland.
6. Under which English king were monasteries and abbeys dissolved?

Chapter 23

1. Who was Torquemada? Which country did he live in?
2. In 1534 Ignatius Loyola founded which religious society?
3. Why was Joan of Arc burned at the stake? And by whom?
4. Name two plays written by Shakespeare.
5. Explain in one sentence each, the meaning of Renaissance and Reformation.

Chapter 24.

1. Give two reasons for the Portuguese exploration round Africa.
2. What was Prince Henry of Portugal's nickname?
3. Describe a caravel.
4. What is the capital of Portugal?
5. Who first rounded the Cape of Good Hope? What was its first name?
6. Name two West African kingdoms of the fourteenth century.

Chapter 25

1. What is the connection between *Zinjanthropus* and 'The Land of Zenj'?
2. Why didn't the Muslims join in the 'exploration race'?
3. Name two towns visited by the Arab traveller, Ibn Battuta. Do they still exist today?
4. Name three Indian Ocean towns visited by Vasco da Gama. What did he find there?
5. Who was 'Monomotapa'?
6. Name three East African exports in the fifteenth century, and three imports.

Chapter 26

1. What nationality was Christopher Columbus? When was he born?
2. Why did Columbus sail westwards?
3. Where was Cathay?
4. What was the name of the first European to see the Pacific Ocean? What does 'pacific' mean?
5. A member of Magellan's crew kept a diary of the journey. They arrived home on a Thursday. Why was the diary-writer astonished at this? What day did *he* think it was?
6. One of Magellan's tasks was to find out whether the Pope's division of the world (p. 143) meant that the Moluccas belonged to Spain or Portugal. With the aid of a globe, can you find the answer?

Chapter 27

1. Name three East African towns taken by the Portuguese?
2. Who was the first 'Viceroy of India'?
3. Why were the traders of Venice alarmed by the new Portuguese forts in the Indian Ocean?
4. Name two sorts of cloth imported from the east in the sixteenth century.
5. In what ways is Goa different from other parts of India?

Chapter 28

1. What did 'Elmina' mean? Where was it, and who built it?
2. Who was the West African king who asked his 'royal brother' to stop the slave trade?
3. Where were slaves from West Africa taken? What work did they have to do?

4. Why is Vespucci famous?
5. Name three different places in the world where the inhabitants are called 'Indians'.
6. Name one new food introduced from America to Africa.

Chapter 29

1. When was the East India Company founded? Where was its eastern headquarters?
2. Which African state was first colonized by the Dutch?
3. Where is Pernambuco?
4. Which island did Henry Hudson discover in 1607?
5. Name two new products that became popular in Europe in the seventeenth and eighteenth centuries. Where did they come from?
6. Why were the Dutch more successful than the Portuguese in the East?

Chapter 30

1. What were the names of the two great peoples in South America whose civilizations were destroyed by the Spaniards?
2. Why have most of the gold ornaments of South America disappeared?
3. What advantages and disadvantages were there in wearing armour when exploring new lands? Would you have worn it if you had had the choice?
4. Name two ways in which the Mayas resembled the ancient Egyptians.
5. Who was 'El Dorado'? How did he differ from 'Prester John'?
6. What was a *quipu*?

Chapter 31

1. Name three Elizabethan explorers.
2. Why were the English enemies of Spain in the sixteenth century?
3. Who was nicknamed 'the Dragon'? And by whom?
4. When did the Spanish Armada try to invade England? What does 'armada' mean?
5. What do you know about Richard Hakluyt?
6. What was an 'East Indiaman'?

Chapter 32

1. Name one great French explorer. Which country did he explore?
2. What did the Indians in North America trade with the French?
3. Which group of people founded the American town of Plymouth? What did they call their colony?
4. What does 'Philadelphia' mean? Who founded it?
5. What new crops did the European settlers in America plant?

Chapter 33

1. Who sailed in: the *Mayflower*, the *Santa Maria*, and the *Resolution*?
2. Why was fruit juice important to sailors? Who introduced it on ships?
3. Name an animal, native to Australia.
4. What language do Australians speak, and why?
5. Where did Captain Cook die?
6. How many years (very approximately) after the foundation of Ur was Australia colonized—1000, 2000, 4000—or more?

Index

(Page numbers in italics refer to maps)